CW00701198

# THE CIVIC CITY IN A NOMADIC WORLD

WORDS & IMAGES BY

CHARLES LANDRY

nai010 publishers

Texts: **Charles Landry**
Sub-editor: **Jonathan Hyams**
Photography: **Charles Landry**
Design: **Hills Design**
Lithography and Printing: **epopee**
Publisher: **Marcel Witvoet, nai010 publishers**

Cover photograph: *Jodhpur, India*

nai010 publishers is an internationally orientated publisher specialized in developing, producing and distributing books in the fields of architecture, urbanism, art and design. www.nai010.com

nai010 books are available internationally at selected bookstores and from the following distribution partners: North, Central and South America - Artbook | D.A.P., New York, USA, dap@dapinc.com Rest of the world - Idea Books, Amsterdam, the Netherlands, idea@ideabooks.nl

For general questions, please contact nai010 publishers directly at sales@nai010.com or visit our website **www.nai010.com** for further information.

Printed and bound in the Netherlands

Paperback edition
ISBN 978-94-6208-388-2

Also available as hardcover
ISBN 978-94-6208-372-1

also available as e-book
ISBN 978-94-6208-300-4

# CONTENTS

*Gazi, Athens*

1

# THE
# WORLD IN
# MOTION

# OVERTURE

We live in awkward times. The world is turning to its darker face. The zeitgeist is one of rising anxiety. The grey zone disappears. Deep fractures are emerging within our world. Our social and our tribal nature and our in-group and out-group instincts are in tension as our world continues to shrink and our cities become more mixed, more nomadic and more diverse. More of us move around for work, for pleasure, for love or to explore and so are influenced by ideas and trends from elsewhere. Some think this is too much and that it must stop, others are excited by the potential of being part of a bigger world. There is still a mix of optimism and pessimism.

*The Civic City in a Nomadic World* has an ambitious aim to start a conversation about the promise of a different urban civilization. This is one where settled citizens of the city and outsiders, often temporary residents, come together to shape and make a place incorporating the best they can both offer. This is a central challenge of the age when the world is increasingly nomadic and people are on the move. Cities need an overarching, positive narrative that binds all people to where they live and where day to day behaviour and activities mesh well with civic life.

In common language today 'the civic' or 'being civic' simply means to be involved with your city, formally or informally, and every person living in a city should share this opportunity. Civic engagement involves participation in mechanisms that make the city work. It is easy to become an active citizen. Being 'civil' implies respect so that conversation and dialogue across differences does not lead to continuous argument. In contrast to such civility, debates have coarsened of late. A great civic city allows space for the civil since civil also implies having inalienable rights and freedoms. These allow us to act relatively free from constraints (within agreed codes of behaviour) and to engage in political, voluntary or other activity as we wish and without being hindered. This gives many cities their freshness. Yet this is not possible in more than 100 countries. The creative tensions between people doing their own thing and our collective endeavours are the lifeblood of city making.

**Cohesion and bonding are core human traits**, but the questions are 'with whom?' and 'how?'. There is often a desire to connect with the different, the strange, the outsider or the other. This feeds

Barcelona Airport

our exploratory instinct – a necessary mechanism for survival. Yet we hanker too after the familiar, the known, the predictable and the settled. So, people too look for and choose the like-minded. Where these things fall depends on how at ease we feel with ourselves and our surroundings. Uncertainty makes people and places cradle themselves back into their tribal instincts and prejudices. The politicians then feverishly feed on these, creating dangerously sharp distinctions between a 'them' and an 'us' or between 'patriots' – who are good and reliable – and 'globalists' – who are bad, confusing and untrustworthy – as if you could not be both at the same time. This is reminiscent of the dark times when 'cosmopolitan' was a dirty word. The demagogues express this division as if a cosmic battle between chaos and order. They are feeding the human urge for an ordering device and a narrative structure for life which comforts and simplifies things. This settles their mind and reinforces a mindset. It provides a mental map and a script they can happily tell themselves. Easy metaphors like good or bad help. This dilemma is the paramount faultline and clash of the twenty-first century.

**We have a stark choice: to close our worlds in or to open them out**. It is not a simple either/or question. There is complexity involved. Closing in when everything across our globe is inextricably interwoven is folly. The default position should be to be more open than closed, more empathy or compassion than animosity - not because we are dreamers, but because we are hard-headed and practical. Having for a long time looked at, lived in and been curious about cities, towns and villages, this is my conclusion. My attempt here is to provide a verbal and visual story of the delights and discontents of the contemporary city – one that I hope touches people viscerally.

Museum of Contemporary Art, Sydney

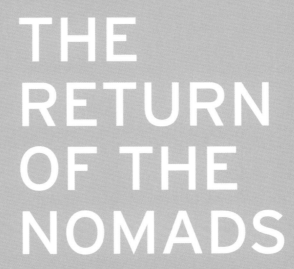

# THE RETURN OF THE NOMADS

The nomadic is both the oldest and the youngest form of existence. It means being on the move. At one time, it was about finding pastures to graze and animals to hunt; roaming was a survival necessity. It shaped existence. Yet now we are nomadic but for more complex reasons.

Everything in **this emerging world is about mobility and movement**, virtually and physically. People move, both rich and poor; ideas, philosophies and ideologies move, the good and the bad; goods move, the shoddy and the sublime; and the displaced move in ever greater numbers. More people for more reasons than before are criss-crossing the globe, from one city to the next in search of better work or life, the excitement of another place, or with no option but to flee from violence, or just to visit friends and relatives or to be tourists. Precise overall figures are notoriously difficult to come by, though we now know that the scope and scale is vast.

The nomadic life and worldview has re-emerged with relentless force. The power of finance capital to shake off its shackles and freely roam the world has intensified its vigour as turbo-capitalism runs its course. It weaves the globe tightly into its net, pervading every aspect of our lives. Yet there equally compelling and powerful other reasons for this restlessness – to feel alive, to explore, to learn and to find meaning.

'A city is more than a place in space, it is a drama in time'. So wrote the polymath Patrick Geddes and it is never more true than today. We are in the **midst of redesigning the world and all its systems** as we witness and adapt to this mass movement of people, products, pollution, pathogens, factories and frenzied finance, ideas and identities in history. Vast flows make the new norm nomadic. Yet there is a yearning for belonging, distinctiveness and identity as the 'anytime, anyplace, anywhere' phenomenon – enabled by digitization – is changing how we interact with space, place and time. So balancing common values of civility and collective involvement with the uncertainties the nomadic world evokes will be a defining issue of the current age.

**Old certainties are crumbling** and systems are breaking at escalating speed. Apprehension is in the air as we seek to invent a different kind of city. Periods of history involving mass transformation can produce confusion: a sense of liberation combined with a feeling of being swept along by events. It takes a while for new ethical stances to take root or to establish a coherent world view that makes the most of our increasingly nomadic world.

Taking an eagle eye view of change-making projects across the world you detect an eager longing. It is bursting out for this 'Other City' where the dictates of finance are curtailed; one that resolutely, yet with imagination and verve, addresses the faultlines and dilemmas of urban change and seeks to **bend the market to a bigger picture and more ethical purposes**. This is a city that: contains the ever-widening gap between haves and have nots; that prefers to open out to the world rather than closing in; that sees the opportunities in problems so might lead the way in creating the 4th clean, lean, green industrial revolution; and that has the courage to deal with the creeping corruption and criminality that pervades so much of public life and erodes the civic fabric.

This is perhaps the Civic City where togetherness in difference meet and mix well. It tries to find a pathway through the major faultlines, dilemmas and potentials of our time – shared lives, inequality, environmental distress, urban vitality, the desire for involvement and engagement and most importantly, at a personal level, the longing for meaning and a sense of wholeness. So, this is a place where we reinvent anchorage, an urban commons, connection, possibility and inspiration. The restlessness and craving for mindfulness that we find are merely symptoms of a larger wave. When everything moves we hanker after stillness.

Simple slogans encapsulate a complex world in motion. Here we witness the flux, the flow and the fluid as well as the rootless and the restless. The combined volume, velocity and variety shifts the amount of movement into a qualitative change. These moments added together flesh out an evolving world. This shifting landscape can feel confusingly foggy. Perplexed we grab onto words like complex, ambiguous, paradoxical or contradictory. We can ask has everything changed. Is it merely the form and appearance or are the tectonic plates moving?

*Thonglor, Bangkok*

Comparing the old and new nomadic world there are revealing differences. We romanticize those that handle animals, we are mistrustful of those itinerant people you might meet in a town thinking they could be vagrants or vagabonds and we are unsure about the new digital nomads. By some they are seen as hip and cool, but their adroitness in handling technology alarms others.

**The older nomadic lifestyle remains in fragments across the globe**. These nomads cling to their increasingly fragile existences, – hunter gatherers, pastoralists and peripatetic peoples. The Mongolian herder culture is dying. It halved to under 300,000 in the last decade as weather conditions changed and many were lured to the attractions of cities, as the stamina for herding livestock started to wane.

# NOMADS: OLD & NEW

The Sami peoples in the Nordic countries are under 100,000 with only half speaking the language and perhaps just 5000 still living from herding. There are around 50,000 San bushmen peoples (the hunter gatherers of Botswana and South Africa). There are a few thousand Berber nomads in the Maghreb and a sprinkling of nomadic Tuareg pastoralists spread across vast regions in Mali, Niger and Burkina Faso. There are 670,000 Aboriginal and Torres Strait Islander peoples, the longest continuous culture on earth, who always were nomadic or semi-nomadic. Now only 9% live in remote and 15% very remote often sad settlements. The well-documented discrimination and injustices against them through time have etched themselves into their psyches.[1]

In India, there may be one million peripatetic or itinerant people whose lifestyles are under severe threat through modern life. They are or were the fortune tellers, conjurers, jugglers, tattooists, drama troupes, minstrels, dancers and story tellers. Here too are the spiritual nomads, with Buddha as a prime example, or the Sadhus (and Zen monks in Japan), ascetic monks who have renounced worldly life. There are believed to be four or five million. They search for insight and teach those to those they meet often by their mere presence. The spiritual nomad, poor materially, yet rich in spirit and mentally, seeks greater understanding of the world.

There are perhaps 20 million people of Roma or gypsy[2] descent spread across the globe of which 10-12 million are in Europe. They originated from the Dalits or low caste untouchables in Northern India and reached the Balkans in the 12th century, and today they represent around 9%

of that population. Traditionally they were itinerant craftsmen who repaired pots and pans or did general metalwork or basket making and horse trading and – especially – they performed music. In Europe they are linked with poverty, crime and anti-social behaviour and so suffer discrimination.

The Irish travellers suffer similar prejudice and are a small sub-group of itinerant people, sometimes known as tinkers or knackers. There are perhaps 35,000 in Ireland and 15,000 in the rest of Britain. Some groups moved to the USA where an estimated 20,000 now live. They survive from breeding dogs, especially greyhounds and lurchers, and horses, and they also engage in casual labour, selling scrap or traditional activities like metalwork.

The journeyman (Geselle) has been prevalent since Medieval Europe, especially in Germany, and was an important step in developing from apprentice to master craftsman. Moving from town to town, they gained experience of different workshops. A small minority of carpenters in Germany today have still kept up this tradition. The institution is seen in a positive light, and the concept has spread from crafts to other occupations, including priests who set out on an extended journey to do research in monastery libraries across Europe. The travellers in the Grand Tour of the nineteenth century had a similar drive to better oneself.

A more recent phenomenon of the 1980s and 1990s is that of the new age travellers, hippies who moved between music festivals and fairs in lorries, vans or caravans converted into homes, and some still exist today. Many do seasonal or temporary work on farms, building sites or factories, pubs or they have stalls at car boot sales. Many of these will have been inspired by books such as Jack Kerouac's cult classic On the Road.

This movement dynamic has even triggered an academic discipline under the awkward name 'mobilities'. The publication of John Urry's Sociology Beyond Cities: Mobilities for the Twenty-First Century in 2000 was key as was his follow up work, such as cofounding the journal Mobilities in 2006. He advocated for and developed a "mobilities paradigm" for the social sciences arguing that the traditional study of society was outmoded in an increasingly borderless world. Perhaps these scholars themselves are in motion as they do their research.

Itinerancy or **moving around and roving makes the settled uncomfortable**, it poses a threat to their society, an implied challenge to and criticism of their values. This lifestyle, like that of circus people even today, has always been a source of suspicion to sedentary people. So would that also apply to the new nomads, the 'global nomads', 'digital nomads', 'existential migrants', 'mobos' or 'mobile bohemians'? The answer is yes and no.

Nomad websites and services are proliferating, such as Nomad Notes, Nomad Capitalist, Nomad Matt, Fox Nomad, Corporate Nomad, Nomad Travel, and the Grey Nomad[3] (for elderly retired people who spend time travelling in a mobile home). Many more without the word nomad in the title include Unsettled[4], a good Medellin start-up in Colombia, and exilelifestyle.com or travelsofadam.com/ whose strapline reads: 'The coolest cultural things to do around the world — and hey it's a (gay) blog'. Many of these references will be out of date by the time you read this as this is a fast changing sector.

Perhaps the most important is DNX[5], the Digital Nomad Exchange set up by Germans Marcus Meurer and Felicia Hargarten. Now a global movement it connects and supports digital nomads with events, boot camps and online services all over the world. DNX's says:

# NOMAD LIFESTYLES

'Shaping the future of work, meeting other cultures and making the world a better place is our biggest passion. We change lives with DNX ... and our vision is that more and more people work location independent, live their true purpose and are free and self-determined. ... we enable you to work from anywhere and regain the power to decide on your jobs, your time, and your life. ... DNX is the #1 event for location independent online entrepreneurs & freelancers.'

The annual Berlin summit is a significant feature of the nomad calendar. For instance at their 2015 summit @levelsio, which is the moniker for Nomadist founder Pieter Levels, who said: 'There will be 1 billion digital nomads by 2035'.[6] Their summits have also been held in fashionable cities like Lisbon, Buenos Aires and Bangkok.

Another contemporary site is www.goingmobo.com: 'The new mobile lifestyle, where an augmented world is available from your mobile device.'[7] One of best of the numerous blogs about nomadic experience is titled Become Nomad: Long term Travel & the Digital Lifestyle[8] where the founder says:

'My name is Eli. I have been a nomad since 2010, constantly changing countries and cities. Until 2010, I was in a stable relationship, maintained a cat, was a rising star in an accounting firm. Since then, everything changed. I move constantly, and have lived in more than 30 countries, while traveling to 60 more. I wasn't too happy that every day of my life seemed like the day before ...  the nomadic lifestyle fits my ideology based on the following pillars: nothing is mine, everything is temporal, life is right now, and it is not serious.'

The extensive website gives advice on everything a modern nomad might need with links to the growing nomad communities and hubs across the world. It describes well the many types of nomads, why they become nomads and the differing ways in which they survive. They all move around, enjoy speedy internet connectivity, an extensive café culture and co-working spaces. The nine-to-five schedule does not exist, weekdays and weekends merge into one and **your laptop is your ever present friend**.

There are various contemporary nomad types. The classic Digital Nomad is dependent on digital tools to make ends meet while travelling and earning money is detached from where you live. They may work for clients or be trying to start up their own business. Remote Work Nomads are employed by corporations and have a secure job, but with an agreement to work remotely either on the move or from home, essentially tele-commuting. This is a win-win situation. The company saves costs and you avoid routine office life. There is an increasing cross-generational number of well educated, influential and affluent professionals in this group, old and young alike. These are sometimes referred to as 'Time Out Nomads' – and are often people that a company values strongly. As the world has a talent crisis, companies are more willing to allow high calibre people to set their own terms and receive special dispensations. This can mean working in intense blocks of time and then taking periods out. Then Half And Half Nomads operate according to longer work/travel cycles as they might have a seasonal job, such as being a tourist guide. This lifestyle makes it easier to travel without needing additional income and only occasional work, say in a bar, is required.

The Offline Nomad is akin to, yet a modern version, of the traditional traveller who mended pots and pans. This is someone who can travel from place to place, doing a job that sustains their lifestyle, perhaps an experienced cook, artisan or barista. Rather than work for a company in the high income world, they are often content with the low wages that are linked to local conditions. They may not have a legal work permit so there is insecurity but nevertheless they are more immersed in the local community.

Rich Nomads are people who have made or inherited money. Travelling from place to place without needing to work can be enriching, yet equally dispiriting as work often provides a purpose in life. They are thus sometimes also Quest Nomads, people searching for meaning in their life. Like others, who perhaps live on more meagre resources, they move around to learn about themselves in the hope too that **'elsewhere helps you find somewhere'**, as being away from familiar surroundings can create the conditions for clarity. This is true too for the wandering tribe of Backpacker Nomads, mostly young and part of the year-out or gap year phenomenon. This is a time-dated lifestyle and more like an extended cheap holiday, but it relies on the same digital resources as those pursuing a nomadic life as an older adult.

Old-fashioned house-sitting is also a nomadic form, force-fed and enabled by platforms such as TrustedHomeSitters and HelpX. The volunteer looks after someone's home while they are on vacation and in return they get accommodation and food. You save money but do not earn any, but also not need a special work visa. You also lose an element of flexibility given the responsibilities involved.

**Nomadism is becoming more organized and perhaps losing its edge**, as entities like Hackers Paradise[9] or Remote Year[10] create extended trips for would-be nomads. They might be software developers, designers, advertising people or perhaps translators. 'Remotes' are vetted before they can join and the 50-80 who are accepted pay around $30,000 (around €25,000) for the year. There is a mix between 'remotes' working for mainstream corporations and freelancers. They live and work in a different city around the globe each month including costs of work space, private rooms, transportation and even attending events like Burning Man in the US. Remote Year gives guidance and resources to get employers on board with remote work arrangements.

Mobile workers come in many forms, with many who do not consider themselves to be nomads living a semi-nomadic life. The catch-all phrase 'peripatetic worker' encapsulates those who work in multiple locations away from a normal work base or indeed without a fixed work base. Some sales people are constantly on the move. Others may be 'fly-in, fly-out' workers on oil rigs, in remote mining areas or construction sites or simply people who cannot find work near home be they an electrician, a carpenter or a music teacher.

Most **digitally-driven nomads share characteristics and needs**. Primarily they seek to balance personal and professional growth. Access rather than ownership is key so therefore the sharing economy is a boon. Work and leisure are blurred. To have a viable lifestyle they need to be seamlessly connected and not lose contact with friends, family and colleagues. They need access to remote collaboration tools such as those from the ubiquitous *Dropbox, Slack, Mezzanine or Zapier* as well as apps that help both work and private life such as *Eatwith, Meetup, ShowAround, Internations'* ('the community for expatriates and global minds'), *SpeedSmart* (assesses internet speeds), *Payoneer* (a payment system), *Upwork* (for bidding for jobs online), *StartupBlink Coworking* (which lists nearly 1,000 co-working spaces around the world) or Teleport (a platform to find the best places to live and work). Plus there are sites for every kind of accommodation level from the cheapest dorms to hostels, couch-surfing and posh places to stay.

They want agile services to deal with financial, administrative and logistical process, such as insurance with WorldNomad. They want the equivalent amenities they had at home and easily. This means sharing from cars, to offices, meeting rooms to accommodation. It might mean having membership access to global co-working spaces and indeed some, like Soho House or Dynamite Circle, are closed member communities who want to encourage exclusivity with membership by application only. The latter also created Tropical MBA. Openness is increasingly breeding a counter-reaction of exclusivity, although co-working is still key and it results in meeting people in a new place. The mainstream has caught onto this group of untethered creatives (are they really all creative?), as brands see them as early adopters and pioneers who are pre-figuring strong aspects of the future.

Finally, the Internet as the largest library in the world provides other untold blog resources, such as 'How to Escape the 9-5 Box and Never Look Back' or 'My life as a 60 year old digital nomad'. Become Nomad lists their favourite blogs as including: Wandering Earl; Making it Everywhere; NeverEndingVoyage; Adventurous Kate;Maverick Traveller; Spartan Traveller; Almost Fearless and two techie blogs Level.Io and Too Many Adapters. Even the names of the blogs conjure up the lifestyles they are talking about. And since everything moves and changes quickly, most of these apps, blogs and services will have changed by the time you read this.

In essence these resources are saying: '**Wherever life takes you, we make you feel at home**'. Co-working spaces are a good starting place to interact with new people. The more ambitious and well-known nomads like Faris and Rosie Yakob have newsletters to keep in touch (exaggeratedly they say: 'Strands of Stolen Genius is our weekly newsletter, where we send you weekly awesomeness'). They also share their schedule on a public Google Calendar. Or Floyd Hayes, who wrote '52 Offices: The Adventures of a 21st Century Nomad' and described the best places in New York for an outdoor office, such as Pratt Sculpture Garden in Brooklyn, Kremville Cemetery, or Times Square.

Nomads need to be tech savvy and many earn their living writing about travel or lifestyle or are all-purpose journalists. Others teach or develop software, do graphic design, help in advertising campaigns or design websites or do translations or professional coaching — all jobs where you do not need a fixed location. Learning the local language is important and many nomads do not.

There are psychological impacts of nomadism, one is exhaustion arising from instability. One issue is building and maintaining meaningful relationships. Crucially **what happens to their lifestyle when they have children and get old?** Can it be maintained? Are job opportunities curtailed?

Expats — a contraction of expatriates — are people who have left their place of birth to live somewhere else. They include some of the nomads already discussed but with the assumption that they will return home at some point. Yet increasingly people find that 'elsewhere' is better than their country of origin and so they stay. People become expats for differing reasons - work, love or the place itself and the group is not homogenous as their motivations and their relationships to the host countries vary enormously. The inference is that someone is moving out of free choice so avoiding the negative connotation of being defined as a migrant (someone seen as not free in their choice). There is often little solidarity between expats and migrants, as if the former has more right to move.

# EXPATS & ATTACHMENT

**Expats fall along a spectrum according to their level of integration** and a primary distinction is whether a person is still working or retired. We can characterize differing types of behaviours. In the European Union (EU) many people from the North want to move South. The weather is better and the cost of living cheaper so even people with a small pension can afford to move and even buy an apartment. The cliché here is of the retired Brit moving to the Costa del Sol in Spain who does not speak a word of Spanish and does not intend to. They want their beer and fish and chips and only communicate with others like them. They contribute nothing to the host environment – they take rather than give. They are not connecting, but can be enjoying themselves. **They are borrowing the landscape** and, as there are no visa problems, moving in and out for longer or shorter periods of time is possible. Another grouping of similarly retired people, perhaps more educated, differs slightly. They speak a good modicum of the foreign language and so can communicate with locals and do so. They engage with the local culture and to some extent integrate into their local community, but are not befriending the social equivalents they might have had at home. If they are a professional, such as a doctor or accountant, their friends and social life will be predominantly with expats rather than the foreign doctor. They huddle together with the like-minded.

A third grouping are people who want to intensively engage with the host culture, they speak the language well and specifically search out equivalents, say Spaniards, to build their social context. This enriches their life. They make their life in the host country with reasons vary

*Alte Munze, Berlin*

from falling in love with the place or with a local. They might have landed there initially on an extended holiday or not liked their land of origin, as did many hippies, who arrived from Europe or North America in Asia and never left. They make their life in the new place often teaching or translating and English here is a considerable advantage. From that other consequences follow. They move on from their typical arrival job and may start their own business where their foreign background becomes an advantage. If they stay they become long-term residents and they may even have children. They are really bi-cultural. Indeed their children may, say, be more Thai or Chinese than English or German. These kids are called Third Culture Kids, brought up in a culture other than that of their parents. When they grow up, the best of them have a wonderful capacity to move from culture to culture and **to be citizens of everywhere and nowhere**, but others can feel lost and unsure about their identity and who they are.

The final stage is to move from being an expat to becoming a citizen. Other variations include economic expats/migrants who as individuals commit themselves to a time-dated or time-negotiable contract. Here the expanding Middle East is becoming a special lure. They need skilled people and income is mostly tax free so it is possible to save money - perhaps to get onto the property ladder at home. Then there are the corporate employees of global companies, who are posted abroad. These postings are steps in a career ladder, although some may then fall for the country. Corporate nomads mostly use chain hotels, global food chains; they tend to hanker after the familiar so their travelling lifestyle is duller than it seems. Perhaps a drink in a faceless hotel bar and dinner at an upscale chain restaurant with a menu that offers few surprises. These latter groupings tend to live in enclaves, some of which are gated communities, and so have little direct contact with the host community. They lead parallel lives. Finally, there is the classic nomad - the diplomat who is often involved with the established institutions in the country of his posting.

Home Nomads are also a category. These are people able to establish a meaningful and self-aware life without traveling; they are nomadic in their mind. Their curiosity helps them to draw on the advantages of being stimulated and feeling alive that nomads receive from moving around. They make every day at home interesting.

*Creative industry centre, Rio de Janeiro*

Researching and studying abroad is a large source of movement and migration and a catalyst for understanding the 'Other'. It is big business and it is growing fast and an unintended consequence is falling in love, since you are meeting a network, doing shared activities with a good amount of free time.

The EU sponsored Erasmus educational exchange programme, the world's largest, is in its 30th year as of 2017. In that time, it has helped nearly four million students and 500,000 academic and administrative staff to teach and learn new practices abroad and its budget is increasing by 19% to €2.1 billion.

# RESEARCHERS & SCHOLARS

The *Erasmus Impact Study* (2014) interviewed more than 88,000 students, teachers and businesses, and found that foreign exchange students were far more likely to have transnational relationships. A third of ex-Erasmus students had a partner of a different nationality, compared with 13 per cent of students who stayed at home. More than a quarter meet their long-term partner while studying abroad. More than one million babies, the study suggests, have been produced as a result. In 2011, the famed novelist Umberto Eco noted the romantic potential of Erasmus:

'The university exchange programme Erasmus is barely mentioned in the business sections of newspapers, yet Erasmus has created the first generation of young Europeans ... I call it a sexual revolution: a young Catalan man meets a Flemish girl – they fall in love, they get married and they become European, as do their children. The Erasmus idea should be compulsory – not just for students, but also for taxi drivers, plumbers and other workers. By this, I mean they need to spend time in other countries within the European Union; they should integrate.'

It leads to other cross-fertilizations. Over half of Dutch research papers are collaborative international research (53%; and Canadian, German, Australian and British are almost half with the US at 30.3% as of OECD statistics in 2015. International co-authorship performs better in terms of their citation impact.

*London Imperial College graduation*

*Aula Technical University, Vienna*

The OECD report 'Education at a Glance'[11] shows the dramatic increase that reflects the speed of globalisation: 1.3 million in 1990, rising to 2.1 million in 2000; 5 million in 2014 and an estimated 8 million in 2025. That is a jump of 380% in 25 years. Going abroad for research or study was once only available for the elite, it is now open to the burgeoning middle classes

40% of international students go to English speaking countries with nearly 20% going to the States and 10% to Britain and the rest to Australasia and Canada. France with just over 5% and Germany just below follow and now Japan and China are on the rise. The latter aims to host 500,000 students by 2020, with large contingents coming from South Korea or Indonesia, who realize that China's economic power increasingly requires more Chinese speakers. Japan, India and Malaysia are equally ambitious as more Asian universities move up the global rankings. Yet China, India, and South Korea combined with 25% still represent the world's leading sources of international students. One in six is from China and Asia accounts for 53% of all students as of 2015.[12]

It has personal, cultural and economic impacts. The net value to the US economy of the more than 1 million international students is estimated a $32.8 billion supporting 400,000 jobs[13]. In Britain the export value of the 440,000 foreign students was £10.8/$14 billion[14] and add to this overall direct and indirect expenditure it comes to £25.8 billion and supports 206,000 jobs In Australia it is the third largest export industry after iron and coal with $US15.9 and supporting 130,000 jobs. One in every six students in Britain is from abroad. In the US it is one in every 25.

The English speaking world has a pre-dominant position so its attributes, attitudes and worldviews have a cultural impact on researchers, scholars or students. It reinforces the position of English as a linqua franca as returnees are then more globally fluent, apart from their personal growth, the help in launching a career, and lets remember falling in love.

Taken together we see different degrees of influence and counter-influence. Depending on where along the spectrum of integration people fall, these nomads are shifting their cultural base and self-identification. In a more permeable world a growing phenomenon is that more people for more reasons relate to more places and sources of identity. They have multiple attachments. They might live in a place short term, they might visit regularly and they might decide that certain places are part of their identity even though they are rarely there. This might be because their parents were born there (thus Berlin for me is special), or it could be that they had a love affair or a study period or work experience.

# SENSES OF THE SELF

Who are these people then, how do we define them? They are more than occasional visitors, so are they tourists, guests, semi-residents, citizens? The distinction between the engaged outsider and the insider is changing and blurring. **Who is more of a citizen, the committed outsider or the unconcerned insider?** Who has more rights to call themselves a citizen? To be a citizen implies being a member of a community and carries the right to participation, it implies too some responsibilities and duties. What if a resident does not care?

So many pre-conceptions about who we are have been thrown up in the air due to the astonishing technical advances that enable us to move and be mobile in every sense. These foster a more nomadic life which allows us to affiliate and identify ourselves in multiple ways, with some connections stronger and others weaker. Nevertheless, we now define and identify ourselves more by our embedded networks rather than classic bonds of a fixed geography. This evolving culture is turbo-charged by internet driven possibilities yet it is still cradled within our deeper-seated cultural backgrounds and the prejudices and interests we bring with us. People look for and choose the like-minded or the useful, forming networks of connection with relative freedom, or they search for new ones that strengthen their interests.

Who am I, we can ask, and where do I belong, who do I identify with? Myself, my friends, my family, my relations, my interests and enthusiasms, my work, my network and connections? Or is it a people, a bond of blood, a race, a colour or a place or places? Perhaps it is just pick-and-choose or mix-and-match that fits so well the culture of individualism and autonomy. Everyone, even if they pretend not to, has

*Video shop, Georgetown, Penang*

many affiliations and identities, they have a string of connections or places of deeper significance. They cannot be easily fragmented and siloed into tidy bits, it all connects. Take myself for example - I am a mostly a mix of German and British with a dash of Italian influences. Predominantly German heritage, but I have mostly lived in Britain. Seeped in the German mindset and manner of thinking, it is not whether I like Germans or not but what they mean for me. Or as described in one of the blogs: 'I am the definition of cultural confusion, I'm a black kid raised in a primarily Euro-American world. I have no idea what's goin' on when i go to the ghetto!'

The challenge is to feel some sense of coherence about the elements that make us what we are. All this shifts dramatically the idea of community or my community. There is always a me and an us or a we. To affiliate with others is a biological need as we can accomplish things together we can never do on our own. Self-interest and collective interest become aligned in cooperation between humans and partly has enabled the species to become so advanced. Yet cooperation is also the central dilemma of human existence as the 'the commons' is always in danger of crumbling. We find it easier to cooperate within as distinct from between groups. Thus, the intercultural city is so difficult to create.

Tribal instincts of the in-group and out-group remain forceful. Strangers seem strange. We need to feel comfortable to relax into the strange, to absorb its differences to let it become part of us and so we have built ethics and moralities to hold differences together. Yet this can be tough.

Community is place specific and is a heavy word laden with too much meaning and expectation and the word is used too easily. The **seedbed of community springs from the soil of a myriad of small encounters**. Our social compost grows from these cells of, often banal, interaction; a flicker of recognition, a brief exchange, a helping hand, doing a favour, borrowing a pint of milk, identifying a common problem or interest. Of course this is mixed with endless non-encounters. Often too it is forced togetherness where there is less choice, being at school, parents watching their children play, getting on at work, visiting the dentist and sharing a joint concern - a piercing toothache.

We have not yet absorbed fully the cultural implications of this dynamic which encapsulates delights, dilemmas and dangers. A core question then for citizens and cities today is: how do we find our sense of self, belonging and meaning in place, in neighbourhoods, in cities? Does belonging merely float across the horizon? Settling here for a moment and then somewhere else in a faraway place? Has physical place and common affinity become detached from each other as we increasingly communicate across the electronic waves? Yes and no. It is simply that place functions differently. In some sense, we are closer to each other and in others we are becoming fragmented and split apart.

The Law Courts

Citizenship is the most powerful and cherished marker of identity. Now it can be bought and sold. Think of the Rio Olympics. 172 table tennis players participated and at least 44 were born on the Chinese mainland, but only six represented China, the rest played for 21 other countries.[15] Bahrain's nine-person athletics team had no Bahrainis and the Qatari handball team had no Qataris – instead between them they had a motley crew of new citizens from Kenya, Ethiopia, Somalia, Egypt and Nigeria. Indeed, Rose Chelimo won for Bahrain the women's marathon gold at the 2017 athletics world championships - she is Kenyan. An even more extreme case was Aaron Cook, the snubbed British taekwondo star who became a citizen of Moldovia, the impoverished ex-Soviet state, in order to be allowed to compete.

# CITIZENSHIP: BOUGHT & SOLD

Athletes on the move, yes, but the global rich are on the move on a mass migration scale. "There is a sudden awakening among the wealthy that they're no longer bound to a certain country,"[16] They are benefitting from this booming $2billion plus global industry to acquire citizenship or residency. They have used their financial and political clout and lobbying strength to create these possibilities.

They look for safety, an escape from arbitrary rule, to avoid political uncertainty, a rule based governance system, less corruption (even if they are themselves shady) as those moving from China, Russia, India and Turkey attest. Increasingly they want more than an island idyll with not much to do and the lowest possible taxes, although low taxation remains a competitive tool. Lifestyle is key together with the ability to run a business unhindered, and access to culture, gastronomy and high-status education. Globally-oriented cities provide this, such as London, New York, Miami or on a smaller scale Nice or Geneva.

In 2016 82,000 high-net-worth individuals (those with liquid assets worth over USD $1 million equivalent  left their home countries, up from 64,000 in 2015. Australia was the prime destination for 11,000 millionaires followed by the US and Canada with 10,000. They are leaving places like China (9,000), Brazil (8,000 - a sharp rise), India (6,000), Turkey (6,000 - a vast increase) and Russia (2,000 - and the many more who left in previous years). Add the millionaires who left in the previous decade this becomes half a million[17]. When former French President Hollande proposed 75% taxes on the wealthy it threatened a stampede out of France.

Fear of the apocalypse, civilization cracking up, is a recent phenomenon causing migratory flows, and New Zealand is the survivalist's destination of choice. It is now taking root in Silicon Valley amongst the tech entrepreneurs and hedge fund managers who want to escape from the volatile world of social unrest exacerbated by toxic divisions, climate change and unpredictability. They are hedging too against the collapse of capitalism and Paypal's co-founder Peter Thiel set the trend. He was secretly granted New Zealand citizenship without formalities with 92 others[18]. Others are buying underground bunkers, isolated islands or anywhere out of sight.

Many and especially **the ultra-rich** have three or four homes and so are rarely anchored in place. Always on the move their rootlessness is dangerous as they rarely build or give back to community **and their empty houses deaden neighbourhoods** with only maids and housekeepers there keeping guard.

Citizenship, once the most valued symbol of identity and primary way of governing populations, is now up for grabs. This is part of the growing investment migration movement. There are lists of 'Where is the cheapest place to buy citizenship or permanent residency?' with the usual suspects from the Caribbean islands at the forefront followed by places like Malta and Cyprus. For even as little as $100,000 you can become a citizen of the Dominican Republic. Most European countries have schemes for non-Europeans where with an investment of between €250,000 and €2 million you by-pass the usual requirements. Often you do not even have to reside for a minimum number of days per year and you gain access to all of the European Union. Countries now compete not only for international talent, but for investors, entrepreneurs, high net worth individuals and even athletes.

Obtaining temporary, flexible, dual or even triple citizenship is now part of planning for wealthy individuals and families. It makes economic sense to be able to operate across multiple territories, to provide security and a bolt hole - a prize migrants or refugees cannot achieve. This mobile citizenship challenges traditional concepts of immigration, citizenship and statehood.[19]

These processes reveal the agility of governments in responding to and resolving a deep contradictory tension. **Global capital accumulation demands open borders**, relatively free movement of goods, services and skilled people across borders. The nation-state and its security systems by contrast were set up and based on fixed borders and populations.

Citizenship confers rights and obligations and in turn engenders commitment and motivation to give back to a place. With national citizenship now malleable it is time to consider how cities with their influx of ex-pats, long term residents or migrants can confer versions of urban citizenship or at least local voting rights, especially since many pay taxes. This would engage them with the fate of the place they live. Both expanding and shrinking cities would benefit. These governance problems will not go away but will only grow.

### VISA POWER

The reasons for buying citizenship are clear especially when you consider how mobile your passport allows you to be. Both the Henley & Partners Visa Restrictions Index[20] and Global Passport Power (GPP) list[21] rank countries by their 'visa free score'. Both advise you on how to improve your 'global mobility score', but it costs. Their numbers differ but they agree on the top groupings with citizens of Germany and the Nordic countries like Sweden or Finland leading the charge. Henley suggests they can go to 175 plus countries out of a possible 218. They are followed closely by those of other West European countries like Italy, France or Spain and then the USA and Britain. South Korea, Japan, Canada and Australasia also have good 'visa free' scores. Britain, until recently, topped the list, but has just slipped down by closing itself in. Brexit with its restrictions on immigration will not help since visa freedom often depends on reciprocity.

The rising stars are places like Peru, the Marshall & Solomon Islands, Kiribati, Vanuatu and Micronesia, who are moving up the echelons. Others rising as their politics become more stable are Chile and even Colombia.

If you want to be a nomad it is better not to be African even if you are accomplished, talented and educated. An African needs to apply for a visa for 100 more countries than a German, and a Russian also has 70 less visa-free countries. Similarly difficult are the ex-Soviet republics like Kazakhstan or Azerbaijan as well as China.

It is extremely difficult to be mobile if you are from the bottom five: Somalia, Syria, Pakistan, Iraq and Afghanistan, with visa-free access to fewer than 30 countries. And North Korea is completely off the scale.

**Global Passport Power tells the story of mobility potential** in one revealing shaded map of the world. Africa is dark as are parts of the Middle East and Asia. So being a nomad mostly means being white and from a developed country. Yet people from some of the countries and places you visit (Thailand, Indonesia, places like Chiang Mai, Bangkok and Bali) cannot enter yours. They need visas for 100 countries more than the top passport power grouping.

*Favela, Rio de Janeiro*

The places the mobile elite cluster in – across the spectrum from the alternative life-stylers, to the hippie-ish, to the high calibre professionals and to the rich – are quite similar. **The hipster listing of most popular nomad cities shifts with fashion** and depends on the criteria used, although the global hubs like New York or London have remained popular through time, but there are rising stars of which Berlin is the most prominent as is Miami. The Nomadlist[22] , a community of around 10,000 people with access to 400,000 more, is a curated list of current trending digital nomad hubs. It assesses places according to any combination of criteria, such as: 'most popular now' or 'most popular', 'quality of life', 'internet speed', 'women's safety', 'cost of living', 'happiness', 'nightlife', 'education', 'cost of Airbnb'. Endlessly entertaining interesting conclusions emerge by playing around with the criteria and the continents.

# NOMAD HUBS & HOTSPOTS

The 'most popular now' (and this might be different when you read this) is Berlin by far, followed by London, New York, Lisbon, Chiang Mai, Budapest, San Francisco, Amsterdam, Los Angeles and upcoming too are Yangon and Adelaide. And the 'most popular' over the longer time has been Bangkok followed by those mentioned and also Paris, Barcelona or Ubud, Bali. Unsurprisingly the least popular places in the world are Pyongyang in North Korea and Kabul in Afghanistan.

Or take 'quality of life' as the yardstick. in this respect, Groningen, Eindhoven and Copenhagen come on top and indeed the Nordic cities all score highly on most criteria such as internet speed. The only thing that lets them down is the cost of living and weather. Many Chinese or Pakistani cities do badly as they do on places to work, especially co-working spaces. The dreamy Male in the Maldives does not do well either. North American hubs from Portland to Santa Monica do well on flexible workspaces. Nightlife's top score goes to Berlin and then some South Korean cities as well. Continental comparisons are instructive such as between the Middle East and South America. The top 13 places for available workplaces are in South America before Beirut appears in position 14. Yet overall Tel Aviv scores highly. Looking at South America the astonishing turnaround of Medellin from murder capital of the world to hipster hub is noteworthy as well as how currently Panama's high internet speeds makes it attractive. Other continental favourites

*Seattle Public Library*

are: New York, San Francisco, Los Angeles, Vancouver, Seattle, Bangkok, Chiang Mai, Kuala Lumpur, Singapore and Hong Kong in Asia and Cape Town, Casablanca, Johannesburg and Dar es Salaam in Africa.

Overheard conversations or chat room comments reflect well the irritating restlessness and attempts to always be where the action is. In that way, the nomads homogenize and bring diversity in equal measure. They flatten language as English takes over, they flatten distinctions as everywhere becomes a hip version of the same: 'Anyone have tips for nice cafés to work out around Prenzlauer, Berlin. I've done Oberholz and thought of trying something new …'. 'Try Spreegold at Schönhauser Allee. After 1hour they charge for the wifi (1eur/h) but I think that's a fair deal.' Or  'I worked out mostly out of Betahaus last time I was in Berlin, but I should check out Neukölln more'. The Oberholz café is a Berlin icon and Neukölln a new upcoming and gentrifying, working class area.

 'Jheeze didn't realise there were that many people into the nomad thing hanging out in Lisbon … I'm going crazy counting down the days until I move there'. Or 'does someone have the details for the meetup? I just arrived and would love to attend!'.

The chat on Become Nomad says:

'Berlin is the hipster digital nomad capital of the world! If you're on a mission to find the perfect combination of a hipster crowd, full of artists, events, good value for money, a strong local start-up ecosystem, Berlin is your place … a word of warning, since it's at the top of everyone's list of trending locations, the city is changing rapidly. Berlin is becoming more expensive and trendy by the minute. As a result, some local pubs and cafes are closing down to make room for chain stores and upscale establishments. So it's better to get there sooner, rather than later.'

This is the gentrification dilemma in that it is, in part, caused by the nomads themselves.

'Budapest is gaining popularity for digital nomads, by the minute. It's a little bit cheaper than Prague, less crowded and touristic'. And 'Barcelona is popular with more affluent nomads.'

'When historians investigate this phenomenon, Chiang Mai will be regarded as the place that launched a global trend. It's a good place to start your nomadic journey ... it has an amazing digital nomad community. You couldn't throw a stone there, without hitting a laptop or an aspiring digital nomad.' 'The problem with Bali is that tourists pack it all year-round and it has unstable Internet.'

'Digital nomads have marked Medellin as a top destination, you will find nomadic friends there quite fast. Colombia offers great value for money and arguably the nicest people on the planet. Crime, terrorism, and drug trafficking are not as big of a problem as it used to be'. 'Buenos Aires is hard to resist with its mix of South American fun with European style'. 'The Chiang Mai of Latin America is Playa del Carmen in Mexico'. 'If you have something major going on or have aspirations to take over the world or are trying to go big, do Hong Kong, Singapore, Munich or London'. And amusingly 'Hi, any digital nomads in Morocco, we're thinking of spending some time digital nomading in Fes later this year.' 'Nope until now we didn't find any digital nomads around here." But then 'I've only stopped through briefly, it seems fairly undeveloped for nomads... The camel burgers at Café Clock are fab... the only really cosmopolitan hangout I came across, but it attracts a few too many tourists'.[23] Hello anyone in Quito, Taipei, Osaka, Accra, Istanbul?

*Socializing in Hamburg*

Building site, Dubai

# THE GREAT MIGRATION

Everything speaks of a world in motion, of migratory patterns triggered by need, stress, conflict, desire or to safeguard your money. Driven by globalization, **migratory tides are a complex web of in- and out-flows** which extend well beyond just those the digital nomads. There is churn and there are returners. The majority of migrants cross borders in search of better economic and social opportunities. Some are well-educated and others are not and note the subtle discriminations of language we use. We tend to call the professionals expats, especially if they are white, and it has a friendly ring to it as if they were 'one of us'. Others less well-off or with a different hue generally we call migrants. There is a tone here of mistrust.

The word migrant too often conjures up negative reactions, such as 'good for nothing', 'wanting to take my job', 'not educated', 'potentially criminal'. In fact, as with any large grouping of people there is great diversity and far more light than shade. My colleague Phil Wood and I explored this in depth resulting in *The Intercultural City: Planning for Diversity Advantage*, a programme subsequently taken up by the Council of Europe.[24] [25] Many migrants are well-educated, alert to the changing world, use mobile technologies with great facility and, like most of us, are only striving for a better life and wanting to contribute to their host communities. Indeed, the consensus is that they make a positive economic contribution.[26] The cultural issues of mutual understanding cause most frictions, issues such as different outlooks on life, differing behaviours towards women, different faiths.

*Relief at finishing work at building site, Dubai*

Many migrant journeys to a promised land are epic. Witness the daily flow across the Mediterranean in unsafe, overloaded boats, many having made their way across the sun scorched Sahara. **Economic migrants are the fastest growing group** and this labour mobility is required to make many economies even possible (think UAE here) and in others to balance declining fertility and ageing populations.

The overall pattern is complex and a few examples suffice. Take the Middle East with its unbalanced demographics. The United Arab Emirates (UAE) has 9.2 million inhabitants of whom 1.4 million are Emiratis and 7.8 million are expatriates (or largely slave workers, if you like). Indians make up 25%, Pakistanis 12%, Bangladeshis 7% and Filipinos 5%. These migrants have few rights and live in camps, whereas the half a million Western expatriates mostly live in the boomtown luxury high rises. Then Qatar has 2.6 million inhabitants of whom foreign workers account for 88%. Indians are the largest group at 25% followed by Nepalis, 13.5%, and 11% Bangladeshis. Throughout the region the treatment of foreign workers has been heavily criticized as abusive and exploitative. On the other side, Russia really demonstrates the churn. Here more than 10 million emigrate, mostly to developed economies, and equal numbers immigrate from the even poorer former Soviet empire.

The main Asian countries are not places of immigration. Their ratio of ex-pats is below 1% in contrast to most developed countries where it is around 10%. China only gave 7,300 people permanent residence among the 850,000 foreigners living in China in 2015.[27] There are some interesting pockets of foreigners there such as the roughly 20,000 Africans living in Guangzhou in an area called Chocolate City or Little Africa, much like the Chinatowns in Lagos or Conakry. However, many of the 5 million Chinese-born people and the approximately 50 million ethnic Chinese previously living outside China have now returned. The in/outflow of Chinese students is increasing dramatically. 550,000 studied abroad in 2016 with 80% returning home. This is projected to rise to 750,000. The predominant movement and feature of Chinese migration are the 282 million rural migrants who have come into cities and now make up a third of the working population – despite having driven China's spectacular economic growth over the last 30 years, they are marginalized and discriminated against and have few rights. In 1989, there were 8.9 million internal migrants and by 1994 23 million. This is a powder keg waiting to explode.

In 2015, Japan has 2.23 million immigrants of which over 20% were South Asian women married to Japanese men and a good proportion are service workers such as maids. Officially these are not immigrants but guest workers. Problems loom for Japan with its ageing demographic and low birth rate: its population is predicted to fall from 128 to 86 million by 2060. With 8 million fewer workers there is pressure to change policy on migrants and refugees[28] , India is home to a reducing foreign population of approximately 5 million,  the vast majority coming from Asian neighbours. The distinction between desirable and undesirable immigrants in all these countries mirrors those found in immigration policies of most Western countries.

Canada with a population of 35 million prides itself as a country of migration, allowing 300,000 newcomers in 2017 of which 40,000 are refugees. Australia is similar welcoming 200,000 including 19,000 refugees. The USA gives citizenship to around one million per annum of whom about 600,000 already are in the country and changing their status. Currently there are 37 million legal and 11 million illegal immigrants in the States. It had given 100,000 refugees shelter in 2016 but that was reduced by Trump to 50,000. Most countries dovetail immigration to their economic interests prioritizing the professional competence of younger potential migrants, regardless of ethnicity.

In 2010, in the EU, around 47.3 million people, 9.4% of the total population, were born outside their resident country. 31.4 million of these were born outside and 16.0 million inside the EU. The largest numbers were found in Germany (6.4 million), France (5 million), Britain (4.7 million), and Spain (4.1 million).

With the Syrian crisis, the total number of immigrants has probably risen to 50 million as more than a million migrants and refugees crossed into Europe just in 2015. This triggered a crisis as countries tried to cope with the influx.[29] [30]

*Text: Safe passage and arrival for refugees, Berli*

اللاجئون
REFUGEES
FLÜCHTLINGE
EINE GROSSE HERAUSFORDERU

AUSSTELLUNG MIT FOTOGRAFIE
VON HERLINDE KOELBL
ERGÄNZT DURCH
„DAS ENGAGEMENT DES AUSWÄ

Wars, conflict, persecution and natural disasters are forcing more people to seek refuge and safety elsewhere. The legacy and trauma of older upheavals still linger painfully – think here of the Pakistani/Indian partition or the North/South Korean conflict

Worldwide a staggering 65.3 million people in 2015 were forced from home. 22.5 million were refugees and asylum seekers with the rest displaced people who did not cross their national boundary. 25% of all refugees came from Syria. This is the highest level ever recorded rising from 59.5 million and 51.2 million in the two years before and 37.5 million a decade ago. Half of these are children.

**There are 10 million stateless people** who have either fled from conflict, including the Rohingya from western Myanmar of whom around 350,000 live in Bangladesh, or the Kuwaiti Bedouins who never acquired citizenship on independence in 1961, or the tens of thousands of European Roma who have not registered themselves – denied a nationality they have no access to the basic rights of education and healthcare.[31]

# ESCAPE & SANCTUARY

In terms of refugee take up, particularly from the Syrian crisis, the main Asian countries do not do well. China has officially taken in 301,000 refugees, but almost all are ethnic Chinese from Vietnam. In 2016, Japan ruled out any relaxation of its strict refugee policy and it accepted only 27 of the 10,901 people who sought asylum there. India, by contrast, welcomed over 200,000 refugees mainly from Myanmar, Afghanistan and Pakistan.

Chinese political ideology does not encourage non-Chinese migrants even though the concept of ethnic diversity is officially recognized, but highlights the symbiosis of the 56 ethnic groups approved by the government. The country lacks the institutions conducive to supporting immigration on a mass scale. They justify this by quoting their non-interference in other countries' domestic affairs, combined with low public support for refugee resettlement, partly due to both faith and official population control.

However, Amnesty International created a Refugees Welcome Index and surprisingly in the survey China came top and Russia bottom on the specific question: Should your government do more to help refugees fleeing war or prosecution? The index ranks nations on a sliding scale of how willing citizens are to welcome refugees into their homes, neighbourhoods, cities, towns or villages and countries.[32]

Europe has received 11.6 million asylum applications since 1985, but 1.3 million in 2015 and that drama of refugees coming into Europe can easily let us forget that Turkey alone has nearly three million Syrian refugees, Lebanon 1.1 million and Jordan officially 657,000 (the government says the true figure is 1.3 million[33]). Leading the way globally on refugees per capita are Turkey, Lebanon, Jordan. Djibouti has large per capita numbers too with strong flows of Yemenis crossing the Red Sea to escape from war. Counterintuitively many Ethiopians are making the return journey using war torn Yemen as a base to get to Saudi Arabia despite the dangers and the tribulations they meet once they arrive. Refugee flows and the reasons for them are convoluted.[34]

The Great Migration is here to stay for decades to come. Imagine and reflect that **more than one billion people are on the move**, that is 15% of the world population not including the tourists and our day-to-day travels and commutes. 740 million of these are internal migrants (2016 and regarded as an under-estimate) and 244 million are international migrants worldwide, up from 175 million in 2000 and 154 million in 1990. Migrants account for 11% of the total population in developed regions and 1.6 in developing ones.[35]

Interestingly once people migrate they want to migrate again. Gallup estimates that 630 million adults worldwide would like to migrate permanently to another country, 22% of first-generation migrants say they would like to move, versus 14% of native-born residents, whether that means returning home or heading to another country.[36] This survey is based on a rolling average of interviews with 401,490 adults in 146 countries between 2008 and 2010. Sub Saharan Africans have the greatest desire to move - 33% native-born people as well as 34% of their migrants.

Those on the move mostly land in cities where economic opportunities lie and whose inordinate pace of growth is immensely stressful. Cities are growing incessantly driven largely by an exploding population and rural to urban shifts. The global population has swollen from 2 billion in 1945 to over 7.3 billion at the current count and of these around 4 billion live in cities. Every week 1.5 million people move to cities; that is roughly 200,000+ a day or 140 every minute.

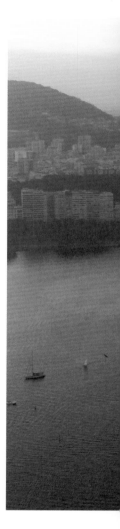

*Is this a better place?*
*Rio de Janeiro*

People are moving around. Where do they go? Surprising places sometimes and where one person dares to move others follow in their footsteps. There are 400 Sikh families working the land in Brescia, a small northern Italian city. There are officially 9,900 Chinese in the Prato conurbation in Tuscany, but including illegals 45,000 working in their 3,500 garment workshops. Most come from Wenzhou and some from Chinatown in Paris. There are 8,000 Roma people in Ghent where the City has been hospitable. They came mainly from Slovakia, whose government strategy was to export what they saw as their problem community by making their life uncomfortable. The dispersion of people surprises. There are apparently over 50 nationalities in the Nordic outposts of Norway, Lakselv and Kirkenes well beyond the Arctic Circle.

# DIASPORAS & DESTINATIONS

There are almost 10,000 Singaporean Hadramis from the Hadramaut region in Yemen mostly by origin seafaring traders, and around 2,000 Yemenis in South Shields, a small town in Northern England. They came over in the 1890s as they were ship workers for British merchant vessels. They are clustered in a small enclave called Rekendyke. There are nearly 20,000 Albanians in Worcester Massachusetts, most of whom came over when the isolationist Communist regime of Enver Hoxha fell in the early 1990s. There are 1.5 million people of Japanese descent in Brazil and half a million in the region of Sao Paolo (325,000 in the City). The highpoint of immigration was between the World Wars when 200,000 moved in search of work as they were excluded from the US and Australia. Many more oddities like these exist each with their own history.

Diasporas have existed for thousands of years. The reasons include overpopulation, religious persecution, lawlessness, conscription, hunger, a bad economy and survival needs, but also conquering armies and colonialists who leave their imprint. In the first Jewish diaspora in 722 BC the Jews fled and in the colonizing activities of Alexander the Great in 330 BC the Greek diaspora was formed and then replenished over the centuries. Think too of the Viking diaspora to Iceland in the ninth century and then to Greenland and even the States. By contrast consider the mass dispersion of people from Africa during the transatlantic slave trade from the 1500s onwards creating an African diaspora in the Caribbean and the States. In the 50 years from 1860 onwards, 40 million Europeans emigrated for reasons of poverty, lack of land and opportunities, and two thirds went to the US and 16 million of these were Italian.

*A group of Roma musicians, Istanbul*

Ireland, the most dramatic case, has a greater diaspora than its own 4.6 million inhabitants. An estimated 80 million people worldwide claim some Irish descent, including some 36 million Americans who say Irish is their primary ethnicity. The Lebanese diaspora is 7 million and the population 5.8. Armenia has 3.1 million inhabitants and between 7-10 million living abroad. Greece has 10.8 million inhabitants and a diaspora of 7 million.  Another large diaspora are the 26 million Italians who have emigrated in the last 150 years whose descendants far outstrip that number. There are more Cape Verdeans abroad than the 500,000 on the islands. The Arab diaspora is an estimated 40 million out of 300 million and most of these favoured South America. Brazil has around 15 million people of Arab descent and most live in the Sao Paolo region; there are substantial settlements in Buenos Aires, Caracas, Baranquilla, and Trinidad apart from the well-known settlements in London and Paris.

**Every war, revolution and large-scale crisis creates a diaspora** like that in Iran, Afghanistan or Syria where in these cases 5 million people live outside their country. They come to arrival cities that mostly adjoin their borders like Turkey or Jordan or the most welcoming countries further away like Sweden or Germany, who have historically been open. They affect those social structures as they need to absorb the incomers, whose children often suffer identity problems. Large inner city schools, often with a majority of minorities may have groupings in them who might despise each other like Serbs and Kosovans or Turkish immigrants and Kurds. That creates tension and in addition the lure of extremist ideologies with their promises of liberation is ever present. Here we take inspiration from the leadership of Leoluca Orlando in Palermo in turning his city from a mafia city to a haven of refugees.

*Immigrant area
of Rio de Janeiro*

The TV programme 100% English, aired in 2006, examined our genetic backgrounds. It involved eight people including personalities and 'ordinary' people who were convinced they were completely English. DNA testing that went back 12 generations showed that in fact none of them were. Mongolian, Turkish, African, East European, Nordic and other traces were found. Who Do You Think you Are, the hugely popular TV series now in its 14th iteration, has also consistently shown we are a bundle of influences, even though some might be dominant. Damen Barks, an 18-year-old trainee soldier and participant of 100% English descent noted: 'For racists to find out that part of them may be what they have discriminated against for years, well that would certainly throw them off their game.' Genealogy, the modern form of ancestor worship, has become fashionable. It has revealed that our notions of nationality and cultural identity are skewed. The truth is **we are all mixed up and related to one another**.[37] Dr Mark Thomas, the academic advisor when asked how many 'English' people currently lived in England said: 'At a rough guess? Er, zero', with the criterion used as a measure of pure Englishness. He noted too:

# THE PURE
# & IMPURE

Since we first evolved in Africa. Migration is not only the norm, it is nature's way of keeping us healthy. The more our genes mix, the better the long-term health of the species – the better we can withstand infectious diseases and the less likely we are to suffer from genetic diseases.

If any place is purer than others it could be Iceland. It is one of the most homogeneous nations on earth with little significant immigration since the Norsemen first settled there in the 9th Century. This makes it a haven for scientists to study genetics. Others argue that Korea is the most racially homogenous society.

*Mixing dance styles at*
*Mannheim hip hop event*

*Goudi building, Barcelona*

# THE SEARCH & EXPERIENCE

'A good traveller has no fixed plans and is not intent on arriving.' Lao Tzu

Tourism creates a dilemma. It is good and bad. It has exploded and it will continue to grow. **Reactions against tourism will become a massive movement** and it has already begun as people fear for their local cultures and see the potential destruction of their cities and nature. We will see places in the future that will self-consciously deter tourists to maintain their local identity. Too many people show too little respect to their hosts – the phenomenon of the 'stag do' and 'hen do' is a prime example, where the about to be married have one more final fling before committing themselves to a partner. Similarly the sex hotspots tend to eviscerate civic life. Tourism is too important to be planned by the hospitality industry alone. Courage is needed to establish when to let it grow and when to curtail and contain it.

Tourism for many locations has been a life saver. When countries have little resources and no chance of creating high value inventions, products and services, what is left but natural assets. Those you dig from the ground, and they mostly leave scars on the landscape, or your scenery, your heritage, your culture. However, we have arrived at a crisis point.

Tourists travel for every conceivable reason and niches cater for every whim and lifestyle: enlightenment, health, sex, sport, sand, spiritual and religious comfort and more. The world is truly your oyster, yet at times you feel you are **trapped in a crazy consumerist vortex**, even though the traveller (so different from the ordinary tourist, apparently) thinks they have 'freed' themselves.

# TOURISTS & TRAVELLERS

There are 130 times as many international tourists today as there were in 1950. Then there were 10 million and today 1.3 billion. Consider the kilometres travelled: many trillions and more. Add to that the billions of domestic trips: 6.5 billion alone in China and India and 1.2 billion in Europe. China and Germany lead the way as the most avid travellers. By 2027, international tourist arrivals are forecast to total over 2 billion, a further astonishing increase. Add to these the vast numbers of people moving to places long-term, searching for work, commuting daily or for fun. The constant ebb and flow of people traversing place and space is overwhelming. It puts a strain on the civic fabric of arrival cities.[38]

Tourism is a powerful movement machine with strong impacts whose dynamic is difficult to curtail given the interests involved. Its contribution to global GDP is €6,528 trillion (10.2%) and forecast to rise to €9575 trillion (11.4%) of GDP by 2027. Travel and tourism support nearly 110 million jobs directly (3.6% of total employment) with projections at 138 million in 2027 (4%). Adding indirect tourism makes 292 million jobs (9.6%) expected to rise to 381 million in 2027 (11.1%).[39] Induced jobs add a further 55 million. In addition, merchandise exports earned €1.08 trillion, 6.6% of total exports in 2016 and this forecast to grow to €1.89 trillion in 2027 and 7.2% of the total.

Unsurprisingly, anti-tourism emotion spills out, especially in graffiti: 'Why call it tourist season if we can't shoot them' in Barcelona or 'tourists are terrorists' in Lisbon and two Berlin favourites 'yuppie scum' and the tee-shirt with 'hipsters are motherfuckers'.[40]

The reasons for travel are numerous and cheap air travel is a significant enabler and catalyst as is the enormous industry attached that seeks to pump up our desire. Merely look at the travel sections of print or programmes of the media: 'Find the place you love'; 'let your dreams come true'; 'discover life'; 'towards the endless horizon'; 'this is where the best begins'; 'see it, feel it, love it'; 'and you think you've done it all'. Tourism's inexorable rise initially focused on sun, sand and sports/sex and centuries of history. Yet once the beach was not enough the city came into its own. So it is 'Come to Paris: the City of Romance' or to Shanghai 'the Paris of the East' or 'St. Petersburg: the Paris of the North'. Look out for 'Edinburgh: Athens of the North' or 'Madurai: Athens of the South' and 'Lexington, Kentucky: Athens of the West'. And Rome is of course 'the Eternal City' and now most famously 'I love NY'. Today you can get tee-shirts for every city you might love. Slogans are now more sophisticated. They have become essentialist seeking to express a genetic code: 'Be Berlin'; 'I amsterdam'; and we are encouraged to discover 'the soul of Seoul'. At times slogans run dry as Leeds wanted 'Leeds, Live it, Love it' that had a surprising resemblance to 'Hong Kong, Live it, Love it'.

The escalating numbers of visitors are **draining and drowning place identity** as people scour the world – all in the name of experience. The most popular places people visit are those most treasured by locals.

Consider the extreme - the death of Venice. The problems it faces are immense as the mass influx of people is triggering a critical situation that its fragile fabric cannot absorb. Its vibrancy is declining by the relentless loss of population, the thronging crowds of visitors tramping its streets, the eyesore and menace of monstrous cruise ships in its harbour who mercilessly dump tourists into Venice's narrow streets and a lack of political will to face these threats. Some parts of the city are unbearably overcrowded and others are becoming ghost neighbourhoods, especially at night when the one-day visitors leave. In 2005 around 15 million tourists arrived each year, in 2017 there are more 25 million. At current rates of growth that would be 30 million in 2020 and 50 million in 2030 - an unimaginable scenario.

Mass tourism shapes the kind of goods offered to people, mostly made in China but pretending to be 'so Venice'. Beyond the splendour of restored churches and palaces, beyond the magnificent façades the reality is dramatic: the survival of Venice as a living and vibrant city is at risk.

Venice is not alone, consider the Spanish Steps in Rome, consider the Florence Duomo, and what about the Boqueria market in Barcelona - hardly a local in sight. The same is true for the gardens of Suzhou in China, Hanok village in Jeonju Korea or Sydney Harbour. Residents rarely if ever go down the Ramblas in Barcelona, the Champs-Élysées in Paris, the Gendarmen Markt in Berlin, the Dam in Amsterdam, or near the charming places in historic European towns from Bruges to Dubrovnik, from Heidelberg to Ljubljana or further afield at Kuta Beach, Bali or Tanjung Rhu, Langkawi.

## BEYOND THE ORDINARY

Three words 'experience', 'explore' and 'love' constantly appear in tourism literature and with ever greater frequency. It indicates a problem. Our daily lives give us too few chances to self-express fully and be imaginative. This leaves us feeling empty in search of the more profound. **Glimpses of the meaningful are too fleeting and rare**. Travel seems to be an answer to create and capture special moments as memories that are etched inside.

Being outside helps you look inside as you are outside of yourself. This allows you in principle to grow, as you self-reflect. At its best, this encounter with the 'other' triggers other things too. You think of lives lived elsewhere and so about your own; how individuals and groups connect across cultures; how shared humanity could work and how to foster common experience; how cultural rituals emerge as common agreements to bind, bond and broker community; and how your own place at home works at a deeper level. **Engaged detachment and distance it seems can clarify the mind**.

Tourism fulfils a deep psychological need. The mind moves, the body wants to move: to move out of routine; to be distracted; to enjoy; to rest and relax; to find distance; to find yourself; and, at its most ethereal, to find the soul, to discover purpose and meaning. It responds both to ordinary desire simply to get away and to deeper yearnings that to be in the here and now is not enough. There are deeper causes here. Increasingly experience is pre-packaged, created by someone else, targeted at you - a specific niche market with identified needs. You are boxed into a category. Chance encounter, discovery, exploration fall by the wayside. Many things we did in the past as part of everyday life are now turned into saleable products. They are monetized. These products, offers and opportunities shout at us. Many of us close in to shield ourselves. Those selling then shout louder, they offer experiences that are more shrill, that are faster, more exciting. Even taking a walk or a tour to see the locals becomes a themed product. By these processes **we are letting ourselves become unfree**.

A while back I asked a group of people working in urban regeneration what shifted their mind and caused a transformative effect so triggering learning and change in themselves. The choices ranged from reading a book, surfing the Internet, watching television, talking to friends or peers, visiting a site or travelling somewhere else with your peer group. The most profound effect was travelling together as a group and then experiencing a project that related to their concerns or life. The key was finding out how the initiative worked, what made it tick and then talking, eating and socializing with the local actors. The distance allowed them to reflect on their work, their own circumstances, their home environment.

Not all travel does this, of course as several examples show. Travelling too much can mean you do not connect at all and there are **vast swathes of the hypermobile**. They are often business people working for global corporates with a punishing schedule. This is true too for famous performers, for example Renee Fleming, who are on a continual roving schedule or chef Gordon Ramsey who has restaurants to tend to across the globe. You are everywhere and nowhere at the same time. Things pass by too speedily. In this blur, there is only the airport, the car, the train, the bus. Getting there and getting out is all there is. Everything can look the same and often you hold onto the familiar, the known, the safe. This can end you up in the ex-pat drinking den with other people like you, the globally branded hotel or seeing a musician you could have seen at home. 'Being in the moment' or 'being anchored' can be lost. Anchored experiences are usually slow, they take time, effort and thoughtfulness.

Travel for most is either bi-annual escapism and recuperation or for business. The **dromomaniacs are a different breed** and they include some of the above. They have a compelling Wanderlust - a constant itch that has to be satisfied. The uncontrollable urge to wander, to move, to go from place to place, this is dromomania, a ceaseless desire to travel. It is pathological tourism, a personality disorder and it is on the rise and linked to 'hypermobility' and 'binge-flying'.

Dromomaniacs are already organizing their next trip although the current one has not finished. 'Getting ready for the next trip I feel liberated like the bars of a cage have fallen away'. Home life may suffer, but anyway there are more friends abroad than at home. 'I miss those people I met, the culture I learned about, the things I did. I need to get back on a plane again soon, even though I wouldn't be going back to the place I'm missing or to see the same people. I just need to feel that high again'.

Like FOMO, the social media disorder, 'the fear of missing out' on that elusive life that is happening elsewhere.

'I needed to develop a self outside of my troubled family of origin, yet it failed to give me the deep sense of belonging that I was desperate to have'.[41]

The solution is to find ways to make daily life as enriching and meaningful as travel life claims to be. Meaning generally is not just given, it has to be achieved. To be curious is a start, or to do something new.

One type of tourism is the vast number of **packaged, ordered and pre-set trips**. Here you can feel herded, timetabled and structured. Organizers are there to shut you off, to give you that two-week window of letting go and having fun, to make you relax, to become soporific. Then you can cope again with life at home you may feel you have little control. Too often it is **a palliative for lives that feel insufficiently lived**. Their contribution to local civic life is largely nil except of course income for the host community. Perhaps that sounds too negative, they are also people like us just trying to switch off and to have an enjoyable time.

Another group are the **cultural tourists**. These are people who, as an important motivation, wish to experience another culture, its history, heritage, its past and contemporary way of life. They want to learn and grow personally by being part of a culture. For them travel is needed to help develop the mind and expand knowledge. A precursor is the Grand Tour undertaken by the European upper classes and intellectuals, such as Goethe. Cultural tourism has grown exponentially and is part of the city marketing repertoire and the urban regeneration agenda, it justifies the huge investments in cultural facilities from museums, to contemporary art galleries and experience centres. It is viewed positively as it involves high spenders, who have cultural capital, and are more educated. They say they are more sensitive to the environments they are in and more willing to learn the customs and language so as to blend in well. Greater levels of education contribute to cultural tourism's popularity as does the nostalgia for things past. Yet there is always more to see and often 'the been there, done that' approach can create **a frenzy to cross things off the bucket list**.

As Rutger Lemm from Amsterdam notes:

[At its best you get] a crossing of racial or linguistic boundaries - one of the most moving phenomena in modern society. It takes courage to try and immerse yourself in another culture. [At its worst] what you get is a one-dimensional experience that has nothing to do with cultural exchange. This way we'll never really get to know each other. You visit my city, take a few pictures and leave. It's as if you're waving at me from a car passing by... Amsterdam becomes a travel cliché, because you, dear tourists, take the easy route. You cling together in the Red Light District and fool yourselves into thinking this is Amsterdam. In fact, we Amsterdammers rarely go there.

GPS research by the Dutch newspaper NRC Handelsblad showed that Amsterdam tourists all take the same routes and stray only rarely.[42]

**Creative tourism** is an interesting response to a shallow world. It builds a bridge between outsider and insider and into the civic life of the city visited. Its philosophy is to engender richer, more fulfilling experiences. It tries to break a mould. At its best it is an **unmediated, direct, unfiltered experience that is not pre-digested and staged**. It involves the active participation of travellers in the culture of the host community, through interactive workshops and informal learning experiences. This tourism seeks to promote an active understanding of the specific cultural features of a place. Here we do things together with locals, live with them, take a cooking class, learn the handicrafts an area is known for or do an archaeology dig. There is no distant, detached observing, there is only living in the now. We merge into a city's emotional landscape and get under its skin, we learn how it functions day to day, how its larger and smaller dramas unfold, we learn about their philosophy of life as well as mundane and ordinary yet important things: going out with the ambulance crew, finding out how they work, hitching a lift with a delivery vehicle, seeing people go to work, waiting in a queue to catch a bus, standing outside the office and smoking, chatting on the sidewalks or watching young lovers canoodle on a bench.

We go deeper into the crevices of a place, with a local guide. How people earn a living, survive, are joyful or sad, how they celebrate their rituals and matters that are important to them. In time as a creative tourist we co-create our experience with them, we share. It can be banal or profound. We discuss commonalities and differences. The more we know we perhaps imagine living there and speculate what it would be like.  Tourism is not only about visiting heritage sites, the icons or cultural events.

Creative tourism involves the lived experience of being there rather than **borrowing the landscape, sights and delights** and keeping them to oneself. We call this authentic and we mean it is of itself and unsullied.  Then as a visitor we can turn into something more than we thought. Perhaps we can feel like a welcome guest, even a temporary citizen participating in the place we are visiting.

*Copenhagen Airport*

Sex is a conspicuous aspect of world travel. It is the darker side as exploitation, human trafficking, violence, drugs and crime are always near the surface. It is most commonly men seeking women, although there is an increase in women seeking men. There are men seeking men and adults seeking children. There are websites for all tastes and ranking lists of the top sex hotspots, for all the kinds of male sex it is more likely to be Asia and for women Southern Europe or the Caribbean.

**Sex tourists generally live in wealthier countries** in Europe or North America and go to Asia, especially Thailand, the Philippines and Cambodia – hungering after the lure of the 'sexual East' and exotic Asian woman – or countries in Central and South America, especially Costa Rica.

# SEEKING SEX
# & PLEASURE

The ethical and legal issues especially concern child sex, the trafficking of women and girls as prostitutes, as well as the disparity between the richer tourist and the poor sex workers who have few options but to sell their body. These women are often migrants from poorer parts of the country and if they had better opportunities they would not be selling sex.

Thirty million people visit Thailand each year. Of these 60% are men and an astonishing 70% of them are sex tourists - 12.6 million guys. Thailand has a reputation for being sexually permissive so prostitution and tolerating other lifestyles are part of Thai culture. Thus the 'oldest profession in the world' has flourished, including the famous 'ladyboy' culture. That is why there are an estimated 300,000 prostitutes in Bangkok and nearly three million in Thailand of whom roughly a third are minors. Here are the global sex tourism capitals like sleazy Pattya, whose sex tourism history started with American soldiers resting from the Vietnam war, or Patong Beach in Phuket. 'Sure it's sleazy, but it's right by the beach, there's a ridiculous amount of women and the night life is insane'. Estimates for the Philippines are that around 40% of all male tourists are there for sex and nearly the same amount for Cambodia, which also has the dark reputation for paedophilia.

The sex image of Costa Rica is described as more differentiated both in terms of class of the prostitutes as well as attitudes and stigma. Anthropologist Megan Rivers-Moore explores this in her nuanced picture of sex tourism *Gringo Gulch*. Many see themselves as care workers believing they are providing a service to humble white men who have run out of relationship options in their homeland.[43] One prostitute said: 'some of them just look for company, they pay for company. I'm very happy to listen, as long as they pay. I'll listen to it all. Cry, whatever, as long as you pay.' The author notes that 'sex tourism here is more complicated than just sex ... the caring aspects, listening to men talk about their problems, making them feel attractive was as important, if not more than the sex'.

Europe has its hotspots too from Amsterdam's red light district window prostitution to Madrid's district which is interwoven into regular streets. In the 1970s, most of Amsterdam's prostitutes were from Thailand, in the 1980s from Latin America and the Caribbean, and after the fall of the Berlin Wall many prostitutes came from Central and Eastern Europe. The various reports suggest 65-75% of Amsterdam's between 8,000 and 11,000 prostitutes are foreigners. Karina Schaapman, a former prostitute and former member of Amsterdam City Council offered the police pictures of 80 violent pimps of whom only three were Dutch-born.[44] Similarly there are more South American sex workers in Spain than Spanish ones.

Men seeking sex tourism is much-publicised. Female sex tourism. By contrast, **female sex tourism has not received much attention** even though it is becoming mainstream. Perhaps it is seen as harmless as they are often middle-aged, overweight and conventionally not attractive (the same characteristics apply to the male sex-hunters). When men seek sex, we think of them as predators, whereas women doing the same is often described as a 'sexcapade' or a form of social exchange, rather than explicitly a money for sex transaction. As with men, many female European and North American sex tourists hold ordinary jobs and they hope to fulfil a need they cannot satisfy back home. For some there is the social status and power that comes from having poorer, younger lovers. Ulrich Seidl's film Paradise: Love is an interesting drama film about a white woman who travels to Kenya as a sex tourist. Kenya, Bali, Phuket, Gambia and the Caribbean are the hotspots for female sex tourism.

The tourism industry's role in sex tourism can be dubious and raises questions about its moral standing, especially in its links to crime, also a mobile industry.

Prostitution in Asia, for instance, may feel relaxed and easy-going as so much happens on the street and in the open. Yet given the profitability of sex, the human trafficking involved as well as drug dealing and crime, there are huge monies at stake and violent people willing to protect their territory. This automatically changes the nature of civic life in most sex focused places. Insecurity on the streets is rife, there is tension in the air, the criminals who control things are always willing to use force and be brutal to get their way. The **daily nuisances pollute community spirit and sex haunts look uncared for,** they are mostly messy, with graffiti everywhere and civic pride is an exception – and not surprisingly. There is a sense of togetherness perhaps amongst those locals not involved in the trade and also amongst the gangs and tribes that run prostitution and drug dealing. Yet looming over everything are the negative rules of order, an order protected, if necessary, by weapons and violence. Naturally the 'higher class' sex business has a more comforting veneer, as it takes place in posher surroundings, although its dynamics are often the same.

This will be true too of sexcam, whose new capital is Bucharest in Romania.[45] Cybersex is an annual $2-3 billion industry and the biggest the Hungarian LiveJasmin has around 35 million users daily mostly logging in from Western Europe and America and supported by 2000 women. The Romanian Studio 20 is the largest studio webcam franchise in the world with nine branches in Romania, with up to 40 rooms each. One is for "cam-boys". Other studios are in Cali and Los Angeles. Hundreds of guys watch a women simultaneously before one goes 'private' and pays for a special so-called conversation. The women in front of the camera are 'models' and the guys watching 'members'. This world of placeless relationships where people are thousands of miles away and do not touch you fits the nomadic age. It is legal.

This sector has a corrosive effect on civic life and the tourism authorities have not taken sufficient heed. Worldwide, the industry thinks that the benefits can be measurable economic factors and they disregard the social and cultural costs. There are insufficient schemes to connect the worlds of prostitution with local community organizations.

Health and medical tourism is booming with citizens of richer places seeking treatments especially in middle-income countries. It is driven by price as treatments can be half the cost or less. It also avoids long waiting lists, at times it gives better treatment and there is certainly a perception of receiving better care. Patients Beyond Borders suggests, as a conservative estimate, that in 2015 eight million people sought overseas heath care with many countries jostling for position.[46] Estimates vary of its size but cluster at around €50 billion for 2015 with predictions that it might grow to €3 trillion by 2025 - an astonishing 60-fold increase.

# BEAUTY & HEALTH

Dentistry and cosmetic treatments are the most popular, though increasingly complex operations are being sought as the industry matures. Some countries have a reputation for specific niches, such as Poland for breast implants and Hungary for dental implants. Dental clinics account for 80% of all foreign patients to Hungary and 40% of the world's dental tourists. Other dental treatment capitals are Mexico and Costa Rica. Both countries have hot spa traditions and these are often combined with other treatments. Thailand has a reputation as the capital of sex reassignment surgery, but offers a wealth of other procedures from cosmetic surgery to traditional Thai medicine. Malaysia specializes in skin diseases and in-vitro fertilization. Go to Turkey for eye operations or hair transplants and the UAE to get rid of fat.

**In 2014 Brazil eclipsed the US as the world leader in aesthetic and plastic surgery**. It is known for liposuction and is home of the 'Brazilian butt lift', invented there by Ivo Pitanguy, the famous plastic surgeon. Brazil has around 5,500 plastic surgeons and performs 20% of global butt lifts. Indeed 2015 was dubbed as another 'year of the rear' since 'procedures focusing on the derriere dominated growth in the surgical industry' with 320,000 buttock augmentation procedures globally - an 30% increase over 2014. The operation involves fat grafting or injection where liposuction removes fat from the abdomen, hips and thighs which is then processed and re-implanted into the buttocks.[47]

Finally, of the economically advanced countries, Germany remains the hub for oncology. Its specialist cancer treatments centres attract patients from across the globe mostly when specialist care is not available in their home country.

Taranto, Puglia

# PARASITES & URBAN LIFE

There are many types of virus. They are all debilitating and depressing. My friends were hit by one last week, but it was not triggered by a mosquito, which had infected their living cells and then multiplied weakening them. No, it was a hacker's virus which infected their website and then inserted a plug-in that scrambled everything. The website weakened, partially disappeared. The things that worked sent false messages. It was the dark web in operation. The immediate response was to change passwords and all security systems. Their tech doctor did a health check and things began to work, they tracked the source in India and tried to close off the attack, within minutes it had shifted to Morocco as they chased it around the world it moved from there to Egypt, down to the Philipines, across to the US and back to Europe to another one of its sources in Russia. Within 24 hours we had wandered the world and a networked group of hackers probably only known to each other electronically were causing havoc on the web. This was the dark web in operation.

Exploring a century of emigre history
in London through the hidden treasures
of the Ben Uri Collections

SOMERSET
HOUSE

Mark Gertler
Merry-Go-Round, 1916
Tate, London 2015

# OUT
# OF
# CHAOS

Ben Uri: 100 Years in London
02 July – 13 December 2015

Inigo Rooms
Somerset House East Wing
King's College London
WC2R 2LS

www.benuri100.org I #BenUri100

LOTTERY FUNDED

KING'S
College
LONDON

100
ART IDENTITY MIGRATION

Diseases are a visible marker of the mobile world and they have spread through the centuries most forcefully through travel, trade and conquest. The more nomadic we are the more likely it is that new diseases will develop and spread. Diseases transmit via the air, water, the exchange of blood, direct contact, and through insects, also called vectors, who carry a germ and infect a human. Disease moves – it jumps from country to country or from animals and insects to humans.

Research is on-going about the deep history and origins of disease with a focus on southern parts of Africa and the initial locations of homo sapiens. Malaria is one of the oldest identified diseases with malaria parasites found in mosquitoes preserved in amber 30 million years ago. It is likely that human malaria originated in Africa and coevolved with its hosts, mosquitoes and non-human primates.[48]

# ORGANISMS & PATHOGENS

Although the geographic origins of several diseases are contested we can establish the first known outbreaks. What we know is that when diseases, such as the plague or smallpox travelled across regions and continents, they devastated populations, given the hosts lack of immunity.

The bubonic plague which ravaged Europe in the Middle Ages jumped from black rats and via their fleas to humans and that rat in turn came from South Asia in the sixth century and the first epidemic was recorded in China in the 1330s before reaching Europe in 1343. Columbus and the European explorers brought smallpox, the plague, diphtheria, typhus, cholera, scarlet fever, chickenpox and many more diseases to the Americas. These diseases killed nearly 95% of the population over 150 years as native Americans had no natural immunity. Some these diseases in turn were transmitted via Europe, although their origins lie elsewhere. Yellow fever originated in West Africa, with the first recorded incident in 1774, and migrated to the Americas via the slave trade. It is said that syphilis came from the New World back to Europe and created several epidemics there. One suggestion is that syphilis existed in Europe, but was not yet identified as a separate disease.

Cholera is first described in Sanskrit writings in India in the fifth century BC and the first[49] pandemics started in India in 1819, travelling eastwards to the Philippines and westwards to Basra in Iraq where a major outbreak occurred and then moved on to Turkey. It first appears

in Europe in Moscow in 1830 and then spreads across the continent before moving over the Atlantic to Quebec and then New Orleans by 1832. A third pandemic is equally devastating and by the time of the sixth in the 1920s it has mostly disappeared from Europe and the Americas.

The extent of damage over time can be immense. Between 1855 and 2005 measles has been estimated to have killed about 200 million people worldwide. For instance, the virus, along with several other diseases, struck Hawaii in 1848, killing up to a third of the native population and it wreaked similar havoc in other parts of Latin America.

**The spread of disease is an unintended consequence** of trade, travel and human mobility. It continues today with new ones making their presence felt and we are just a plane ride away from exposing ourselves to an infectious disease we are not very immune to. This came into the spotlight with zoonoses, viruses and bacteria transmitted from animals especially birds to humans. These dispersed across the world like SARS, MERS, HIV or avian flu and most famously recently HIV/AIDS which is said to have jumped to us via a chimpanzee sub-species pan troglodytes. In the 1980s, HIV took the world by surprise and the roots of the virus were soon discovered to lie in Africa. It spread rapidly around the globe, particularly in the West

*Manama, Bahrain*

and especially North America. Eastern and Western Europe differed in how it transmitted the virus with sex prevalent in the West and drugs use in the East. That changed once the Berlin Wall fell and then the causes merged. Interestingly those European countries with higher connections – Britain, France and Switzerland – also had high incidences of the virus.

Vectors, such as mosquitoes, are living organisms. They transmit infectious diseases between humans or from animals to humans by sucking blood and ingesting disease-ridden micro-organisms. The diseases often travel inadvertently by transport vehicles or commodities especially perishable ones. For example, the Asian tiger mosquito, a dengue virus vector, was introduced to North America on rubber tyres shipped to Houston and tyre dumping grounds are important breeding sites for these mosquitoes. Equally some think mosquitoes can cross oceans by riding in airplane wheels. One hypothesis is that in 1999 the West Nile virus came to New York City in this way and then crossed the continent. It emerged near a major international airport and near some of the most ethnically diverse districts in the world.

Another debilitating disease is crime. **The globalized economy has its parallel globalized illegal, dirty and dangerous crime economy**. It is largely an urban phenomenon. Often called mafia from the Sicilian dialect mafiusu meaning swagger or bravado, these fluid organized crime networks coalesce wherever profit can be made and some are immense. They know no borders or rules. They transcend geography and so cultural, social and linguistic boundaries. Their main activities are drug dealing, human trafficking, prostitution, smuggling migrants, extortion, money-laundering, selling weapons or counterfeit goods, stealing cultural property and cybercrime. Wherever crime is present it fractures civic life and it is mostly in cities, it creates an overall atmosphere of potential violence, visible exploitation and the smell of danger.

# CORROSIVE CRIMINALITY

None of the groups is afraid to put a bullet into your head, stab you to death, to smash your limbs or injure you beyond repair. Some make a point of looking fearful, others come across as fake genteel.

Organized transnational crime operates in varying ways involving clans, gangs or crime families and partnerships who might collaborate with each other across borders, which makes tracking them complex, especially as the leaders insulate themselves. They exploit differences between countries to avoid detection often by bribing officials and politicians.

Organized crime revenues are notoriously difficult to estimate and they hide what they make in shadow companies or launder it into legitimate activities. Criminal groups range from vast drug cartels to a handful of car thieves, but any group of substance operates internationally. According to Fortune[50] in 2014 the biggest crime organizations by revenue are Solntsevskaya Bratva with $8.5 billion, one of the Russian mafiya groups. Its 9,000 members include many ex-soldiers or KGB agents and its tentacles reach strongly into the US where white collar crime is one activity. Apparently the shadowy Semion Mogilevich is the boss of bosses, who has extensive contacts with the Russian political class and he lives undisturbed in Moscow. It specializes in drugs, especially heroin, and human trafficking; yet it is not averse to selling nuclear arms or organizing giant global hacking campaigns. It is highly decentralized and made up of 10 separate semi-autonomous divisions run by a twelve-person council. Rather like in *The Godfather*, they meet across the world disguising their gatherings as private celebrations.

Then Yamaguchi Gumi is one of several groups that make up the Yakuza, a highly organized crime collective founded centuries ago in Japan. It operates on a highly tiered pyramid structure. Like all the other big syndicates it has links to criminal affiliates in Asia, Europe, and the Americas using front companies in legitimate industries – like construction, real estate and finance – to launder money. Kenichi Shinoda is the current 'supreme kingpin'. It is rumoured to have 55,000 members and a revenue of $6.6 billion. Drugs, gambling, the gaudy pachinko parlours, extortion and 'dispute resolution' are their mainstay.

The Italian mafia started in Sicily in the early 19th century and having spread to America still has many wings. The biggest is the Camorra from Naples with a revenue of $4.9 billion and the Sicilian arm is now relatively weaker. The 'Ndrangheta from Calabria has a revenue of $4.5 billion and gained influence by building close ties with the South American cocaine cartels and now controls 80% of that trade into Europe.

The Italian-American mafia has been severely weakened in recent decades, but still has bases in North-Eastern USA and instead the Russian mafias, the Chinese triads and Mexican drug cartels have grabbed a share of business.

The Sinaloa drug cartel is Mexico's largest with $3 billion revenue. With many other cartels, it acts as the intermediary between the South American producers and the American market. They have an equally brutal sister organization Bario Azteca in El Paso on the US side of the border.

This list just scratches the surface.[51] Consider the effect the 1.4 million gang members that the FBI estimates operate in the US[52] and their impact on US neighbourhoods. Consider the many fangs of the triads from Hong Kong and their mainland associates. Add to these their global affiliates wherever Chinese reside across the globe from the States to Europe and beyond. Consider the D-Company from Mumbai founded by the shameful Dawood Ibrahim, a terrorist, contract killer and drugs trader. He helped organize the Mumbai bombing spree in 1993 with associate Tiger Memon that resulted in 257 deaths and over 700 injuries (they say in retaliation to the killing of Muslims). Consider the unrelenting brutality of MS-13 gang, who practice merciless revenge and cruel retributions. Having fled the civil war in El Salvador they arose out of the immigrant gang culture of Los Angeles and spread back into their homelands.[53] Known for their fearsome tattoos, see the referenced images,[54] they operate in both places. One cause for celebration in the small El Salvador was national news. No murders reported for a day in January 2017, the first in two years.[55]

**These cartels and those in other countries help to shatter the social fabric** with their corrosive effect on public morality and corrupting influence apart from terrorizing communities and killing those who seek to expose them.

Let us remember two brave heroes from Mexico as examples: Javier Valdez and Miroslava Breach. She used to say that corrupt politicians were more dangerous than drug traffickers. For almost 30 years, she investigated cases where authorities and criminals worked together in her native state of Chihuahua, in northern Mexico. She was then killed.[56] Valdez, who himself was later killed. said: 'Let them kill us all, if that is the death sentence for reporting this hell.' He wrote too:

The omnipresent narco is everywhere. Inside me there is a pessimistic bastard, distressed and sometimes sullen, who feels like a somewhat bitter old man with watery eyes, who is bothered by having his solitude spoiled. But he dreams. I have an idea of another country, for my family and other Mexicans, that does not continue to fall into an abyss from which there may be no return.[57]

Detailed numbers on crime's overall impact and the people involved is hard to come by – certainly not its corrosive effect on communities, social capital and the negative direct and indirect spin-offs. The only comprehensive data available are those of the United Nations Office on Drugs and Crime (UNODC) and it is purely economic. In 2009, it estimated that transnational organised crime generated $870bn a year, close to 7% of global exports.[58] It is likely to be much more now. Drug trafficking at 40% was the most lucrative, with cocaine the largest element, and the subsequent money laundering is skyrocketing with one estimate at $1.4 trillion per annum.[59] The cybercrime epidemic is predicted to grow exponentially and to cost business $2.2 trillion by 2019. It is often orchestrated by crime syndicates.

*Poster on Nervion river walk, Bilbao*

The International Labour Organization (ILO) estimated that in 2005 there were around 2.4 million victims of trafficking at any given time with annual profits of about $32 billion. Of these 600,000 to 800,000 people are annually trafficked across international borders each year and 80% are women and girls and nearly 50% are minors. Add to this at least 20.9 million people are victims of forced labour worldwide and 2012 research estimated trafficking victims making up 44%. In Europe, according to UNODC estimates, there are 140,000 victims at any one time with an annual flow of 70,000.

The costs of smuggling migrants according to UNODC vary. A boat trip from Turkey to Greece might cost $100, as would a trip from Africa to Italy, getting from Afghanistan to Central Europe $12,000 plus and from Mexico to the States around $3,500. Given that several million people are smuggled globally each year $billions are earned between recruiters, transporters, hoteliers, facilitators, enforcers, organisers and financiers and corrupt officials including the police and border guards.

Odd to note that organized mobsters, especially Italians were glamorized rather than seen as unsavoury. Hollywood's love affair with the mafia started in the 1920s. Prohibition's black market helped solidify organized crime as it grew out of small criminal groups. Since prohibition was unpopular, the criminals who stood up to the law were seen as heroes. Books like Mario Puzo's The Godfather and the subsequent film promoted the mafia as people who cared for their communities and as people who lived by a code of honour and conduct.[60] Fortunately that glamour is fading as crime's impact in spreading havoc on civic society is becoming clearer.

Frankfurt Airport

# POPULATION MATTERS

There is an elephant in the room. It is a dramatic problem that dares not speak its name – population. Both for its size and its growth. And this is most intense in cities, where now 4.1 billion people live. They represent 55% of the global population (7.5 billion) in 2017. Population has risen by 325% since I was born in 1948.[61] This expansion creates absorption problems as well as environmental, resource and social stresses. Population size and demographic movement shape cities' futures. It has been discussed from Confucius (551 BC – 479 BC) through Thomas Malthus and to climate change scientist James Lovelock, who says 'this is the beginning of the end of a peaceful phase in evolution'.

To discuss how population growth can be curtailed and overall numbers sensibly reduced is not about euthanasia or eugenics, but about solid education, behaviour change and addressing cultural issues, including religious reasons for why people are not having fewer children.

David Attenborough attests:

'There is no major problem facing our planet that would not be easier to solve if there were fewer people; and no problem that does not become harder – and ultimately impossible to solve – with ever more. And yet there seems to be a taboo on bringing the subject into the open.'

**Scientists and politicians are frightened to spell out the consequences** or are too tentative. One devastating study concludes cautiously: 'We want to make it clear they are not advocating government controls or intervention, they simply want to make people aware of the environmental consequences of their reproductive behaviour'.

# CITIES & THE ANTHROPOCENE AGE

Another study: 'We recognise these are deeply personal choices. But we can't ignore the climate effect our lifestyle actually has'. Sustainability advocates equally have paid too little attention to the overwhelming importance of the issue given how having more people creates exponentially more consumption.

Discussing population creates moral dilemmas, especially for Catholics, the only religion explicitly against family planning. Then it creates economic dilemmas for the swathes of African people for whom having more children is a survival policy that ensures the elderly are looked after. The Western city dweller wants children less as having children in cities is increasingly less easy. Then in some cases it can be political. Iran, once the poster child of family planning reversed its policy in 2015, now exhorting its women to have more children. It is the major Shia Muslim country in the world and it wants more adherents for its faith and there is power in numbers. Similar thinking affects Jews and Mormons. Previously Iran achieved the fastest fertility rate decline in the world, from 6.6 children per woman in 1970 to 1.9 in 2010. It was a model for the world as it did so by giving women control over their own fertility and coincided with a dramatic increase in the educational level of younger women. Contraceptive use across the world is revealing, with China first (89%), followed by Vietnam, Iran, Costa Rica, Peru, Cuba, Russia and with Morocco in eighth and Zimbabwe tenth (59%).[62]

To say there are too many people on the planet is an understatement. Just what 'too many' is has to be defined, yet figures speak: the planet cannot sustain itself. More people are moving and trying to get into more developed cities to escape hunger or battles caused by the conflicts over water, rising food and oil prices and inequality. Urban rioting will become the norm. It sparked the insurgencies in Rio, Istanbul and the Arab Spring and, as food prices spiked in 2008 and 2010, so too did the number of food riots in cities throughout the world. They are just a foretaste of what is to come as yields reduce with rises in temperature. There will be less to go around.

The most effective way of reducing the carbon footprint is having one less child, as t**he impact of an extra child is almost 20 times more than other environmental actions**. Yet, according to a study by Oregon State University, in government advice about sustainability high impact actions like having one fewer child were never mentioned. The next best actions are selling your car, avoiding long flights, and eating a vegetarian diet. These reduce emissions many times more than common green activities, such as recycling, using low energy light bulbs or drying washing on a line.[63]

Each child in the US and its legacy descendants adds 9,441 metric tons of carbon dioxide, about 5.7 times the lifetime emissions of the parent and 160 times that of a Bangladeshi, whereas the child's lifetime emissions alone are 40 times more. However, given Bangladeshis shorter lifespan the overall impact is less. Over-consumption is a major part of the issue. Put another way carbon emissions must fall to two tonnes of $CO_2$ per person by 2050 to avoid severe global warming, but in the US and Australia it is already 16 tonnes per person and in Britain seven.

Hell bent on favouring ideological politics over global responsibilities for women, population balance, urban harmony and climate change, the Trump administration has reinstated the 'Global Gag Rule'. This withdraws any support to family planning programmes, which even utter the word 'abortion'. Public health advocates across the globe warn this will have grave consequences and ignores decades of research. When family planning services and contraceptives are easily accessible, there are fewer unplanned pregnancies, maternal deaths and abortions. And when women have control over their reproductive health, it improves the long-term health of mothers and children and creates lasting economic benefit.[64]

**Future population growth is highly dependent on the path of future fertility**. This is why women need more power. Small changes make big differences when projected over several decades. If fertility is half a child more, the world population would reach 10.8 billion by 2050 and 16.6 billion by 2100. If it were half a child less, it would lead to a population of 8.7 billion by mid-century and 7.3 billion by 2100, marginally less than we have today.[65]

Whilst fertility has declined in virtually all major areas of the world population growth is rampant. Africa has a rate of 4.7 children per woman as of 2010-2015, a fall from 4.9 in 2005-2010. This will create incredible pressure as **literally hundreds of millions of sub-Saharan Africans will try to push into the borders of Europe**. In 2010-2015, Asia's rate is 2.2; Latin America 2.15; North America 1.86; Europe is 1.6 children per woman. In Europe, 24% of the population is 60 years or over and that demographic is projected to reach 34 per cent in 2050. Other continents currently have smaller proportions, around 12%, yet these will rise to around 25%. Elderly people number 901 million in 2015, rising to 2.1 billion in 2050 and to 3.2 billion in 2100. The over-80s are projected to rise seven-fold by 2100 to nearly one billion. Believe it or not there are some naysayers who are transfixed by the spell of the technological fix[66] or who believe the problem is under control and that the population will peak, since education drives lower birth rates. Their mantra is that although humans take more resources from the Earth than the planet can safely produce we can "dematerialize". That is – reduce the amount of materials needed to produce the same goods and services. A MIT-led study called 'A simple extension of dematerialization theory'[67] contradicts the naysayers.

It finds that technological advances alone will not bring a sustainable world via dematerialization. They found no evidence looking at 56 materials, goods, and services from basic resources, such as aluminium and formaldehyde to hardware and energy technologies like hard disk drives, transistors, wind energy, and photovoltaics. There was no overall reduction in their use, despite technological improvements to their performance. They identified only six cases of materials usage declining, but these were mostly toxic chemicals such as asbestos and reductions were via government intervention.

There is a stark choice, population growth can only stop in one of two ways: either sooner, the humane way, by planned containment and fewer births involving family planning backed by policies to make it available and encourage people to use it. Or later, the 'natural' way, by more deaths – famine, disease, rioting and war.

## THE CONTAINED CITY

Denial and our dulled senses make it hard to imagine and viscerally grasp the impacts of this Anthropocene age. Cities have a pressure cooker effect. They can become dysfunctional if they grow in chaotic ways or too fast. Cities are consumption hubs and exacerbate the global resource pressures. T**he 'too much' effect is prevalent**, with too much crime, too much noise, too much mental illness, the effects of increased density which exacerbate the situation. There is too much loneliness, now regarded as an epidemic even though there are more people in cities and they are more connected than ever.[68] We express this mostly by generalizing about the stresses of urban life, rather than being more focused on whether the numbers matter. Population matters should be at the heart of city making debates, and indeed national policy, but they are not.

There is a flipside. Cities can be an ameliorator: people are more educated in cities - a major factor in reducing growth; it easier to administer birth control programmes in cities; they are an accelerator of problem solving with great minds working together, and so are intensifiers of human thinking and inventive solutions. Cities can be the laboratories for solving the problems of their own making.

A vision of place, less reliant growth can get you to imagine alternatives. This can lead to experiments in thinking about and living without population growth. Can Western lifestyles then be maintained or can a lower population improve lifestyle? Or would poorer places get better. Imagine the experience of Kolkata or Delhi with 25% less population and traffic. There is a template in the shrinking cities movement, think here across the US rustbelt from cities like Baltimore or Chicago or the many in Europe especially Russia.

The struggle is difficult given the addiction to growth. Take Melbourne – 'it can only get better as it gets bigger and it approaches the 4.0 Fourth Industrial Revolution.'[69] This is the threshold and optimum size argument. It raises critical mass issues. **When does size lead to cities becoming dysfunctional**. What then happens to urban cemeteries? Are cemetery skyscrapers the next thing? What are the incentives to reduce population? Remove government incentives to population growth, such as child benefit (heresy even to ask the question, many will say). We could ask too - would 60 million people in Britain best be accommodated in six cities of 10 million each or 120 cities of 500,000 each? The latter would be small enough to be intimate and big enough to be cosmopolitan. Which is best for the people, for sanity, the environment, the economy?

Biennale, Venice

# CITIES & THE CULTURE MIX

Ideas evolve, survive, reproduce and die just like living things. They also reincarnate, they can jump generations and continents. The most powerful become memes so they disperse and are imitated. Meme goggles[70] are useful to understand how ideas spread from the trivial to the profound, from the safe to the dangerous, from the practical to the spiritual. That lens helps us decode fashions. It explains why we suddenly like Mexican tapas, Chinese wontons, Japanese sushi or Italian spaghetti. Cultural diffusion might lead to a fusion, but also confusion before they are assimilated.

Ideas, habits, customs and inventions move when people move, trade or invade another culture. They mingle with the host culture but diffusion processes are not one-way. There is influence and counter-influence. This is true of the distant past as it is today. Think of the spread of Greek culture under Alexander the Great and its ultimate effect on Islam, or the Islamic conquests of the Iberian Peninsula, or Sicily and its transmission of Greek knowledge to the West. Think too of the impact of Eastern philosophy on California or the Californian McDonalds culture on Asia or the impact of Western culture itself on most the world. Cultural colonialism is one driver and it imposes itself — such as when the Spanish, French, English and Portuguese forced the aboriginal populations of Asia, the Americas and Africa to become Christian.

# IDEAS &
# IDEOLOGIES

Along the way we receive new things like paper or gunpowder from China or African music. Yet there are unintended consequences in the long run which can turn out as positive or ambiguous. See here the use of English in India as a national binding device. French-speaking Africa has perhaps more cultural resonance than it might have if it had only communicated with its tribal languages. Their domestic culture might also shape their version of French, the vocabulary and the rhythm with which French Africans speak then enriching French as a whole.

**Most of what we think, know and do has come from somewhere else**. Cities are the hubs of this mix and mingling, they are powerhouses where cultural diffusion meets. Witness the many Chinatowns or Italian quarters as in New York, the French Quarter in New Orleans or German one in Qingdao.

## DISCOVERIES & INVENTIONS

Discoveries, inventions, scientific insights and ideas can move quickly and they come in different forms and many change how we see the world, what we can do or how we want the world to be. Some scientific discoveries shifted our understanding — think of the Copernican revolution, the recognition that the Earth orbits the Sun (and not vice-versa) or Darwin's theory of evolution by natural selection and the idea of the survival of the fittest. Or quantum theory that deals with the smallest things, and relativity theory that deals with the largest things like space, time and the universe itself.

**Techniques that create workable solutions can travel at speed** and be adopted more or less immediately and be transformative. Michael Faraday's contribution to developing electricity in the early 1800s set in motion the conditions for our nomadic world. Samuel Morse's development of the electrical telegraph in 1837 takes this further. Alexander Bain's electric printing device created in 1846 later becomes the once ubiquitous fax. The American Oliver Evans is credited with designing the first refrigeration machine in 1805 so that food could travel without perishing. Elisha Otis invented the modern elevator in 1852 when he came up with his safety brake in Chicago. It made skyscrapers possible. Penicillin was invented by Alexander Fleming in 1928 and it contains disease thereby allowing safer travel. All this made the world in motion possible.

Then there is the World Wide Web invented by Tim Berners-Lee. Yet even that had a pre-history. The seventeenth century German philosopher, Gottfried Wilhelm Leibniz, speculated about calculating machines, and the polymath, Charles Babbage, is credited with developing the first mechanical computer in 1821 or Alan Turing, the crypto-analyst and computer scientist in the 1940s or John von Neumann, the mathematician in the mid-1900s. The invention of the computer would not have been possible without parallel developments in other fields like philosophers dealing with logic. This reminds us that dramatic transformations are a collective endeavour coalescing and cross-fertilizing inventions from across the globe.

They played their part in the information age. This is the breathtaking move in human history that shifts the basis of the industrial age towards the digital revolution. Its incredible speed of information transfer force-feeds hyper-globalization and allows us to escape the tyranny of distance. It allows us to be placeless. Only then can we truly enter the nomadic age. To be more nomadic is less an ideology and more a way of life and being. It links to a powerful idea that connectedness trumps rootedness.

These possibilities join up with other ideas and one of the most powerful has been the notion of sustainability, whose implementation itself benefits from digital capacities. In spite of the existence of climate-change deniers, it has spread and shaped how we think the world should develop.

## SOCIAL CONCEPTS

Social ideas are alive and can equally disseminate like a virus. These include concepts like empathy, justice, equality, even humiliation, and some of those are very old and have infused our mindscape. Some are big political theories like democracy, the free market, communism, socialism, fascism, human rights, seen as universal rights, such as the right to life or the right to freedom of speech. This spread after the French and American revolutions. Equally, feminism, which critiques our imbalanced power relations of explicit and implicit discrimination, and so reinterprets the world through a gender lens. These are notions that have changed the world and will continue to do so, often in intense power struggles.

These are ideas about how our social organizations or government should work, or what our ethics or morality should be. Belief systems, such as philosophy, religion, and political theories have a deep impact on how humans organize. They provide the overall texture through which our world thinks. They become an ideology when they embody a system of concepts and become the source of policy and action.

The free market is an economic idea that over the last decades spread like wildfire, so shaping politics as an ideology. It is indelibly linked to the notion of the market's 'invisible hand' and Adam Smith, the eighteenth century Scottish philosopher, and his The Wealth Of Nations, first published in 1776. Arguing that self-interest is the basis of all economic transactions, he thought individuals acting in a self-interested way would benefit society. What is often forgotten, as we mostly remember the slogan 'the invisible hand', is that Smith did not believe self-interest was the only principle that should structure economic life – governments should intervene where necessary and behave morally, as a completely free market could destroy society. The neo-liberal notion of economic rationality has diffused, yet it is imprisoned by its thinking that by default we are selfish. It has spread so deeply that we do not remember it is only an idea invented by humans and not necessarily intrinsic. Humans have other altruistic motives. Evidence is the vast and lively civic world where we think beyond ourselves.

Communism and socialism inspired many through time and responded to injustice and exploitation as it crossed cultural boundaries. Although some of their recipes, especially those of the former, have been discredited, the core issues they address of fairness, justice and equality remain powerful motivators of action. Achieving those aims today, say of fairness, will have different manifestations. One of these is the notion of the urban commons where resources are shared and jointly managed. With divides between the rich and poor escalating there remains a fertile soil from which it will grow, allied too to hope and to a vision of a different future.

**A significant idea is humiliation, widely shared by those who have suffered from the imperial legacy**. Its most virulent form is seen in the way some Muslims feel historically and currently endlessly humiliated.

Scott Atran notes in quoting Al Baghdadi:

'O soldiers of the Islamic State continue to harvest soldiers, erupt volcanoes of jihad everywhere and dismember enemies ... to liberate mankind from the satanic usury-based global system leached by the Jews and crusaders.'

As he says this is an appeal that resonates with many, and stirs at least some to atrocity. Or as one young ISIS lion cub Abdullah says: 'I will be the one who slaughters you, O Kuffar. I will be a mujahid, inshaallah. ISIS attracts converts as it dreams of a glorious purified past and its caliphate. Atran suggests we must offer youth another personal dream to create a life of significance with a concrete chance of realization and offer them the chance to create their own local initiatives.

This is the battle of ideas par excellence between a more inward-looking religiously-inspired view of world and one motivated by the secular values of humanism, or where there is a recognition of a shared humanity. Can the nomadic world find a way through this quagmire?

The English language is a good example of diffusion. **English, in what feels like the speed of light in evolutionary terms, has come to dominate** how most of the world communicates – it has become the Lingua Franca. An Italian speaking to a German may do so via English as might a Dane speaking to a Chinese or a French person to a Kenyan. In this process, English hoovers up useful foreign words too like entrepreneur from French or Zeitgeist from German. This is hugely convenient. Remember too how President George Bush once famously said that the French have no word for entrepreneur.

International political, economic and scientific life is increasingly conducted in English as are the major conferences. In the EU, there are 24 official languages but it is English and then French, Spanish and German that dominate. In Asia or the Arab world any event of international significance has English present.

# LANGUAGE & DIFFUSION

There are in fact many more Chinese native speakers (1.2 billion) and more Spanish native speakers (400 million) than English (360 million). Yet English is spoken to a relatively good degree by 1.5 billion people in the world. Let's not forget the power of the Internet. Although more than 75% of the global population does not speak a word of English, over 50% of the Internet's content is in English.[71] Yet an interesting sign here is that 20 years ago 80% of Internet content was English.

**China understands the cultural power of the Internet** and has fiercely protected its own content and search engines. The question is whether 'The Great Firewall' blocks cultural browsing and so ironically isolates China. The French Academy has attracted notoriety by attempting to protect French from importing foreign words, especially anglicized ones, and its latest campaign is to create French equivalents for 'hashtag' or 'selfie' as well as developing a French language computer keyboard.

The dominance of English as a language is crucial as this reinforces the soft power of Anglo-Saxon or American culture and its embedded ideas. Even though there many counter-examples in cultural life such as Brazilian tele-novellas, Japanese manga, Korean K-Pop or the world music scene. Clearly the issues are not simple.

However, language, spoken and written, is perhaps the primary means of communication or expression through which we grasp, negotiate and create meaning out of our world. And equally through which we deal with the practical exigencies of life like legal documents, trading or verbal conversation.

*Collaborations Conference, Toronto*

Of course, many ancient cultures used symbols to pass on their history or stories, and of course music and dance convey powerful meanings, and of course blind people express themselves through touch or deaf people through signs. And non-verbal symbols like smiles, frowns, winks, waves, are constantly used. Crucially too we are witnessing an epochal shift from the verbal to the visual, the impact of Instagram being an example here.

Yet for a majority of cultures it is language that is the prevalent way to transmit founder myths, history, identity, information and knowledge. Think here of the Nordic sagas or Finnish Kalevala or the Hindu Vedas and Upanishads. Think of the role of literature in defining nationhood and identity.

Language death[72] is a matter of rising concern. Only 600 of the around 6,000 global languages are safe. It worries not merely anthropologists and linguists, but anyone interested in cultural identity and expression as the world continues its globalizing march. Just like we talk of bio-diversity as a form of protective resilience, so too we must with language.

We are in the midst of dramatic transformations which is causing something of an identity crisis for many cultures. Their ability to express themselves is being reduced at times critically. Our cultural scaffolding is fragile often without a tarpaulin to protect it. Globalization exerts immense power. It has provided untold opportunities. Yet **the promise of globalization was diversity but the result seems to be sameness**.

Vienna

# INVADING SPACE & PLACE

Think back 50 years ago when practically none of the global restaurant chains or fashion houses existed outside of their home territory. Today their octopus tentacles reach nearly everywhere. Food and clothing are two of the most important markers of identity and local distinctiveness, yet the globalizing drive of chains is causing that to erode. There is, of course, influence and counter-influence and **not everything is travelling just one way from the power centres towards the periphery**. The Napolitano pizza captured the world and now has many variations, of which the Chicago deep-dish pizza is perhaps the most famous. The fashion industry too continually scours the world for inspiration, borrowing and twisting local designs to its purposes.

Consider a thought experiment. Play a game and map places across the world where you do not see global brands. Globalization promises greater diversity of expression or variety, yet the reality differs. The numbers I will throw at you will shock and they evidence a decline in distinctiveness.

Coca-Cola open happiness
Coca-Cola open happiness
Coca-Cola open happiness
Coca-Cola
open happiness
Coca-Cola

FOOD & DRINK

Coca-Cola is everywhere and is the world's most valuable and most globally known brand, recognized by 94%of us, – now in just over 200 countries. Indeed, the logo has a special beauty. The drink was the first to expand globally in the 1920s. It sells 1.9 billion servings a day and in a guestimate of 30 million plus outlets, 500,000 restaurants, and, in 2010, it had 2.8 million vending machines. Stacked up, this is the size of four Empire State Buildings or 4.25 million cubic metres of space.

Coke is everywhere, but not in North Korea or Cuba which for political reasons have banned its drinks (although some slip through in Cuba). Bolivia also tried to ban Coca-Cola unsuccessfully in 2012.

# THE BRAND
# & THE BLAND

Following droughts in 2017 in Tamil Nadu and in Kerala, home to 110m people, the government with the backing of traders sought to ban Coke and Pepsi. They alleged it was depleting ground water resources in the drought-stricken region. It also wanted to help local products get a better foothold. This reminds us of how in the 1950s the French who coined the phrase "coca-colonisation", staged protests overturning trucks and smashing bottles as protesters saw the drink as a threat to French culture. Coca-Cola became a symbol of capitalism during the Cold War and a faultline between capitalism and communism. Now it projects friendship, family, happiness and other fuzzy associations.

The battle between Coca-Cola and Pepsi Cola is legendary, which Coke has won as it controls 42% of the total carbonated soft drinks market compared with Pepsi's 30%. We must remember that Coke also owns Sprite, Fanta and Minute Maid and that Pepsi owns 7Up, Tropicana and Gatorade amongst a vast collection of drinks. Yet Pepsi is a larger company given its other non-drink products, and it too sells Pepsi in more than 200 countries.

Among the food chain outlets, it is hard to find a chain-free well-developed country. Iceland and Bermuda stand out and Bermuda has a law - the Prohibited Restaurants Act 1977. There are no outlets of McDonald's, Subway, Starbucks, Burger King, Dunkin Donuts, Pizza Hut, Taco Bell, Wendy's, Domino's Pizza or their Canadian or European equivalents. One KFC slipped through as it was there before 1977, but it is Bermuda majority owned. By contrast, there are several Bermudian

*Coco Cola exhibition in Ghent*

fast-food restaurants. Iceland had no McDonald's or Starbucks as of 2016 although the former is thinking about coming in. Other places like Iran or Macedonia have no chains, nor do the more impoverished places. McDonald's is present in 120 countries, Subway in around 110 and Starbucks in over 70, but not in Greece or Turkey. Italy is Starbucks free as of 2017, but that changed in 2018 when the first opened in the historic Palazzo Delle Poste building in central Milano with another 200 plus to follow in the country. The backlash has begun: 'If I ever went to Starbucks, I would feel like a number, not a customer....... and do they ever pay their taxes.'

The latter is good news for Americans and tourists comforted by the familiar watery coffee who cannot handle local specialities and serious coffee culture. Tourists too often decrease distinctiveness, preferring the branded, bland restaurants, hotel chains and shops. It is bad news for the rest who like to have some sense of local culture. There is an amusing infographic on the Quartz website that outlines the geography of Starbucks.[73] With the exception of a few locations in Morocco, in Egypt and some recent openings in South Africa, there are more or less no Starbucks in continental Africa.

Also spreading their invasive tentacles over the world are around 45,000 Subway outlets (a large portion are in the US), 37,000 McDonald's, 25,000 Starbucks, 20,000 KFCs, 15,000 Burger Kings, 14,000 Pizza Huts, 11,300 Dunkin Donuts, 11,000 Domino's Pizza, 7,300 Baskin Robbins, 7,300 Hunt Brothers Pizza, 6,500 Taco Bells and 6,500 Wendy's. Most of these are franchises, the quickest way to grow. Few wealthier nations are Big Mac or Frappuccino-free.

**The chains are large and powerful and entrench their positions in the public imagination** by immense advertising budgets (McDonald's $1.5 billion in the US in 2016 and $500 million for Subway).

Another game is to speculate how long a road would be made up of the 180,000 outlets of the top ten chains. I estimate, if on average they were a fraction more than 10 metres wide each, this would make 2,000 kms, (though in fact the average McDonald's is wider). Or if we take the 240,000 that belong to the top twenty chains then the distance increases to say 2,500 kms. Then adding some chains like the 9,600 US CVS pharmacies and 13,200 Walgreens Boots Alliance or the 11,700 global Walmarts of which 3,500 are supercentres, 1,800 Targets or 2,300 Home Depots, we get to around 4,000kms. Appropriately this is the distance between New York and the unreal world of Las Vegas.

Let us also consider the surface area covered by the bigger chains in the world. The fast food chains average around 250 sq. metres per outlet and this covers roughly 60 sq. kms, exactly the size of Manhattan. Add to this the total space covered by all Walmarts in the world and that makes a further two Manhattans and then you have the Costcos, CVSs, Walgreens, Targets, Home Depots and so on - probably

*Coca Cola is everywhere... Delhi,
The Maldives Mexico City, Buenes Aires,
Abu Dhabi, Berlin, Athens, Phnom Penh.*

another Manhattan equivalent. All the IKEAs in the world take up 9.4 sq. kms. the equivalent of four-and-a-half Monaco principalities.

The highest density of Starbucks is in Midtown Manhattan, where there are now also 171 Manhattan Subway sandwich shops − versus 147 subway stations. Per capita, Canada tops the list with one Starbucks for every 35,000 Canadians followed by the US, Singapore and South Korea. Seoul has most Starbucks (284) with New York second (277).

McDonald's was historically synonymous with fast-food and the focus of anti-capitalist protests. It operates 36,899 restaurants worldwide of which 14,267 are in the US. It employs more than 375,000 people (2016)

*Melbourne Airport*

and serves 68 million customers each day. The US has the highest McDonald's density at one outlet per 22,000 inhabitants, followed by New Zealand with one per 27,000 people. There are 7,920 McDonald's locations Europe, with Germany the most at 1,472 restaurants, France at 1,386 restaurants and Britain 1,262 restaurants. China has 2,000, Russia 550 and Brazil 800. Even Andorra has five, Liechtenstein three, the Northern Marianas two. as does New Caledonia. For all its anti-American rhetoric, Saudi Arabia has around 230.[74] McDonald's is persistent and its latest battleground is Florence where it announced in late 2016 that it was suing the city for €18 million after it was blocked from opening a restaurant in the historic Piazza del Duomo.

To make the point about how a few branded organizations cover the globe another category is convenience stores. Here 7-Eleven is the largest and just opened its 60,000th store, followed by Family Mart with 23,600, and Lawson's at fourth with 11,500. Behind their English names are Japanese owned companies and they have spread their wings. Japan has a convenience store culture and in fact, many are rather creative miniature emporia that are Wi-Fi enabled, with post office facilities, cash points and printing services apart from foods. OXXO from Mexico is the third largest with 14,500 outlets.

We **are witnessing the decline of distinctiveness**, and wherever you are you tend to see the same thing.

## FASHION & CLOTHING

Looking good and always different is the fashion industry mantra. It creates a mood where you feel you are nearly always out-of-date and so therefore bored with your clothes. So off to the charity shop with last season's best seller and let me be beguiled and ensnared by the latest colour or style.

In a perpetual give-and-take, fashion influences and is influenced. Few fashion houses can survive without a global reach whether at the low, mid or high end. This is reflected in the scale and **scope of the production supply chains that criss-cross the world** to make the fashion system work. Most outsource production to the cheapest hubs in Asia. After intense lobbying by organizations like Fashion Revolution and the Ethical Consumer, companies are increasingly being pushed to make these production chains transparent. H&M, Inditex (which includes Zara and Massimo Dutti) and Levis are doing best according to the Fashion Transparency Index, and the luxury brands are doing worst. The Rana Plaza disaster, which killed 1,134 people in a garment factory collapse in Bangladesh in 2013 highlighted the dreadful and exploitative conditions within which much of fashion operates. Carry Somers, co-founder of Fashion Revolution notes: 'Shoppers have the right to know that their money is not supporting exploitation, human rights abuses and environment destruction as lack of transparency costs lives.'

Inditex is the largest fashion company and its Zara subsidiary manufactures half of its clothing – the most fashionable – in a dozen company owned factories in Galicia, northern Portugal and Turkey. Inditex operates in nearly 100 countries and has 7,385 stores of which 2,200 are Zara, 740 Massimo Dutti and 1,000 Bershka. H&M, with 3,700 stores, is the second largest and is the biggest buyer of clothes made in Bangladesh. Third is Uniqlo with 1,800 stores. It is the brand name of the Fast Retailing Company in Japan and makes the majority of its clothes in China, where a report called *The Road to Dystopia* criticized its labour practices. Gap, the fourth biggest, has facilities in Cambodia, Bangladesh, Myanmar, Colombia and more. Less known is the South Korean Cheil, the fifth largest fashion company and owned by Samsung. At the lower end, there is TK Maxx (or TJ Maxx) that operates over 1,000 stores.

Nike is vast and predominantly a shoe company but involved in clothing and it produces in 430 apparel factories operating in 40 countries with China, Vietnam, Thailand and Indonesia in the lead.

Floating between mid-range and high-end fashion is Armani with its nearly 3,000 outlets focusing on Giorgio Armani and Emporio Armani stores in 60 countries across the globe.

At the high-end, Louis Vuitton is part of the world's largest luxury group LVMH. Its products range from clothes to perfumes to champagne. It makes 20% of its bags in France and has factories in Spain and California, although many of the components, such as buttons, rivets or zips are produced in Asia and elsewhere. LVMH with Dior, Louis Vuitton, Bulgari and Fendi and Kering with labels such as Gucci, Stella McCartney and Alexander McQueen are the big hitters. Gucci makes most of the products in Prato, mostly by 45,000 Chinese people living in the wider district. For them, like most of the high-end luxury companies, clothing is a small proportion of their output and essentially a marketing exercise for their perfumes and accessories where the real profits are made.

The brands are visible everywhere, especially at airports where travellers will see them clustered. Overall there are 200 plus Dior boutiques, 550 Guccis, 600 Pradas, 460 Louis Vuittons, 500 Burberrys, 310 Chanels,

320 Dolce & Gabbanas, 300 Hermes, 200 Fendis, 110 Ralph Laurens, nearly 100 YSL/Yves Saint Laurent and 70 DKNY stores. All of these luxury brands are present in the thousands in other locations too, such as in the more exclusive department stores like Selfridges in London or Mitsukoshi in Ginza, Tokyo.

The top of the fashion pyramid is haute couture, very expensive handmade garments that often set a trend or create a look, as these are bought by celebrities or the very rich and whose style then filters down into high-end fashion. Their look in turn often but not always trickles down and then appears in mid-range and cheaper clothing that is frequently copied overnight after the major catwalk shows most famously in Paris, Milan and New York. It is claimed that only around 2,000 women worldwide buy haute couture and of those just 200 are regular buyers.[75]

This part of the system is **necessary to activate and inflate craving, lust, desire and emotion**, for which also an immense advertising machine is required. Content is less important than marketing. Condé Nast's Vogue March 2016 edition had 405 advertising pages. Hearst's Harper's Bazaar ran second that month with 336 pages and Elle's was third with 315 pages.[76] Not surprisingly companies like LVMH, the 19th largest global company, has with €4.2bn the fifth biggest advertising spend.[77] This means the ratio of production cost to sales cost is disproportionate and growing. If a Gucci or Fendi bag costs €1000 in a shop a quarter might be the production costs (machinery, labour and location) and €750 on marketing and selling. Another example is NIKE. It is the 18th largest global company, but has the 14th biggest advertising spend at €2.75bn. A €100 NIKE sneaker costs on average €30 to produce, although the labour costs are far, far lower.

Once, the fashion cycle was two fashion seasons a year: Spring/Summer and Autumn/Winter. **The agitated frenzy for the ever novel; the now**; the trend; and not missing out has created a monster. The fashion industry in essence churns out a micro-season every week. The fast fashion business model is enabled by big data that helps monitor sales patterns by the minute across the globe with the 'fast fashion' companies, led by Inditex, H&M and Uniglo, responding instantly with their just-in-time production methods. This is why Inditex is vertically integrated, so as to control the whole process from idea through production to sale. What was once ridiculed as disposable fashion is now the mainstream.

To keep the feverish, frantic system going **the industry employs a world of 'what nexters' or trend forecasters** looking at the next colour, the next length of garments, the next width, the next neckline, the next must-have accessory. And then there is the look. So one moment its tribal or savannah chic, then gypsy boho, then city sleek, followed by ethnic authentic or space age mechanical, the drugged up orphan look, the emaciated waif or pretending you are a poor immigrant. However, you are paying extortionate amounts for torn tee-shirts or jeans.

It is ironic to hear a mission statement from one of the fashion behemoths, 'Our mission is simple: we exist to help customers look and feel good while making a positive contribution to people and the planet'.

There are longer or shorter patterns within this overall scheme like the dishevelled, floppy look that has been here for a while. There are variations, of course, with some still promoting the Ivy League preppy look and others understated classics.

In this crazed ever changing, restless dynamic it is not surprising that minimalism is **a new consumption trend, where less costs more** – remember, how the smaller bikinis also cost more. The brands are also projecting overall lifestyles so they have seamlessly moved from providing clothes, to accessories to home design to hotels and holidays and ultimately shaping your whole life. Think here of Bulgari hotel in Shanghai, Tommy Hilfiger hotel in Miami or Armani hotel in Dubai.

Interesting and seemingly contradictory human emotions play themselves out here and the higher-class brands have to do a fine balancing act. First there is the 'snob effect', where people search for the exclusive

and where price is seen as if it were quality. The second is the 'bandwagon effect', a psychological drive for people to do something primarily because other people are doing it. This has to be both encouraged and controlled.

Inevitably this ever-moving super-structure requires a complex logistical puzzle to orchestrate the people rushing around the world for photo shoots (and always in the most 'exotic places') to attend fashion shows and promotional tours. Think here of the designer, the models, photographers, prop and set designers, art directors, hair stylists apart from the truckers, visual effects and lighting specialists and especially those who create spectaculars.

*Jeepney racing to Manila Airport*

# THE FRENZIED FLOW

Place names and those of eateries tell us about the inexorable movement of people and cultures. There are 29 Londons in the world and 15 are the US, 15 Amsterdams with 10 in the US, 14 US Birminghams and 4 Rotterdams. Look at a a busy high street in Amsterdam, New York, Caracas, Johannesburg or Shanghai. You see Shanghais in Paris and Paris in Shanghai. There was even a Shanghai restaurant well beyond the Arctic Circle in Kirkenes. Consider all the Milanos you meet in New York: Café Milano, Caffe Milano, Milano Pizzeria, Milano Bistro, Milano Restaurant. Or those in Frankfurt: Ice Bar Milano, Pizzeria Milano or simply Milano and many more. Or all the Istanbuls you find wherever there are Turks. Simply called Istanbul Kebab house, Istanbul Grill, Istanbul Bistro, or Istanbul Restaurant. A quick check brought up Tokyo, Buenos Aires, Cape Town, Seoul and Sydney.

Yet there are more flows than people, consider: Money, goods and even our sense of reality.

'Money makes the world go round' is one of the great clichés of the age. It is an astonishing lubricant acting as a proxy for value since it enables seamless transactions in nanoseconds across space and time zones. More than anything **finance makes the constantly moving nomadic world possible** – how would people otherwise get paid in relatively simple ways. It is becoming increasingly abstract from bartering live cattle or material objects to coins to punching in a set of numbers. Once backed by notional equivalents in gold the physical note or coin now has marginal value and these are being phased out. It is what it represents that counts - the trillions of 'promises to pay'.

# FINANCE & ITS ESCALATING SPEED

It is spinning around the world ever faster, both the velocity and the volume. Consider the new ultra-fast fibre-optic data connections. 200 finance companies paid $2.8bn between them to build the straightest possible cable between Chicago and New York (a distance of 827 miles) to save 13 milliseconds.

The Bank of International Settlements (BIS) calculated that on a typical September 2016 day $5,100,000,000,000 in currency was traded – I put in the zeros for impact rather than saying $5.1 trillion. The US Federal Reserve estimated that $14,000,000,000,000 of dollar-denominated payments were routed per day through the US banking system. The largest 20 stock exchanges globally traded about 6,631 billion shares in January 2015, or 315 billion shares per trading day and with other smaller exchanges this might come to 350 billion.

The World Federation of Exchanges calculated the value of share trading worldwide. It was $114 trillion in 2015 compared with $81 trillion in 2014. The total number of trades in 2015 was 23.7 billion up from 15.3 billion the previous year. Most is attributable to rising trading activity in the Asia-Pacific region, which is now nearly 50% of global trading.[78]

Global currencies ease these processes so the dollar's pivotal role is crucial as is that of the Euro or as will be the role of the Chinese Renminbi. I remember the time not so long ago that British people were only allowed to take £50 of currency with them and any financial transactions were arduous and complex as indeed was just making a phone call. A **modern nomadic lifestyle would have been difficult then**.

The conveniences and opportunities that easier money flows allow are incredible, but of course they get misused. The financial crisis of 2007-2008 is one instance where the money world got itself into a frenzied collective madness in its search for profits. Money criss-crossed the globe in and out of finance centres, tax havens and back again with such speed and complexity that they themselves could not trace what was happening. People argue about the total cost with estimates varying between $30-50 trillion. That is a cost of between $40,000 to $55,000 for each human being in the world.

This crisis was helped by deregulation in the finance industry, yet that process also helps the world flow. But authorities allowed banks to trade in derivatives. These are financial products that derive their value from the value of another underlying asset, such as the value of a mortgage, a currency or a commodity. Things are one step removed. For instance, 1,000 mortgage debts are sold profitably on to a hedge fund, who in turn might also sell it on. Two steps removed, and with more selling on things became three, four and more steps removed. In a merry-go-round, banks then gave out more mortgages to continue selling profitable derivatives. Interest-only loans were the lure and so became affordable to less well-off, subprime borrowers. Then insurance companies insured against risks by providing 'credit default swaps'. So much money was being made that banks did not focus on their core business of helping business. Only 8% of all money that banks created went to non-finance businesses. Initially this raised house prices so everyone was happy, but a blip made the whole house of cards fall as poor people failed to repay their loans.

Rolling Stone magazine famously described the process citing Goldman Sachs, one of the main perpetrators. They are like a 'great vampire squid wrapped around the face of humanity, relentlessly jamming its blood funnel into anything that smells like money'.

CHINA SHIPPING
中国海运集团
CHINA SHIPPING
中国海运集团
中国海运集团
中国海运集团

Logistics, that seemingly unattractive, invisible activity, lies at the core of the world in motion and is one of the biggest industries in the world. It keeps things flowing. It is complex. Most of us are not aware how crucial it is. Without logistics, how could we bring events to cities, materials to large construction sites, a parcel to your home, to export and to import goods – and all on-time. Logistics companies are everywhere so we forget to think about them, but we should. Together with finance and retailing, these are the largest global industries. **Logistics keeps people and products on the move from origin to end-user**, combining or connecting different means and modes of transport: roads, rail, air and water, with trucks, vans, cars, bikes, trains, planes and ships. These are linked to hubs, interchanges, ferry ports and airports in complex supply chains managed by sophisticated software systems, to track and to manage inventory, flow of information, order processing, warehousing or material handling.

# THE LOGISTICS OF THINGS

The figures impress and a few will suffice. The global market in terms of revenue was valued at 7.18 trillion euros in 2015 and is expected to double by 2023 or triple by 2030, an annual growth of around 7.5%. And more things are moving around. It was estimated at 55.0 billion tons in 2015 and projected to nearly double by 2024. 11 million people[79] in Europe alone are employed in transport services.

It accounts for 5% of EU employment and contributes nearly 5% of GDP. There are nearly 1 million companies in road transport alone. Airports and airlines employ 670,000 people, and 3.2 million depend directly or indirectly on the air sector. European shipping employs 300,000 seafarers and another three million in related jobs. Add to this the EU's 8 million automotive sector workers and we start to grasp the extent. This includes the 23 million shipping containers in service, of which at any given moment 14 million are travelling and the same number out of service and used for multiple purposes, as well as 6 million that never go to sea.

All vehicles travelling in the USA went around the world the equivalent of 25 million times when their combined total hit the 5 trillion kilometres mark in 2015. Consider there are around 140 million commercial vehicles and 3.5 million heavy load truck drivers. Or that Britain has 4 million vans as of 2016, up from 3.6 in 2011, of which 57% are white. Van to van that would be 18,480 kilometres long. The combined British

Soho, London

payload volume adds up to 26.2 million cubic metres – the equivalent of 10,483 Olympic swimming pools. Take Asia where similar trends are happening, India where the extended logistics sector employs around 16 million and where demand is expected to grow to 28.4 million people by 2022. There are similar stories from China and Japan.

And let us not forget the daily travel movements of working people or their business, shopping and leisure trips. Consider the astonishing fact that the 1.2 billion cars, vans and trucks in motion are perhaps clocking 45 trillion kilometres annually; imagine the 3 million train locomotives, railcars, and coaches trundling to their destinations clocking up 12.7 billion kilometres in 2013 and this is 25% up from 2001; ponder the 48 billion kilometres a year the 20,000 strong commercial airline fleet cover and predicted to double in 15 years. And let's forget cycling and walking, the most common form of movement.

EU citizens spend around 10 hours a week travelling an average daily distance of 34.7 km. 13% of expenditure goes on transport-related items.

The global transportation industry has substantial problems. There is an ageing workforce and driver shortages in many countries, putting pressure on keeping things moving. Given the image problems of the industry – largely male dominated – companies are already struggling to find workers with the requisite skills to handle the entire supply chain. They need more women in every sphere. This puts pressure on developing driverless vehicles and **a big 'robots versus truckers' battle lies ahead as automation takes hold** - automated material handling equipment, warehouse control software, biometrics and RFID are new technologies.[80][81] The Silicon Valley start-up Otto promises to retrofit vehicles with driverless capabilities for just $30,000, when the average trucker's wage is around $40,000 per year.

Many of the largest logistics companies are German. The top five are led by German Post's DHL with 325,000 employees and a €57.3 billion turnover the largest, followed by UPS with €53 billion and 440,000 employees; Fedex with 400,000 employees and €44 billion turnover; DB Schenker a subsidiary of German Railways with 95,000 employees and €20 billion; and Kuehne + Nagel with 70,000 and €20 billion turnover. Internet shopping has increased their revenue with the volume of parcels growing immeasurably, exacerbating the mass movement of vans and smaller pick-ups throughout the world. On December 20th 2016, UPS's busiest day, it handled 15.8 million packages and FedEx 9 million on that same day. This outstrips Amazon which ships 1.6 million packages a day. There will be some e-substitution but shipments of parcels will grow, for example in Britain from 1.8 billion 2016 to 2.3 billion in 2023.

Add to these astonishing figures the size of the global mobile services sector. Its turnover in 2017 was just over €3 trillion euro with mobile ecosystem employing 28.5 million people directly or indirectly. The scale and scope is clear. In 2014 a threshold was reached. There were more mobile devices (8.6 billion) than the 7.1 billion people. Those devices are expected to skyrocket. In 2016 44% of the global population (3.77 billion) had a smartphone – a phone with internet access, and an operating system capable of running downloaded apps. More than 50% of the global population have portable devices to communicate and interact and 37% use social media with WhatsApp, WeChat, Facebook Messenger and Instagram users running into billions. 22% of the population use e-commerce.

This mobility industry and the mobile services industry combined make it even vaster. **Interdependent, together they underpin our nomadic world**. The first involves activities, products and services to optimize the movement of goods and people. This requires the manufacture and running of all the transport hardware, including storage, and then there are intense cross-sector linkages to computer, electronic and electrical product manufacturing and associated information and communication activities. The latter sectors allow us to interact through conversation, data access and content services harnessing voice, image, internet, SMS, text, or big data.

Yet remember there are challenges ahead to be able to cope with this nomadic world. We receive between three to five times as much information than we did 25 years ago and this pales into insignificance with the 100+ fold increase in what we churn out. 295 exabytes of data are floating around the world – that is 29,500,000,000,000,000,000,000 pieces of information[82] representing apparently 315 times the number of grains of sand on Earth. The vast information mass that makes up the evolving digital universe is made up of texts, images and videos on mobile phones, You Tube uploads, digital movies, banking data swiped in an ATM, security footage, recordings on highway tolls, calls zipping down digital phone lines. It is predicted to grow by 40% each year over the next five years and is barely charted and evaluated with only 3% tagged and 0.5% analysed according to IDC.[83]

## SELF-STORAGE & MOBILITY

The unprecedented growth of self-storage reflects the rise in workforce mobility as well as its other reasons like downsizing, increased divorce rates, rising rental costs and shrinking space and their small business use. Since the first facilities were created in the States in 1958 it has grown year in, year out and has been the fastest growing segment of the commercial property market over the last 40 years. In 2014 gross incomes of US self-storage companies were $27.2 billion with the

*Docklands, London*

54,000 storage facilities accounting for 230 million square metres of space; that is nearly 2 square metres for each American. This represents 229.5 sq. kms of self-storage - nearly three times the size of Manhattan.[84] The largest global companies are not well-known, such as Public Storage who owns the biggest storage facility in the world in New York with 4,000 units on its 12 floors with 25,000 square metres of rentable space. Others include Extra Space, CubeSmart, Life Storage and U-Haul. 9.5% of Americans have storage facilities, far more than any other country.

The 2,700 European facilities are miniscule by contrast to the US whose capacity is approaching 8 million sq. metres, 30 times less than the States or, put another way, the average number of storage units per million of population in Europe is just under 4 compared to 163 in the U.S.[85] Australia per capita is the 2nd largest place with 1,100 facilities and 2,6 million sq. metres of space.[86] The average number of times an American moves in their lifetime is 11.4 and for British people 8 times.[87][88] However, American millennials are moving less annually (11%) than they did at their post-war height of over 20% in 1948. The 2008 economic crisis is a major factor[89] here as job opportunities are a prime motivation for moving and these are now more modest, so an impetus is lacking as is another incentive for moving to a new home. Home ownership for younger people is at its lowest level in at least 40 years. The above does not contradict the overall argument about the nomadic world as moving home is only one aspect of the nomadic life. In addition, for lifestyle reasons some people move more and others less.

The three big game-changers supplanting material resources or location are: big data; the Internet of Things; and intelligent objects. And we have only seen a glimpse so far of the potential of artificial intelligence (AI). Rarely is the cultural landscape sucked in by the gravitational pull of dynamic technologies and the ideas they engender - digitization is one. **It is the dominant cultural force of the twenty-first century**, twisting everything into its orbit. A paradigm shift, it shapes the world in its image, affecting all forms of communication or culture and art: how words and texts are written, used and placed, how we relate to each other, how cities are experienced, such as in the dynamic world of Web 2.0, a social web that fosters collaborative processes or blogs, chat rooms, message boards, of Wikipedia, Facebook or Twitter. And Web 3.0 is on its way that will have elements of an independent intelligence.

# THE VIRTUAL & THE REAL

The interactive, immersive force of digital technologies allows us to work with great sophistication from anywhere and to feel a co-presence even though one person may be in Mumbai, the other in Shanghai and the third in Cape Town. It allows us make artefacts or art in new ways and to **experience the city as a dynamic, moving, responsive interface** where nothing is static. Here there are vast opportunities, for instance, to imagine, to communicate and to interpret museums, galleries or performance spaces in different ways, breaking out of their physical confines and spreading their tentacles into public space. The same applies to heritage sites. The world of advertising and marketing is already grasping the opportunities.

The capacity to simulate and virtualize experience is one of the most crucial topics in the contemporary world – a mental and social transformation created by our new electronic environment that blends and mixes the 'virtual' and 'real'. Simulated products, services and augmented reality experiences are a cyber-world that is extending everywhere, even creating virtual social networks, relationships and feelings, let alone currencies like bitcoin.

*Sign outside Dublin Library*

# Waiting Time

## About 15 Minutes

## from this point

INCHEON AIRPORT
IMMIGRATION OFFICE

INCHEON AIRPORT IMMIG

The world in motion requires more to consider, more choices to make, more decisions to take, more experiences to digest, more peoples to adapt to, more opinions to assess and more worldviews to absorb. It encourages speed as this 'more' happens in the same time frame and time cannot stretch. There will always be 3,600 seconds in an hour. We talk faster and now average 170 words per minute, up from 145 a decade ago, while our brain works best at comprehension at around 130. We think we are thinking faster, when in fact we are grasping subtleties less. We walk faster, 10% quicker than 25 years ago; we eat faster, largely because processed foods do not make us feel full. Of course, we travel faster; going by horse and carriage in 1800 from New York to Detroit was 450 times slower than by plane today.

# MORE MOVES & FASTER & FASTER

The equivalent car journey is 70 times faster, allowing for legitimate speed limits. We hope too to digest faster as we absorb more information faster, often doing so on the move with portable devices, and responding to messages while we walk. This **addictive info-mania can divide attention when texts, tweets, and gizmos demand an answer**. Our brains relax into the surfing, drifting world that navigating the internet encourages. Its versatility has unleashed powerful potential and is immensely convenient most of the time, yet increases restlessness as it can scramble thinking. We face the dilemma of losing depth as we gain the breadth of possibilities. Where does calm fit into this picture?[90]

You do not have to be a nomad to be absorbed into or be dependent on a nomadic world. It is etched into our everyday lifestyle. Consider the food you eat, the coffee, tea or alcohol you drink, the flowers you grow, the trees you plant, the wood you use, the fridges, dishwashers, washing machines, computers, TVs you buy or the trucks, van, or cars you drive. At any given moment ships are traversing the globe with 14 million containers filled with commodities, and 550,000 kilotons (kt) of dry goods like grain, 390,000 kt of liquids, 62 million cubic metres of gas and 10 million kt of vehicles. They are producing 152,000 tons of carbon.

Then too there are the films, videos or ads you see, the software in your computer or the device itself, or video games you play, the fashions you wear, the ideas you have, the philosophies you follow. Mostly they come from elsewhere.

2

# THE
# CITY IN
# MOTION

*Previous page: View from
Oscar Niemeyer's building,
Sao Paolo*

*This page: Taipei*

# THE PAST & THE FUTURE

The settled and unsettled meet in cities, and so we shift our focus. A world in motion is a world of cities in motion. Everything meets in them. The world is turning in on itself and towards its next phase of closure and containment, but the nomadic cannot be contained. We can make it more difficult. We can put up trade barriers. Terror organizations can make the city unsafe and a place of fear as they are both drawn to and frightened of the nomadic impulse. Its way of life is too flexible and insufficiently black and white. None of this will stop people, ideas and goods from moving – predominantly to cities. There will be counter movements to calmer smaller places and even escaping to rural retreats, but those numbers will be relatively insignificant. The urban is the dynamic of the age.

The nomadic instinct has existed through time and represents the exploratory impulse in action. The far horizon can have an allure. It leads people to move in their mind, to speculate, it is the drive that innovates the world to move physically as well as to escape from pressure, to survive better or to begin afresh. And they mostly end up in cities. **Cities are the accelerators of opportunity and exchange**, but also of the problems of living with difference.

The overarching unfolding nomadic context will affect cities across the globe, whether in deepest Congo, the highlands of Malaysia, the outer reaches of Russia or the landscapes of Patagonia. In many ways, cities will look the same, but how they operate will change and this will require physical settings and infrastructures fit for the coming age - the nomadic age. Our ideas of owning things will change: why lumber yourself with too many goods when you can share instead. You can have an office share or even do your work in a café. People will behave differently, perhaps treating city centres as if they were at an exhibition or experiencing travel through virtual reality goggles.

The changing circumstances, such as a blended virtual/real world, require deep psychological adjustment. It can be both unsettling and invigorating to have vast waves of people coming in and out of cities. In some inner-

city schools, up to 90 languages are spoken, and some of those kids have witnessed harrowing circumstances. Do they get on or do they mistrust each other, do they feel integrated in their host communities?

TWO NARRATIVES

The predominant narrative for cites focuses on their triumphant achievements[1] and there are excitements and direct contributions that the fleet-footed nomadic operators and well-connected make across the world. Yet there is a less told darker side to this narrative - a lack of awareness of the looming threats cities face from a series of interlinked environmental, cultural, social and financial crises, mostly out of their control. This new global pattern[2] of risks is global in scope with tightly intermeshed mega-crises forming a collective systemic crisis. It cannot be dealt with by a business-as-usual approach. To avert the worst a shift in power towards cities is required, as cities can act more nimbly in delivering an integrated response. They are the natural magnets to drive the necessary innovations and they have the critical mass to implement them. But significant changes need to be made in the relations between cities and nation states and our cultural mindset to allow this to happen.

The **greatest mass movement of people in history we are witnessing** and the inordinate pace of growth of cities exacerbates pressures (even though some cities are shrinking in certain regions). This growth requires elaborate infrastructures, well-functioning institutions and networks for cities to survive and flourish. The predicted growth in cities suggests that $100 trillion needs to be spent over the next 15 years on infrastructure, such as roads, airports, sanitation systems or housing and public space – imagine the energy output of all the steel and cement required and their effects on climate change.

Gostiny Dvor, St Petersburg

Dramatic decisions need to be taken to ensure cities continue to survive well into the current century. Cities acting on their own will have little impact on these systemic problems whatever good initiatives they undertake. They will need to network and collaborate with other cities they respect. They do not have the authority to create the necessary incentives and regulations regime to allow them to act forcefully in implementing solutions. But **cities are closer to their citizens and so have more legitimacy with them**. As these crises feed off each other, interacting often in dangerous ways, they require collective, connected solutions executed with vision, resources, determination, strong will and the ability to generate behavioural change.

## THE COMPLEX THREATS

The primary threats to the stability and well-being of cities are: climate change, food security, health, lack of resources, poverty and inequality, security, and lack of finances largely due to austerity policies since the financial crisis.

Add to these a growing population which exerts pressure on everything and this global passage of people can cause the identities of cities to shift, often with explosive impacts when fundamentally differing views about how life should be lived collide. The inability to grasp the complexity of these threats and how to deal with them causes an intense governance and management problem. There is urgency and limited time to act within this pressure cooker atmosphere, which is a crisis in itself. This is the risk landscape cities find themselves in – they encapsulate their vulnerabilities. It is an interlocking interdependent chain – a risk nexus.[2]

My colleague Tom Burke and I wrote about this extensively in The Fragile City.

Living together in relative harmony within our differences is a dominant theme of urban life. Of course, similar questions arise in rural areas, but it is the sheer numbers in cities that make a difference. This is why the concept of the civic and the citizen ultimately emerged - you have both rights and responsibilities in your city. These shape how cities are built, look, feel, are organized, and how differing groups interact. Assessing the varied urban histories through time can be perplexing. Yet with imagination we can envisage how what we now call civic life – a life engaged with your city – was structured and unfolded. We detect easily the battles between power, order and control and liberation, between freedom and empowerment, and the constant balancing act between individuals and the group.

# HISTORIES & HERITAGE

We see too the difference between how insiders and outsiders were treated and the struggles of the disenfranchised to make their voice heard. Stratification and keeping distinctions are constants. Each type of city has responded to these differently. In a few of the oldest cities we can still detect the layers of history and imagine how coexistence worked (think here of Rome, Constantinople or Xian, and how women, men and slaves, classes and trades lived separately and together, and how foreigners will have been clustered in their own settlements).

It is important to understand the bigger backdrop to the nomadic age to see where we have come from and where we might be going. **Without that historical trajectory we can lose perspective** and drift into simplistic thinking. Here follows a simple sketch to consider what urban forms might have supported a collective social life. A constant throughout is conquest, discovery, trade and insider/outsider exchange and conflicts which together lead to cross-fertilization. This is why it is **nigh impossible to find someone whose bloodlines have not been mixed up**, simply because of the movements of people over periods of time.

There is the 'Imperial City' built on an unquestioned hierarchy, order, power, control from above and the threat of random violence. Its emblem is perhaps a hill top palace. The civic as we understand it today – all the people coming together as equals or citizens – does not exist. Meanwhile the 'City of Religion' equally stresses an order, but is united by reference to a higher being and a moral code, with a temple, mosque or church centrally placed. It is around religious practice that life together is expressed. Think here of Madurai in India or Mecca. A variation is the Medieval City, typically walled and protected, with orders, guilds, classes or castes defining a person's place and potential interactions within the overall structure. The 'Renaissance City' builds on this, but an independent citizen begins to emerge with linked associational structures. Their power is expressed physically, say, in the burger houses or palaces of Venice and Florence. It was seen too in their markets with traders from the German lands to the North or dominions to the East that they once physically controlled. Attached to these was a hospitality infrastructure for travellers and itinerants. Crowd scenes in paintings of the time around the 16th century, say in Venice, Lisbon or Antwerp and the Hanseatic cities later, show the actual diversity of places even then. You see black people, Chinese and Indians. The movement of peoples and inevitably too of goods and ideas is ever present. **This criss-crossing stimulates inventiveness**. The world and cities in motion is evolving with pace.

The central square, variously named piazza, plaza or maidan in different cultures, is the main gathering place and assemblage point. Think of Siena's Piazza del Campo, Jemaa el-Fnaa in Marrakech or Naqsh-e Jahan in Isfahan, or the more modern incarnation in Helsinki's Senate Square or the many virtual social media based, deterritorialized town squares today. Here the different buildings reflect the powers coming together - the political buildings, the learning institution, commerce and religious power. They face each other. Or think of the ideal renaissance city, Pienza, where the collective gathering places and the view or vista and the horizon is seen as crucial.

Of course, these meetings are stratified and status is key. There is an underclass and significant exclusions as in the 'Bourgeois City'. This city has largely broken the bonds of the feudal and begins to create forms of affiliation, fellowship and social life with coffee houses, clubs, salons or society circles. Within this historical process Gutenberg's printing press is as revolutionary as the Internet was 30 years ago. Privileged knowledge escapes out of the monasteries. **It is the speed and relative ease at which books can be produced that force-feeds exchange**. It brings the known world to wider audiences and this taps their exploratory instincts. Their minds wander and one would have met people that today we consider nomads.

The idea of the public sphere emerges, initially defined by Jürgen Habermas[3] and helpfully elaborated and expanded by subsequent thinkers. The public sphere can be a physical space or an open-minded environment or both together – here difference comes together. Gerard A. Hauser calls it 'a discursive space in which individuals and groups associate to discuss matters of mutual interest and, where possible, to reach a common judgment about them'. Nancy Fraser calls it 'a theatre in modern societies in which political participation is enacted through the medium of talk'. She highlights too how it is men who dominated this public life then, with women pushed back into a private and domestic role. She encapsulates this clearly: 'a repressive mode of domination shifts to a hegemonic one'[4] and this has not changed in some countries, like in the Middle East, even up to the present. Think then of Paris in terms of activities and physically how its buildings began to exude a confidence, boldness and style expressed ultimately by the Haussmann interventions in the 19th century. Think of London and its coffee house culture.

Later the Industrial City required vast movements from rural lands to the city, as is happening in China today, and some of these in Britain will have crossed over from Ireland escaping the potato famine. And the move of 40 million Europeans to America begins to gather pace at that time, again mostly escaping from wretched conditions. These are familiar themes repeated today as people push, for instance into Europe, from sub-Saharan Africa or the Middle East.

Harsh and relentlessly forbidding, industrial society focused on cities and speeded up trade, establishing the routes by which economic and colonial power unfolded. Dominated by the privileged and wealthy, there are continual micro and larger movements between classes. Even within the working-class, a station-master would regard themselves as higher than the porters, and a butler felt superiority over the maids. Many working-class people aspired to join the middle-class. Others escaped overseas in the mass movements of the time to avoid the hierarchies in their own society. **To become your own person, as for many nomads today, is a common theme through time**. Another way of escaping from dominance was to form social structures like working-men's clubs or trade unions that fostered the solidarities based on shared experiences.

In this period, cultural institutions as we now know them formed, with the public library the most popular and emblematic. These open the eyes to a wider world, bring knowledge from across borders, allowing people to let their minds wander and so gain knowledge of different ways of living. By origin, libraries are our most democratic institution even though in the past the Corinthian columns implied that you as a citizen should humbly go to the fount of knowledge —contrast this with modern libraries, transparent, accessible, open, where participation is encouraged and you can hang out, as many digital nomads do. Another eye opener are the Great Exhibitions the first of which is regarded as Crystal Palace in 1851, with its sub-title the *Works of Industry of All Nations*, or the Paris Exposition *Universelle* in 1855. There had been others before but not so global in scope. Here the world came to you so you could marvel at other continents. Now you can see those on the internet which brings the world to us through virtual reality.

Ebenezer Howard's 'Garden City' that tried to harmonize the virtues of town and country conceived the town centre as a neutral territory where communities of difference would connect. There is a garden ringed with the civic and cultural facilities including the city hall, concert hall, museum, theatre, library, and hospital from which six broad main avenues radiate outwards.

The 'Radiant City', Le Corbusier's dream, fragments the criss-crossing urban complexity out of which we now know urban vitality flows resulting in dynamic diversity. It is a rational, ordered place that segregates functions and zones activities. Mixed uses and mixing, which lie at the heart of the civic, when defined as places where difference meets, can suffer. Indeed, by physically dispersing people we encourage sprawl and degrade public spaces thereby often fostering loneliness. Other contemporary urbanisms, like New Urbanism, seek to maintain the best of the past for the future. Its principles are a design template to change the built environment so it promotes community interaction and reduces isolation by smaller walkable blocks and human-scale design. The many other urban priorities that emerge, such the 'Green City' with its emphasis on carbon neutrality or the 'Creative City' with its focus on being part of shaping, making and co-creating the city, create conditions within which it is more likely for people to interact.

And there is another dream - a dream of the new Aerotropolis promoted by John D. Kasanda and Greg Lindsay. He believes that just as railway stations often formed the hub around which the city was built we now need to build the heart of our cities and all its logistics around and close to the airport. This will allow us to arrive and escape with greater ease and speed and be connected to the wider world. This is the embodiment of the city in motion.

Following the same trajectory but through the lens of planning we can explore 'where next' with planning in a nomadic age. Self-conscious planning for the nomadic world did not and does not exist in the way we might plan for a more sustainable or more creative city today. Foreign traders were segregated even before the Jewish ghetto in Venice founded in 1516. This had more extensive, enforceable rules. It is a type of planning by default, exclusionary in its aims and actions. Ghetto is now used to describe any urban quarter where a majority of minority groups live and often in poverty like the banlieue in Paris. Many variations of the ghetto, both externally imposed or self-created and visible, exist in cities. The diasporas gather as in Chinatowns, Greek Towns, Italian or Indian Quarters in multi-cultural cities across the world.

# TIMELESS THEMES

Others are based around the like-minded, such as gay ghettoes, most famously once in Castro, now in San Francisco, or gated communities for the wealthy. The latter apart, these are mostly permeable, although dominated by a group, there is inflow and outflow, as people might want to experience differing cultures especially cuisines or an atmosphere.

The interplay between structured versus organic development, between public or private space, or insider and outside space, and the choice between the desire to zone or to mix — all still shape the possibilities of how people can come together today. They are the constants of planning that have built a repertoire over time.

Order vs. chaos has always been at the heart of planning including for 'the first urban planner', the Greek Hippodamus (498 – 408 BC). He proposed a sense of order and rationality to what were then confusing, intricate places without apparent structure (Athens). Hippodamus reflects his time and place, and his ideal city consisted of 10,000 men and 50,000 women and slaves, with its public life highly stratified.

There is a clear sense of the insider and outsider. Mass expulsions and ethnic cleansing campaigns are so frequent throughout history – and **this is a danger par *excellence* of the nomadic age if stereotyping of outsiders is not checked**. One of the first recorded was the extermination of the Jie people in 350 AD described in ancient Chinese texts suggesting 200,000 were massacred, in part because they looked different. There were continued expulsions, especially of Jews, but also the forced resettlements throughout history. Think of the African slave trade from the fifteenth to the nineteenth century; the compulsory

Turkish Greek population exchange in 1923; the German expulsions from the Soviet Union in 1945; and the Soviet expansion of Russians into the Baltics and elsewhere from 1945 onwards. The ethnic cleansing process across the world continues in the name of purification in an attempt to reverse the mixing process - Sudan's cleansing of the peoples of Darfur, the Bosnian-Serb campaign, or the Karen in Myanmar. Even today we push people out we do not want. More than 2.5 million American illegal immigrants were expelled under the Obama administration with more following under Trump. Many of these illegals move back and forth.

Religious proselytizing inverts expulsion as it seeks to get the outsider to become the insider or it enforces conversion. Most widely known is that of Christianity, but even though the Koran states: 'Let there be no compulsion in religion', Muslims do, in essence, convert. When the Ottoman Turks invaded what is now Bosnia you had a stark choice: convert or get nowhere. ISIS has taken it to an extreme. Pay the jizya, the tax on non-Muslims or convert and if you do neither be killed. Converting from Islam is punishable by death in many Muslim countries and even owning a bible in the Maldives – those islands of romance, apparently - is severely punishable. Take the Saudi Arabian case and its zeal to proselytize its extreme version of Islam – Wahhabism – across the world. Hugely hypocritical, it demands the right to propagate, yet is utterly intolerant of any other faith in its own country. It has funded hundreds of mosques across the world, but no churches or temples of other religions are allowed in Saudi Arabia and a 2014 decree brands all atheists as terrorists. An important effect of Saudi proselytizing is to slow the country's evolution into the more diverse world, and its promotion of literalism[5] undermines pluralism, tolerance and openness in the Islamic world. **This contrasts starkly with the high points of Islamic culture** and its astonishing contributions to global civilization. These issues will cause deep ructions with more open countries, especially if those places dare to spell out the unbalanced relationship.

Certain Christian churches still today convert with vigour as seen in the wandering troops of Jehovah's Witnesses, or Mormons who see it as a duty to travel the world to convert. This creates riches. The vast Watchtower headquarters of the former in Brooklyn, New York sold for a $340 million in 2016 and the Mormons property portfolio in Salt Lake City, their headquarters is extensive.

There is also an important balance in how the public and private sphere is divided - a strong theme of planning and city makers. What public social space means and who is part of it has gone through a trajectory, with real restrictions of access in the past. A woman, a lower-class person, or a servant might be physically present, but not fully able to participate. They were often hidden from view. Think here of stark differences in urban form that reflect cultural attitudes. Arab cities with their high walls and enclosed environment ensure you cannot see women. In Dutch cities, by contrast, there are mostly no curtains and you can see right into personal space. This urban culture is saying 'we have nothing to hide'.

It is only with empowered citizens and an open cultural context that these spaces can properly act as the commons of all people and be active political, economic, social and cultural arenas. This is the ideal of a democratic urban commons. It is astonishing how little of this in its full sense exists today.

These gathering spaces were mostly centred around a hub, such as a market, a plaza, a religious setting. It is here that travellers meet, liaisons evolve, interchange occurs. The trading of the goods, services and skills local inhabitants need is what fosters this continuous flow. **The world in motion meets in markets** and their placement was and is always crucial in urban planning. Civic life also unfolds (or not) in ordinary, less significant places. A cursory glance of everyday spaces we move through and linger within across the world show how this does or does not work. The mix between men and women, young and old, and different income groups is rare. That coming together, regardless of difference, happens in major festivals or special days. And still women are mostly less visible, noticeably in Muslim countries, or men and women keep to themselves.

The planning repertoire widens as other realities cause priorities to move centre-stage. Often crisis is the trigger, such as disease and that disease was often brought in by travellers – think here of the plague and later cholera. Another trigger is destruction, a natural disaster or a fire. This creates urgency and action and a chance to think afresh. Crisis then becomes opportunity and at times creates bold ambition. Health is an example. Jumping ahead to the nineteenth century, the polluting industrialized cities finally demanded action as the evils of urban life for the working poor became clear and that agenda stays with us. This finally led to urban planning as a discipline and a profession as we know it today with the Town & Country Planning Association formed in London in 1898 and the first university planning course in 1909 in Liverpool and in the same year the Housing & Town Planning Act. This compelled local authorities to introduce the principles of the 'garden city' as its guide, blending town and nature, and placed them into coherent systems that ensured construction conformed to building standards and codes. Then the professional disciplines of surveyors, architects, engineers, land use planners and lawyers began working together on planning the city. **The focus was more on getting the physical conditions right rather than how people can mix**. The words and concepts like multi or intercultural did not exist. Societies then were more ethnically homogeneous.

Another common theme of planning has been whether or not to zone. Modernism goes to one extreme. Having come into fashion it completely changes the urban landscape with its tower blocks and division of functions, the aim then to separate living from work and the clean from the dirty. Yet **removing the mix of activities sapped vitality from communities** as they were isolated out. It both made the city fit for the car and encouraged its use. The car both helps give access, but creates an urban form that does not encourage the blending of work and play and public life, the kind of environment the nomadic world seeks. Counter-reactions to this type of city-making happened quite quickly. The clean lines on the drawing board were often mirrored in the sanitized urban landscapes that followed. A lack of human-scale was perhaps its greatest weakness.

In quick succession new priorities emerge about how to create and plan good cities. The New Towns Movement was one. It often had social democratic leanings emphasizing facilities within a zoning framework, including schools, health and cultural centres. The Development Corporation in Milton Keynes in Britain in the 1970s, for instance, not only planned and developed the city but also invested in social life. Another example is the environmental movement triggered by Rachel Carson's The Silent Spring later the Club of Rome report. It impacts on how we think and build and as a consequence environmental departments come into being from the early 1980s onwards. It is now common sense. The climate change agenda has highlighted the effects of flying around the world, but not yet explicitly linked it to an overarching focus on the nomadic world by, for instance, suggesting more strongly how to reduce movement such as that meetings or conventions could happen virtually.

These accretions like health or environment enrich, but **some insights or trends have been left underdeveloped or left out**. The feminist lens on cities could shift city making strongly, yet has not had sufficient effect on how cities are thought through, made and managed. It might have developed a softer less aggressive aesthetic, and that in turn might have affected our behaviour. The creative city notion, whose essence is how you unleash the potential to create better places to live, has had some affect especially in highlighting the power of third places (neither home or work and mostly in the public realm).

Changing perspectives over time are reflected in the language of planning. Transport becomes mobility and then movement and ultimately seamless connectivity. The first conjures up the objects as with cars, trains and planes and the associated infrastructure like roads. Seamless connectivity highlights the processes of getting from A to B and invisible systems like Wi-Fi and our networking capacity so that you move without hindrances multi-tasking along the way.

**Seamlessness is what the both settled and unsettled want. Ease of connection** wherever they are, good walkable public space, public transport always available nearby, ease of transition from one transport mode to the next and continuous Wi-Fi. Who then is responsible for overall connectivity? Thus urgent priorities can slip through the crevices as they have no department. What department is responsible for the psychological state of the city, its atmosphere, its social connections or the link between permanent and temporary residents?

*Villeneuve, Lyon*

# THE PRESENT & THE DREAM

What shall we call this emergent city? Language matters. Words, concepts and perspectives have power, they resonate, they can be compelling or contentious: garden city, green city, learning, knowledge or innovation city, network city, sustainable and now resilient, city of well-being, smart city and creative city or city of nomads. Each implies a differing priority, a vision and a focus. Yet of course we need elements of all of them. What comes next – perhaps the 'civic city', a city of engaged citizens. Here the notion of urban citizenship in a nomadic world becomes a central question if we want to create commitment and involvement. The idea of **a rich public sphere is helpful in thinking through 'the civic' and 'the nomadic' together**. It implies a cultural context where people, of all shades, and authorities can meet and have critical discussions and influence each other about matters of joint public interest. These act as a counterweight to classic political authority. That sphere happens in face-to-face meetings, from the formal, such as official meetings, to the informal, such as in cafes, in the media and in the wider cultural realm. The idea and reality of the public square is emblematic, both as a place of physical encounter and its varied virtual forms. Addressing these issues becomes the template and goal for city planning.

The notion of the public sphere, although initially conceived as connected to the emancipatory drive of nation building, has equal relevance to cities or even across nations as it can describe a general set of cultural and organizational attributes. At a city level, organization is easier, but transnationally it is immensely hard.

Concepts, sharp encapsulating slogans, and principles can drive processes and change reality – and they have. Think of words like democracy – wars have been fought over it – or sustainability or a more recent favourite, resilience. They can express aspiration, provide inspiration, encourage a different way of looking at the world, describe the existing in a way so it is better understood. The effect can be to demand, guide or create change. In a short-span attention world, snappiness has weight, but it also means things go out of fashion as people get bored and think about the next big thing. A throwaway world chucks things out, and often they are good. Sometimes old things once discarded come back - think here perhaps of holistic thinking.

# THE POWER OF CONCEPTS

The question is whether the terms 'civic city' or 'the city of citizens' have sufficient energy and complex simplicity to drive change. Words like 'green', 'smart' or 'creative' are easier to immediately understand. 'Smart' has a double sense of being tech savvy with a sub-text that you the individual are smart, so it feels like the word is praising you. 'Creative' equally has a positive ring to it. It signals that you have imagination, that you are interesting, attractive and stimulating. Everyone feels they can be involved. To say you are 'civic' has a worthy, old-fashioned ring to it. To add being civic to a nomadic world gives the bank of ideas a more contemporary feel. Some will argue though that it is a clumsy mouthful. Yet my aim is the give the idea of the civic a renewed urgency and power.

Can the notions of civil and the civic be brought back to life and given traction especially in conjunction with nomadic or do we need an even deeper crisis and social fracturing to make the idea feel viscerally relevant? Any overarching concept for city making needs to be strong and catalytic. It needs here to address the delights of being nomadic and what is worrying about the movement, such as the fractures in cities, the decline of distinctiveness, the blandness of cities, the tensions of gentrification – and ideally all in one.

What are the qualities of a good, catalytic idea that can drive a process and becomes a roadmap to move forward? **A great idea needs to be simple but complex in its potential**. A good idea is instantly understandable, resonates and communicates iconically – you grasp it in one.  A good idea needs to have layers, depth and be able to be interpreted and expressed creatively in many ways and involve many people who each feel they have something to say about it and to offer. A good idea connects and suggests linkages. It is dynamic. It breathes, it immediately conjures up in the mind multiple dimensions and possibilities. With a good idea creativity and practicality come together. A good big idea focuses attention. Ideally it should touch the identity of a place and so feel culturally relevant. Indeed it should support, build on and create it. In this way it should speak to deeper values and ambitions. It should be significantly powerful and be implemented in many ways.

Many cities around the world, for instance, say they are going to become the 'educated city' or 'innovation city'. This idea is narrow; it implies and feels as if it is only the education and tech sector that is involved. It excludes most others. In spite of everything it is the idea of being a citizen in a city who wishes to be committed, involved and proud of their place that remains powerful.

## THINKING BIG & BOLD

All over the world there are towns and cities called Utopia, Paradise or Heaven or Heart's Desire (surprisingly when I went there in Newfoundland I passed a settlement called Dildo on the way). They all reflect our desire from the beginning of time to create more ideal places where the world is good to you and we live in harmony with differences.

The yearning for better community in the material, cultural, social and spiritual sense is older than recorded history - it is a cross-cultural phenomenon. It is re-emerging with force today. Consider from the past the literature of faith from the Vedic to the Biblical in secular reform from Plato's 'Republic' to Thomas More's 'Utopia' to Ebenezer Howard's 'Garden City' to Le Corbusier 'The Radiant City'. Utopian dreaming is an expression for our hopes of a better future and happier life for our self and the world at large. There are also darker versions that mostly want to purify us like Hitler's Germany or with ISIS and its return to the lost caliphate where apostates are eradicated.

Thomas More first used the word 'utopia' to describe the ideal, imaginary island nation whose political system he described in Utopia, published in 1516. Here there is communal ownership of land, private property does not exist, men and women are educated alike, there is almost complete religious toleration, and there is no army. Incidentally there are only two places of significance without an army, Costa Rica and Iceland (apart from 20 mostly small islands like Vanuatu). Utopia is a Greek pun on *ou-topos* [no place] and *eu-topos* [good place]. What is the nomadic city ideal? To shape this city is our challenge today.

To think about ideal cities and dream settlements was common in the Italian Renaissance, as in Pienza, Lucca, Sabbionetta and Palmanova. There were the industrial utopias such as, in Britain, the Sunlight settlement in Liverpool, Bournville in Birmingham or Saltaire Village in Bradford. Elsewhere includes Canberra, Australia's capital which was conceived as an ideal, Seaside in Florida, the New Urbanism icon, Celebration, the utopia built by Disney near Orlando, Christiana, the hippy community in Copenhagen, and Freiburg, Europe's major green city focused on solar energy. In exploring all of these a central theme, Canberra apart, was an attempt at human scale and legibility. Though, the contrast between Pienza with its vistas, Celebration with its cloying traditionalism and Christiania with its destructive drug culture is stark.

Today we more commonly use the word 'vision' – the capacity to imagine, but with more clarity than dreams, giving direction, providing a focus and an aim. Most contemporary visions are not city-scale or comprehensibly transformative in scope nor do they provide a thorough going alternative view. Here the 'Garden City' concept of more the 100 years ago stands out that has been revived in the eco-cities movement today. Typical larger visions over the last two decades have been the dockland redevelopments, such as in East London, Melbourne or Puerta Madera in Buenos Aires. **There has been an inability to think big** and we must, yet with subtlety. It will be immensely difficult. The fast speed and escalating impacts of a world in motion requires responses across many spheres, for instance: how to deal with too many tourists in some cities; how to dampen negative aspects of gentrification in others; how to take land out of the speculation dynamic as global capital races around the globe; how to avoid some places becoming no-go areas. All these issues causes tension.

The popularity of vision-making is directly related to our dissatisfaction with what we have. The most recent global city vision to address the evolving world is The *New Urban Agenda* agreed at UN-Habitat III in Quito, the 20-year summit on cities. A substantial part of this was *The City We Need*, a global advocacy process organized by their World Urban Campaign who created a series Urban Thinkers Campuses (UTC) involving all interest groups from business to trade unions to citizens groups. These involved 26 cities across the world and over 6000 people with each city choosing a theme to shape the UN's new urban paradigm. They concluded that cities should be: healthy, regenerative, affordable, equitable, economically vibrant, walkable, well-designed and well-managed at a metropolitan level, and crucially distinctive. To which others added later putting the 'public interest centre-stage', the 'common good' and 'justice'. Clearly good aims, but these worthy objectives have not been met. Why are the obstacles to achieving these globally agreed public purposes not sufficiently highlighted in global fora? Unless the potent issues of power, inequality, monopoly and dominance are tackled head on it is unlikely that the aspirations will be realized. The Mannheim Assembly with its theme *Urban Citizenship in a Nomadic World* [6] was part of the UTC initiative and re-affirmed that cities at their best are open and this openness makes them cradles of civilization. Openness is the key to a successful city making that is vigorous, fair, transparent, diverse and accessible. This entails being against discrimination of all kinds. It is the lively democratic, humanistic and more secular city that creates the rules of engagement for people to share and live together within their differences and diversity, and to adapt to a more nomadic world.

**This civic conception of openness is not universally accepted** and there are increasingly negative reactions across the globe. In the fast and relentless dynamic of urban change with its disruptive economic forces that create a sense of anxiety and uncertainty, the alternative has been to appeal to a politics of fear, hatred and exclusion. The Assembly argued that the response must be not to demonise but to understand and engage with those who worry about openness. The new nomadic norm is here to stay, whatever the ups and downs. The vast flows of refugees we are witnessing will remain a permanent feature over the next decades and already seriously affects over 30 countries globally in the North and the South. The Mannheim Forum suggested that cities should act as models of this 'Other City' and highlighted the three major themes of land ownership, the dilemmas of participation, and city autonomy.

With a helicopter view of change-making projects across the world, you detect a desire for somewhere, some city, to offer an alternative – one that is achievable. Broader visions seek to inspire, to get people on board so that they form alliances and partnerships in order to generate the energy, motivation and will to change and to bend the existing dynamic. Usually they come back to nevertheless important though similar themes: harmony, balance, justice, fairness, equality, sustaining, and community. Visions inevitably reflect their time and place. So today a strong ecological dimension is a given, future visions will have to address how to make the most of the potential of the nomadic world.

Too few urban visions and their associated strategies seek to tangibly heal the fractures, such as between rich and poor, between those of different backgrounds or world-views, in a courageous way. These are elements of a civically-minded nomadic city vision which would need to include a changed idea of urban citizenship, changed conceptions of permanent ownership, and be heavily focused on real sharing economy ideas well. beyond cars, apartments and holiday homes. Capitalism as it currently operates cannot achieve these aims We stand at a crossroads and many of the issues we need to address fall into the soft realms rather than the hard physical sciences, yet **the soft is the hard**. This will require a shift. In city making it is those concerned with the hard that have higher status and authority – architects, engineers, surveyors, the construction industry and their supporters such as accountants. Do they really understand what it is that drives people and cities? We know that **accountancy-thinking cannot make great cities**, as it is the non-monetary extra that creates the trick. This implies giving higher recognition to the people-oriented disciplines of anthropology, psychology and those who get social dynamics. Remember too that many of the great influencers on how cities work were mostly not architects or planners by origin – Jane Jacobs, Manuel Castells or Saskia Sassen, for example.

## CITIZEN & NOMAD PLANNING

Distil the best from the best practitioners and the classic urban design gurus or writers like Kevin Lynch or Jane Jacobs in the past, or practitioners like Jan Gehl from Copenhagen or Rob Adams from Melbourne or even Andrés Duany. You then have the physical template of the city or neighbourhood that both citizens and nomads would like. There is little difference. An irony is that they try to retrofit the things we got rid of, such as the mix of functions – living, forms of work, shops, hang-out places and relaxing. We now recognize explicitly that finding differing reasons to interact creates the complexity that brings urban vitality, chance encounter and serendipity. Yet there is a lead-and-lag process in terms of policy and rules - with the rules often lagging behind the lived experience or desire. **The cities we love we cannot build anymore as the rules may forbid it**, even though they often fostered civic connections.

They all confront basic physical planning ideas like grids, straight or curved lines, streets aligned at right angles, star-shaped layouts from which streets splayed out, avenues with long interrupted views, enclosed comforting squares, well-aligned city blocks, building types and scale. This has evolved into a canon as to what makes good urban design, but it is the fine grain that counts.

What is described below is not easily achieved. It involves more than physical planning and many difficult conversations with interest groups along the way. It includes: Walkability: pedestrian-friendly street design, hidden parking lots; garages in the rear; narrow, slow-speed streets; the car is curtailed and some streets car free. Connectivity: an interconnected street grid network which disperses traffic and eases walking and to create interest there is a hierarchy of narrow streets, boulevards, and alleys. This balances awe and intimacy. Specialisms: areas or clusters of activities and retailing reflect the distinctiveness within the place - some more grand others more neighbourly, this balances the conventional, the slightly off-beat and the weird. Mixed-use and diversity puts together a mix of shops, offices, apartments, and homes. There is a mix of independent and innovative locally owned retailers and markets. Global brands are there, but do not overwhelm. There are 'third spaces' such as cafes for meeting and mixing and a variety of learning facilities. There is mixed-use too within neighbourhoods, within blocks, and within buildings.

Avoiding too much ghettoization encourages a diversity of interaction between age, income, culture, and race. Mixed housing leads to a range of types, sizes and prices in relatively close proximity. Urban design creates a sense of place by emphasizing beauty, aesthetics and human comfort. Ordinary and extra-ordinary architecture is commissioned aimed at a human-scale with nourishing surroundings that lift the spirit. Civic uses, cultural hotspots and significant sites are placed carefully within the community. The neighbourhood structure establishes clear centres and edges interspersed with public space and park areas of differing sizes.

The overall structure highlights proximity and differing densities with more buildings, residences, shops, and services closer together for ease of walking, to enable a more efficient use of services and resources, and to create a more convenience. The applies from small towns to large cities.

The movement and mobility system ensures there are trains, trams and buses to connect neighbourhoods and other towns and cities. Pedestrian-friendly design encourages people to use bicycles, rollerblades or scooters as well as to walk. Principles of sustainability and healthy urban planning are embedded. Respect for ecology, the value of natural systems increases energy efficiency leads to more local production, greater use of eco-friendly technologies and reduces environmental impact. Taken together such places will be psychologically more enriching as they are people-friendly and have a strong sense of community, they are vibrant and vital as they provide choices and opportunity, and they are culturally stimulating. They have heritage, history and tradition without being nostalgic and they combine intimacy with well-orchestrated grander gestures.

Twenty five or so cities typically come on top of the varied rankings for good places; Copenhagen; Vancouver; Munich; Amsterdam; Zurich; Vienna; San Francisco; Bilbao; Barcelona, Helsinki; Stockholm; Melbourne; Paris; Montreal; Berlin; Barcelona; Auckland; Fukuoka; Portland; Singapore; Hamburg. The rankings more focused on corporate expats like Mercer's or The Economist differ from the rankings of Monocle.

*Collective city making in Ivano-Frankvisk, Ukraine*

*La Défense, Paris*

# THE PLACE & SPACE TRAJECTORY

Urban transformation is complex. A simple approach I use to think through urban dynamics over the last 50 years is the notion of 'The City 1.0', 'The City 2.0' and 'The City 3.0'. This helps schematically characterize the different phases of urban development from the 1960/70s onwards. Along this trajectory we begin to understand the rise of our restless nomadic world, the tensions and opportunities this creates and how our ideas of civic togetherness transform through time. Once you start a number sequence, of course, people like to add others, such as 'The City 4.0'[7] and then sometime there will be '5.0'. 'The digitizing city' section describes the full impact of the world of digital disruption, the blending of physical and virtual and the rise of artificial intelligence (AI). This impacts on governance, management and financing.

The historic city we have inherited in all its variations is 'The City 0.0'. Those historic cities differ from continent to continent, culture to culture their purpose for being, their origins and their ideals. Differing spatial forms and anchor points predominate in each and they in turn encourage or discourage varying forms of togetherness.

Every shift in how we organize or create wealth forms a new social order, a new type of city, a new politics, new ways of learning, new ideas about life and new art or cultural institutions. Each requires different capabilities.

### THE CITY 1.0

The stereotype of The City 1.0 is: a large factory, its main symbol, and mass production; the mental model is the city as a machine; the management and organizational style is hierarchical and top-down; structures are siloed, vertical with strong departments, partnership is rare; learning is often by rote and repetition; failure is not tolerated; work, living and leisure are separated; aesthetics is not highlighted. The parallel planning version of 1.0 focuses largely on land-uses, comprehensive development and civic participation is low. Transport 1.0 makes the city suitable for the car, with pedestrians less important. Road infrastructures are mostly ugly.

# THE CITY 1.0, 2.0, 3.0...

Culture 1.0 is shaped by its civilizing mission with a predominantly elite audience who feel entitled to determine quality and programming. It is top-down, concentrating mainly on traditional forms in cultural institutions which highlight excellence and whose architecture can resonate with this haughty approach. One thinks here of German theatre, European opera houses or the Edinburgh Festival (and not its fringe). It assumes a right to public funding as well as relying on patronage. Popular elements to bring people together at times emerge or coexist. Think of the Edinburgh Fringe or even Fête de la Musique, the French culture minister Jack Lang's massive 1981 celebration of music. now held on the 22nd June across Europe. Libraries throughout remain the most popular cultural space and begin re-assessing their mission. 'Official' culture is seen as detached from commerce.

Overall this is the rational, ordered, technically-focused and functionally-divided city. It is a hardware-driven urban engineering paradigm for city making. It reflects a mental attitude and approach to life. It had its highpoints from the 1960s to the 1980s. Residues of this approach still exist both in how people think and work and in their focus on the physical fabric.

### THE CITY 2.0

The City 2.0 by contrast shifts priorities and evolves from the 1990s onwards. Its industrial emblem is the science park and high tech industry; its management ethos has flatter structures; partnership working rises as does collaborative working; learning systems open out.

There is greater awareness of needing to integrate disciplines as the mental model sees issues as more connected. The urban form is more aware of how the software and hardware of the city interact. Urban design becomes a higher priority. It begins to focus on the emotional feel of the city and its atmosphere.

The nomadic *starchitect* emerges and cities become more spectacular using bizarre architectural forms. Gleaming glass towers proliferate, bold shapes break out of traditional patterns of the square box; skyscrapers explode onto the landscape, some with good public spaces. Vast retailing, entertainment or cultural centres try to bewitch, enchant and seduce you; citizens become more like customers and consumers.

There is a move too to reflect human need and human scale. How people interact rises up the agenda. The city becomes a canvas and stage for activities. Planning 2.0 is more consultative and sees the city in a more rounded way. It links the physical, social and economic and the notion of transport 2.0 is more about mobility and connectivity. The city is less car dominated, walkability and pedestrian friendly street design become a priority; as do tree-lined streets or boulevards. This 2.0 city seeks to reinsert mixed-use and diversity of shops, offices, apartments, and homes.

Respect for ecology and natural systems rise as do the use of eco-friendly technologies and energy efficiency. More local production is in evidence and more emphasis on distinctiveness, aesthetics, human comfort, and creating a sense of place.

Culture 2.0 shifts focus. The diversity agenda — of people, ages, income levels and cultures — rises to the fore. It reaches out, more voices are heard, community concerns are stronger. The creativity agenda spreads as does greater awareness of the power of creative economy sectors and the link between the arts and their role in the broader economy. Cross-fertilization between artistic disciplines becomes a deep trend as with science, technology and the arts. Culture becomes a competitive tool, it is used to encourage urban revitalization, spectacularizing the city and the economic growth agenda. The European Capital of Culture award is one scheme used. The spillover effect of arts on attractiveness, image building and tourism is highlighted so increasing the popularity of museums, galleries and arts in public spaces. Activating street life and promoting festivals becomes part of the cultural repertoire. Equally, community-driven arts projects proliferate as part of a growing movement towards engagement and inclusion, forcing institutions to open out. Arguments for and rationales of the impact of arts proliferate, such as how involvement in art fosters health. In this phase, an instrumental view of what arts and culture can do overrides the focus on the intrinsic value of art.

## THE CITY 3.0

The City 3.0 goes one step further, it takes on the needs of the City 1.0 and the virtues of City 2.0, and tries to harness the collective imagination and intelligence of citizens in making, shaping and co-creating their city. The aim is soft urbanism as it addresses the full sensory experience of the city and the emotional impact of the built fabric. The public realm, human scale and aesthetics are a priority as blandness and ugliness are felt to weaken a city. The mental model is to see the city as an organism. Organizationally it is more flexible; horizontal and cross-sector working and linking disciplines become the norm. A culture of creativity and experimentation is more embedded and tolerance of risk — and thus failure — is more accepted.

Learning and self-development is vital to the City 3.0. In the City 1.0, knowledge institutions were more like factories for drilling in knowledge rather than communities of enquiry essential to unleash, explore and harness talent.

The City 3.0 sees entrepreneurship as a crucial resource to make cities work. The economy 3.0 fosters imagination, innovation and a start-up culture. Open innovation systems often drive business as do collaborative competition. Micro-businesses and SMEs have greater importance in a more tech-savvy world.

The urban form seeks to create cultural and physical environments which provide the conditions for people to be creative, to meet and to be together in public space. This can be a room, a building, a street, a neighbourhood. Typically anchored around a rejuvenated old building, they resonate as they exude memory and physically their spaces are large, adaptable and flexible. The emblem of a City 3.0 is its creative zone or creative quarter. 'Third places' - neither at home or an office – are important to work on the move. The 'here and there' and 'anywhere and anytime' phenomenon is a characteristic of the age. This world thrives on flexibility and has a pop-up culture. We are in the nomadic age.

Planning 3.0 moves on from a strict land-use focus. It is more integrative, interweaving economic, cultural, physical and social concerns. Mixed use is crucial to its planning ethos. It knows that **planning is more concerned with mediating differences between complex issues** such as fostering urban growth and yet containing the downsides of gentrification. It works in partnership and seeks citizen participation in decision making. It takes a holistic approach to identifying opportunities and solving problems. Being eco-conscious is part of a new common sense as is being intercultural. This City 3.0 recognizes talent attraction and retention as vital, thus immigration laws are adapted to attract the best from the world. It is outwards more than inwards.

City 3.0 is experience driven and at times is shrill, using smart technologies and immersive, self-regulating, real-time and interactive devices. Smart grids and sensors, open data platforms and apps for city services make this happen. It seeks to have a complete and integrated view of city systems such as energy, transport, health and employment by analysing, gathering citizen feedback and leveraging information across all city agencies and departments to make better decisions. Seamless connectivity is the watchword and cross fertilization the norm. The aim is to anticipate and react to problems.

In moving towards a City 3.0 we can increasingly see the interconnection between culture, creativity and the city. Culture 3.0 increasingly sees people make their own culture. As less passive consumers they challenge their own expressive capacities, even if many still wish to watch rather than engage. The relevance of mainstream and alternative culture is re-assessed as is the balance of funding between them. The classic institutions remain powerful, but are challenged to open out so as to widen audiences. Culture is performed in more unusual settings, the city is more a canvas and a stage – the street, a local café or a pop-up venue. Here tactical urbanism projects (from guerrilla gardening, to flash mobs or artistically inspired street makeovers) mushroom in this event driven culture. Artists are more like curators, designers or makers. To weave things together and bring out the best connectors and intermediaries become more important. The rich cultural life is increasingly the aim and so culture's connection to health and well-being is a natural fit.

These overall trends within the City 1.0, 2.0 and 3.0 are clearly schematic and they overlap. We need City 1.0 attributes like good hardware, but the world increasingly needs to operate at City 3.0 level. This remains a struggle because working in silos can be comforting.

The major faultline in cities is mostly the misalignment between an evolving 3.0 world and its economy, culture and social dynamics where the existing institutional set up and operating system still has several 1.0 features. **Many institutions originating in a 1.0 world coexist with people who live a 3.0 lifestyle**. This can create tensions and misunderstanding and this disconnection needs to be overcome. That is a creative act.

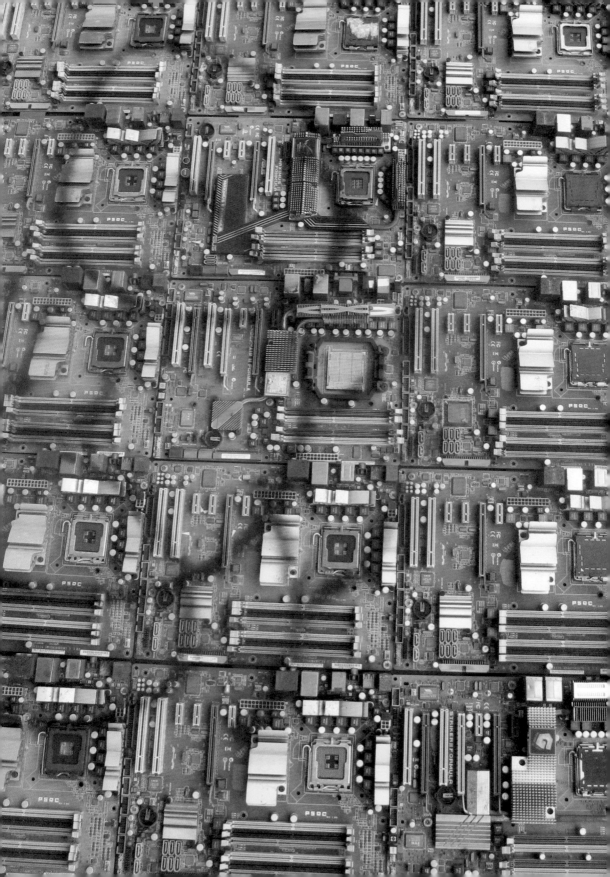

Overriding everything is a digitizing world[8], it makes turbocharged nomadism possible. Some may wish to call this the City 4.0. It is the infrastructure for the nomadic age. The digital and the nomadic are intertwined. Our culture is digital and the digital shapes our culture. It is omnipresent, like the air we breathe and the electricity that flows. It shifts the understanding of time, space and place. The new nomadic world could not operate without it. It is both a catalyst and an enabler. The digitized city is already with us and a dramatic and phenomenal global transformation is underway. It impacts both on the more and less developed world. Yet it needs a jointly created cultural and political vision of where next. Cities including Helsinki, Amsterdam, San Francisco and Boston started to harness its possibilities early on, but the smart cities of Nairobi, Accra and India are grasping the opportunities, along with many now in China and South America, following in the wake of the pioneers.

# THE DIGITIZING
# CITY: INFLUENCE & IMPACT

### ADDRESSING PROBLEMS & POTENTIAL

The digital can do more than allow the tech savvy to lead a more nomadic lifestyle. It can be relevant to every goal of global urban agendas. Typically these seek to empower people, to make decision making processes transparent, or to contain profligate resource use (as in the UN 2030 *Agenda for Sustainable Development*[9] or UN Habitat's The City We Need'[10]). Devices can help monitor health. Sensors can measure and help reduce resource use such as water, energy or consumption patterns. Digital tools can help us to understand natural environments and make our physical infrastructures safer, more reliable and effective. The internet can empower people by giving access to a vast knowledge store.

Applications are increasing exponentially, both in the developed and developing world. In the latter, cheap smartphones are a diagnostic tool to check many health conditions; the collapsible Luci Solar Lanterns give light at night; the Lifestraw sophisticated water filters kill 99% of bacteria; the BRCK battery-powered modems give access to the internet; Hello Tractor low-cost smart tractors with GPS antennas can track soil conditions; the Power Pot portable electric generator doubles up as a cooking pot, generating electricity from the cooking process.

---

This text draws on my book *The Digitized City: Influence & Impact*

*ipei public art
tech district*

Digitization represents a tectonic shift. The disruptive potential is changing cities, society and social life, connectivity, the economy, cultural institutions and cultural life. Its impacts and influence will be as powerful as the climatic changes that swept through our world with the Industrial Revolution 200 years ago, yet it is more invisible, driven by algorithms etched into small screens. This engenders fear of a world racing ahead uncontrolled but also creates excitement around the opportunities unfolding. Those who make decisions, the digital settlers, have mostly migrated into this world, whereas for the young digital natives, it is all they know. This highlights a misalignment as, **for the first time in history, the young are teaching the old** rather than the reverse.

Every new means of production changes the physical and mental landscape and how our systems operate. Its drama is clear when the world's largest taxi company, Uber, owns no taxis; when Facebook, the world's most popular media-owner, creates no content; when Alibaba, the most valuable retailer, has no inventory; and when Airbnb, the world's largest hotel chain, owns no hotels.

## DATA-DRENCHING THE WORLD

Digitization, through its power to connect, communicate and manipulate data, is driving transformation on a scale that changes the foundations of business and public service, affecting every facet of our lives. This data mining revolution is an innovation accelerator, a Gutenberg 3.0, transforming how we work, manage and organize, what we do, and how we create and think. **Digitally-driven tools and technologies enable placelessness** and shape the cultures we produce, consume and how we experience the world and especially cities.

The digital rides on its third platform: a combination of cloud computing, mobile devices, social media and big data technologies working together. Here, mobile devices and apps extend capabilities, the cloud acts as an outsourced mechanism, big data enables ultra-fast analysis to interpret data and gain insights, and social technologies bring interactive human dimensions into digital, automated processes. Combining these disparate technologies simplifies working environments and is turbocharging digital commerce, information analytics and the development of intelligent infrastructures. Once artificial intelligence (AI) is in full swing, a fourth platform will emerge. The scope, scale, pervasiveness, ubiquity and speed of evolving technologies is astonishing. As of 2015, there are 3.2 billion internet users worldwide. Of these, 2 billion are from the less developed world. This means **the world is a tightly formed electronic net, and not being connected is disabling**. At its simplest we interact by texting messages, and with more complexity by managing household electronic devices from a distance or by running businesses from a faraway café in an isolated place.

Here, technology is like oxygen and is increasingly easy to use. Unavoidably, we are pulled into its thrall with its fluid, malleable, remixed content, where we graze (the digital form we once called browsing) and dive deep with its permeable boundaries seamlessly sliding into endlessness. The watchwords are open, flexible, interactive, co-creative, agile, connective, instant, immersive, ubiquitous, enabling, sharing, integrative, multitasking, simulated, virtual, fragmenting and constantly online. These are the words of the nomadic world. The interactive, immersive force of digital technologies and the ability to feel a co-presence across the globe

## REDESIGNING & REVERSE ENGINEERING

We are in the midst of redesigning the world and all its systems - legal, moral, political, economic  physical – and infrastructures for a digital age, with information and communications technologies (ICT) as one backbone. This has immense psychological and cultural implications. Yet our **built environment has been designed for how we lived and worked 50 years ago and more**. To adapt to the digital empowered nomadic age, a reverse engineering process is necessary to create new intelligent infrastructures, sensing technologies and objects that live within its hard-engineered fabric. This is The Internet of Things that allows urban objects to communicate, from fridges to dog collars, adding to our vast data mountains. This is big data and only a tiny fraction has been tapped to enable algorithms to interpret the chaos. Sensors help cities respond in smart ways from the simple to the complex: when is the next bus or metro coming, where is a free car parking space? More powerfully, we can control how a city works from a distance, or with apps that help the sighted and the visually impaired to find where they are, or self-regulating mechanisms to control energy use, monitor levels of pollution or adjust light levels.

The 'sharing economy' becomes possible, built around sharing human and physical resources. Innumerable apps foster swapping, exchanging or joint purchasing with car-sharing technology, such as ZipCars. It makes Uber or Airbnb possible. Opening up data creates easier feedback loops between citizens and city decision-makers, helping to reinvigorate local democracy and making collaborative governance models possible. Perhaps the city is software, as its operations are completely software-driven. The open source movement has accelerated the digital world, enabling collaborative activities between disciplines and to break silos. These processes have been brought about by disruptive technologies and once artificial intelligence gets into full swing, another phase of disruption will occur (self-driving cars, for instance).

## HUMAN VALUES CENTRE STAGE

A human perspective should drive technologies rather than the reverse. Technology fever and innovative apps make one forget that it enables and is a servant to our bigger aims, such as encouraging more empowered citizens. Crucially, the innovative impulses unleashed should solve old problems with new possibilities for the economy, such as addressing inequality or creating quality jobs.

**Decision-makers have a once-in-a-lifetime opportunity to rebuild our cities differently**, including harnessing social media capabilities, interactive platforms or open data to deepen democracy, so making it more responsive to desires and needs. Sending feedback on a pothole in a street is one thing, shaping the whole electoral process another. The crucial question is whether the public interest be given centre stage. Facebook is redefining democracy in potentially negative ways. It is an electoral weapon that can micro-target numerous specific audiences with repetitive messages and by using psychometric profiling predict likely preferences or prejudices. The British Brexit campaign and that of Donald Trump claim Facebook helped them clinch their electoral victories.

Cities must remain alert to ensure their priorities and values are acknowledged, as the digital industrial complex has discovered the city as a major new market. Crucially, we should not only talk about new hardware infrastructures but also of empowering people to be 'smart citizens'.

Undeniably, untold promises and opportunities to improve our quality of life are possible by making life more citizen-centric, more local, more convenient or efficient and seamlessly connected. As with all new technologies, these positives mesh with dangers. They are both liberating and potentially invasive. The most pressing threats include control by algorithms or the watchful eye of surveillance, suffering overload from constant data cascading over us, or unemployment created by intelligent robots.

The communications revolution has broken the public sector data monopoly, as everyone has access to knowledge on their devices. The digital unleashes the ability to mobilize opinion and movements, of which the Arab Spring, the Occupy movement, the Five Star Movement in Italy, and Podemos in Spain are examples. Tactical urbanism projects, such as 'parking day', 'restaurant day', 'better block' or 'guerrilla gardening' stem from the same ethos. Social media-savvy, they enable citizens to unite while not meeting physically. They change how the city and citizens communicate and make decisions - these are the radical civics in action. This harnesses community intelligence whereas, historically, community responsibilities were outsourced to public administrations, which were service production engines. This implies a culture shift with transparency permeating the culture.

## THE URBAN EXPERIENCE

There is a seductive quality to this digitized city. It draws you softly into its interactive web where with a swipe and a click you can be gratified – mostly instantly. Here is ubiquitous Wi-Fi, where we move easily between the worlds of 'here and there', that is local, global, real and virtual. Mobile devices provide mobility so we can work on the fly, be up-to-date and where our vast library of the internet provides untold knowledge resources. Every social group is participating, yet those operating completely on the move without any kind of base form a growing minority. Most jobs can be done from home or a workplace and bus and truck drivers, nurses, shop staff, dentists, museum attendants or construction workers also have digital resources. The role of physical meeting places has adapted. It is often more about touching base than being there continuously.

The volume, velocity and variety of instantly available data streams combined **with the 'anytime, anyplace**, anywhere' phenomenon changes how we interact in space, place and time. Yet place matters more than ever, in spite of increased virtual interaction, as people need physical place to anchor themselves. The public realm rises dramatically in importance and as working patterns change, gathering places and especially third spaces have renewed relevance. This sensorized city largely looks the same, but operates and performs differently. Think of how Airbnb, Zipcar, Uber, Lyft or Bridj have re-conceived hospitality or urban mobility.

This city communicates through every fibre of its being. It is dynamic: signs move, billboards tell stories, info boards inform. It has a filmic quality; you sense you are floating. Yet the buildings still have solidity. Serendipity is consciously orchestrated as meeting places and third places grow, strengthening connectivity. This changes our work environment, with portfolio working becoming more dominant.

The digitized cityscape enables global brands to dominate our sensescape and visual experience. This has emotional and psychological effects on urban dwellers given the dangers of sense overload and overstimulation. Some cities like São Paolo, Paris and Tokyo are now seeking to control this proliferation in the public interest. Increasingly, artists are engaged to create the installations and events that generate this urban experience. We see buildings transform, occasionally with sudden subversive, temporary elements to keep public attention. This urban branding process has special power at night. Public entities struggle to compete in projecting useful information from transport timetables, pollution monitoring, weather conditions, events or alerts. Mexico City has begun to use artworks as billboards to reduce the clutter.

## THE 'SMART' CITY

The 'smart city' notion has a powerful rhetoric and involves using information and communication capacities to increase performance and reduce resource use. It was initially promoted by big tech companies who identified the city as a major market and bulk purchaser of products and services in order to make life more convenient, efficient, secure, self-regulating and predictable. Companies were criticized as they did not initially focus on citizen engagement. This apparent free-for-all digital landscape is largely patrolled by what Hill[11] calls the 'Urban Intelligence Industrial Complex' led by IBM, Cisco, General Electric, Siemens, Philips and search engines like Google or Yahoo.

The 'smart' word is in danger of over-use, but there can be no smart city without smart citizens.

Smarter cities are inclusive places that use technology and innovation to empower, engage with and capitalise on citizen participation. Engaging citizens goes beyond the uptake of technology: it extends to co-creating ideas and solutions by encouraging new governance and transparency tools such as living labs, integrating citizen input in urban planning with spaces and support for start-ups. Successful smart cities facilitate this participation, co-creation and co-production with citizens and other local partners. (Eurocities, 2015).[12]

Eindhoven's intelligent lighting strategy creates responsive streets that help dementia patients through innovative aids. Amsterdam's 'social sensing on demand' allows citizens to provide feedback on emerging conditions from potential flooding to broken pavements as do Curitiba's water depollution devices. Barcelona's smart bins project helps garbage trucks to only pick up full bins as sensors communicate to drivers.

Every medium of communication changes the city and how we interact with it. Each transformation has increased sociability or the capacity to network with the ability to catch a train, drive a car or make a phone call. It has not declined with the increased options offered by the internet and social media. The issue is the quality of interaction. Does online social life, catalysed by permanent connectivity, complement our offline world by enriching our overall life experience or replace it, leading to some loss? Communication in the flesh gives us the physical and emotional contact that we need.

The desire for community has not changed; what has changed is how it is expressed - less bound in the fixed physical spaces of traditional community limited to family and a few outsiders. Our more nomadic life allows us to affiliate and identify ourselves in multiple ways, defined more by - and embedded in - our networks than classic bonds. Networks define community in a nomadic world. The downside is the negative networks where undesirables can find each other more easily.

**In this shifting landscape place matters** - it provides anchorage, belonging, opportunity, connection and, ideally, inspiration. Here online and offline, cyberspace and local space combine to make identity, shape interests and generate a meaningful life. This manifests itself in how cities work, are designed and navigated. The public realm, from pavements to benches, pocket parks and well-designed covered areas, rises dramatically in importance as do third places, like informal cafés (Oldenburg, 1999)[13]. These are essential for community-building - communal yet homely but always with free Wi-Fi. Greater connectivity and faster internet have liberated people to work from home as telecommuters or on the move. Third places are key as welcoming, accessible spaces. **There is power in being alone together**. The collective urban experience will take on added importance in the future. With fragmented communication channels as the norm the importance of collectively shared experiences is growing. Thus the culture of festivals and spectacular events which are artistically driven, form an increasingly significant part of urban culture. Third places exist too in the virtual realm with online communities, whose qualities mirror those of physical communities and where relative freedom from social status is a bonus. There is a genetic basis to our tendency to be social and the addictive qualities of increasingly visually-driven social media. The world is dramatically transforming from the dominance of word and text-based communication to the visual, and scientists highlight the 'picture superiority effect'. Advances in pattern recognition software linked to artificial intelligence and self-learning systems make manipulating the visual easier. This explains the rise in image-based social media platforms and the power of infographics - merging visuals and text. The internet engages us in untold worlds, but can encroach and invade, creating cognitive overload and breaking concentration, fragmenting attention and disconnecting us from life. Storytelling is then a powerful tool that puts the whole brain to work, stimulating a desire to connect threads and narrate a causal sequence of events.

Digital technology is a revolutionary force and it needs guiding towards what we as citizens and cities want from its power. This needs an ethical anchor to guide politics, policies and investment, which should be about solving the global and local problems that really matter. To keep the best of this innovation dynamic requires policy priorities within a governance and incentives framework that harmonizes fairness, transparency, public access and the right to privacy. This balancing act must navigate between sanctioning, enabling and supporting and containing, curtailing and controlling. It includes: safeguarding privacy and allowing people to manage their own data; being continually aware of balancing public and private benefits; fostering a new civic culture to be co-creative; creating rules and codes for the sensorized city, the city of interactive surfaces and immersive digital environments[14]; creating a mixed partnership 'thinking brain' with an agile organizational form that learns to understand weak signals on the horizon; most importantly, instigating a dramatic digital literacy programme. Ninety per cent of jobs require ICT skills, but we need not only functional IT skills but richer cultural learnings to adapt to the digital enabled nomadic world and to understand its pitfalls.[15]

*Waiting for redevelopment, Lisbon*

# THE RETURN OF THE CITY

Weaving all these elements together you have a city you could call nomadic. The city has always been a centre of transactions, power and intellectual resources. Yet in the context of the nomadic age it is now hard to imagine that in the 1970s there was a fear that the city was in such a decline that it might not recover, as city centres hollowed out with business and commerce leaving in a flight to the suburbs. The result was urban wastelands as also industry declined and began to move to the Far East. Remember, New York barely avoided bankruptcy in 1975.

A significant phenomenon emerged in the transition to a knowledge driven economy from the early 1980s onwards. This prefigured the digitally enabled world. **The city was 'rediscovered' and began again to exert a gravitational pull**, because of its resources in learning, its capacity to help exchange and make transactions, its cultural institutions and richer artistic life and vibrancy, its stock of buildings and infrastructure and its transport links. The city was seen as an accelerator of possibilities. The city is a dense communications system that is not easy to replicate in other settings.  These were things pioneers wanted and they are what locals as well as the more nomadic desire. Within that context the 'creative city' concept emerged, which described how in a dramatically changing world it is possible to create the conditions for people to think, plan and act with imagination in order to find solutions for intractable problems or to discover opportunities. It focused initially on the value of creativity, culture, heritage, the arts or design for city development. Once the urban focus re-emerged a vast urban regeneration process began with the tearing down of the past to make the city ready for professional services related industries, offices and residential developments that frequently pushed out older tenants as a result of the price hikes - in essence the gentrification process. Often the results were negative in that older communities were torn apart or displaced.

Kaohsiung, Taiwan

Getting the balance right within gentrification processes is one of the most difficult dilemmas for urban development.

City planners and property developers then self-consciously tried to create urban developments which **tried to mimic and recreate the urbanity** and qualities of well-functioning cities with their mixed uses and intense interactions. The industrial period had fostered segmented land use planning in order to separate dirty or less healthy functions from living and recreation. In the cleaner knowledge economy this separation was less necessary and mixed uses and new configurations for living and working have emerged.

Simultaneously, an extensive retrofitting exercise began. **World-wide, several hundred old warehouses**, breweries, train, bus or fire stations. cement, coal, textile, tobacco or steel factories, old markets or military barracks or older working class districts, were transformed into culture or experience centres, incubators and company breeding grounds and as hubs for wider urban regeneration. Trendies call them industrial chic. Think here of the Creative Factory in Rotterdam, Ler Devagar in Lisbon and its linked complex next door, or the Russell Industrial Centre in Detroit, the Cable Factory in Helsinki, the Spinnerei in Leipzig and the Toy Factory Lofts in Toronto. The creative professionals and the nomads across the world, the graphic designers, software engineers, app developers, artists or actors, are drawn to these places. Their mere presence made them the vanguard of regeneration, a process that is well documented, but also led to gentrification and as costs spiralled often pushed those creatives out later. Indeed some property developers specifically enticed and incentivized artists and other creatives to move into declining areas in effect using them to trigger the regeneration process. Typically then cafes and restaurants move in attracted by the bohemian atmosphere and cheaper rents followed by younger professionals which over time change the ambiance. This process was first documented way back by Sharon Zukin in New York in the 1970s.

It is strange that those same places that had had **horrible working conditions began to be celebrated as places for the new and the hip**. Why do these structures resonate? They exude memory and the patina of ages in an age where novelty erases memory increasingly and of course, physically their spaces are large and allow for flexibility and interesting structures. As the celebrated Jane Jacobs noted 'new ideas need old buildings'.

The problem is that these old buildings have mostly been refurbished or destroyed across the world. City planners have a renewed challenge to create these atmospheres without the physical substance to work with.

Four personal experiences bring the gigantic global gentrification question home to me - living in London, working and living in Berlin, and working in Lisbon and in George Town, Penang. Gentrification up to a point is good, it can get a development dynamic going and improve environments, but when a tipping point is reached it can swing into the negative. In part it is brought about by cities attracting expats and becoming nomad hubs.

A Financial Times article on Brixton on the 14th July 2017 was emblematic. It explains the gentrifying processes we witness in Berlin, Lisbon and soon Casablanca, but also in Kala Ghoda in Mumbai, Fitzroy in Melbourne, Songshan in Taipei. Or as one typical blog says:

'In San Francisco it's the Mission, in New York it's the East Village, in Berlin it's Kreuzberg, in Seoul, the booming capital of South Korea, it's Hongdae – the go-to neighbourhood and anything a hipster could want.'

Yes, really, this is why I was amused to see a tee-shirt in Berlin with 'hipsters are motherfuckers' on it.

# TRANSITION & CHANGE

## BRIXTON, LONDON

I lived near Railton Road in Brixton, London in the early 1980s, near where David Bowie had been born. It was then called the frontline, a place you did not go to. Brixton has a rich history, it has been a centre of black culture since 1948 when the Windrush ship brought migrants, ex-service men mostly, to Britain to do jobs the British did not want, such as on the metro and rail.  This Windrush Generation built a strong community, they met in Windrush Square. That generation saw hardship and their children often discrimination. Their chances were limited and drugs took their toll. Later there were regular eruptions around the frontline given unemployment and police discrimination against black youth. It blew up first in 1981 and then again in 1995 and in 2011 given the social and economic instability.

Around the corner was a place called Poet's Corner with streets named after Milton, Spenser and Chaucer. Now it is a hotspot. There are co-working spaces and incubator centres like Impact Hub nearby with digital nomads in force. Started in London 2005 it now has approaching 100 centres worldwide and 15,000 members. Now in Brixton, good two bedroom apartments cost £550,000 and houses around £1.5 million. In the last 5 years property has risen by 76% and it is still going up. As with everywhere where gentrification is moving fast, locals complain of being priced out. They believe the place does not belong to them anymore. For the better off young professionals or successful actors it is cheaper than elsewhere in London and very accessible to the financial heartland. To get onto the property ladder many need a helping hand from parents. They bring in a wave of posh cafes and speciality pubs and swanky restaurants, and then the old fish and chip shop closes. 15 years ago, people would not come here easily or happily, though the posher Clapham nearby was alright.

Local distinctiveness is declining as Brixton High Street Homogenizes, despite the presence of people like Tom Shakhli, who founded Atlantic Road Café and instigated the Brixton Pound, a local currency like those of Bristol and Stroud (near where I live now). Brixton's is accepted by 200 local businesses.

Beyond the obvious chains like Starbucks, there are others less obvious coming in, as the FT reports. They look independent but are not, like Franco Manca, that has 38 outlets. It started in a covered market and has now been bought by the ex-Pizza Express chief executive. Effra Social looks unique, but is part of a chain of 44 bars run by Antic. 'I love the arty, independent, cultural vibe', comments one restaurateur. Yet this is the nearly unavoidable dilemma. You want and need some gentrification to get development processes going, but once it reaches a tipping point prices escalate and you often destroy what you set out to experience.

### TAKE BERLIN

The city's greatest marketing coup was the fall of the Berlin Wall in 1989. Equally important were the cheap prices of property with hundreds of empty buildings especially near the no-man's land straddling the former border. Around 120 of these were initially squatted before they were legalized. A creative bureaucrat, Jutta Weitz, is an unsung heroine here. She was responsible for dealing with industrial properties on behalf of Wohnungsbaugesellschaft Berlin-Mitte (WBM) and was keen to help the artistic community. The idea of *Zwischennutzing* (temporary use) was key to the strategy, and so many interesting structures ended up as hotbeds, one of most famous of which was the Tacheles complex, a mix of studios, workshops, a nightclub and a cinema. The garden outside had an open-air exhibition of metal sculptures. This and many other initiatives helped create the vibrant alternative culture scene that enabled Berlin to become Europe's hotspot for artists. And of course, as development proceeds 25 years later, new places emerge. Nearby Leipzig, with its cheaper rents is now called Hypezig, with the Spinnerei as one pole of its attraction.

*Urban regeneration workshop, Detroit*

**A major often forgotten factor** was that already on the 20th June 1949, the US military governor General Frank Howley had agreed to a proposal by Obermeister Heinz Zellermayer, the speaker of West Berlin's hospitality sector, to initiate 24/7 licensing. Howley then persuaded his French and British counterparts of the idea. Thus Berlin was then and has become the only major European city where you could party and drink for 48 hours on the trot. This attracted the club culture that mushroomed dramatically and especially once techno had been brought over to Berlin from Detroit by Dimitri Hegemann, who founded the important club Tresor, with others like Berghain following in quick succession. Even today you find planeloads of people coming via Easyjet or Ryanair from the outreaches of Spain, Italy, the Nordic countries and further afield to 'let go'.

Scroll forward 20 years. Berlin is Germany's capital and settling into its new role, scroll forward another 10 and it is essentially the capital of Europe. The city has moved on from the slogan 'Berlin ist arm, aber sexy' (Berlin, is poor, but sexy) proclaimed by the then mayor Klaus Wowereit. Whilst it does not have the economic vigour of a Munich, a Hamburg or a Frankfurt the world is taking notice. Berlin's history and heritage and vast investments in its cultural facilities is one reason, another is its attraction as a start-up centre and being a political capital is also key. But a crucial issue is that $20 trillion worth of global capital is floating around and searching for a home and where better than trendy Berlin. This includes money seeking a safe haven as it escapes out of Russia and China as well as the Middle East. The impacts on the ground are powerful: rental prices have increased by seventy per cent in the 10 years to 2016.[16] More and more people are buying apartments, squeezing out low-income renters, and investment groups are making more large-scale portfolio purchases.[17] Property prices have more than doubled on average over the last decade and even more in select areas like Prenzlauer Berg, Charlottenburg or Kreuzberg.[18] Some say that Berlin is an Eldorado for property investors, with many buying tranches, site unseen.

Then there is the sharing dynamic that is shaking the property market to its foundations, such as Airbnb, which has reduced the availability of affordable housing in the city. Some professional hosts control dozens of properties; in Mitte, a government study found that in one building on Wilhelmstrasse, 280 out of 300 apartments were rented to short-stay tourists as short-term rentals are more profitable. That reduces the housing available for local residents, driving overall rents up. Berlin authorities estimate that 15,000 apartments have been taken off the market to be rented to tourists and so, in 2014, they instituted a law to ban short term rentals – called *Zweckentfremdungsverbot*, a misuse of ownership.

People can still rent out rooms in their homes, as long as they do not exceed half of the floor space. Landlords can apply for official permits to rent out entire apartments short-term, but must include a convincing explanation why they need to. Crucially those that are approved can be rented for no more than the average rent per square meter for the local area. The Berlin law, designed to curtail the runaway growth of Airbnb home-renting has been challenged in the courts, but Berlin's administrative court upheld it, saying what to some will feel revolutionary and to others a relief: 'the ownership guarantee provides no claim for a residential property to be used with the expectation of making a profit.' **The rest of the world will be looking at the longer term outcomes** and what types of regulation are possible within the sharing economy logic, yet simultaneously encourages its energies. At a European level the Commission of the European Union wishes to lift legal roadblocks to the sharing economy, yet when that equally destroys community it stands at the horns of a complex dilemma. Yet it will be difficult to monitor as Airbnb tries to slip around the rules as Steven Hill writes in The Globalist.[19] The airbnbvsberlin.com[20] website provides a wealth of evidence and infographic detail about how Airbnb works in the city.

Berlin still has laws in place that dampen the kind of rampant property investment that exists in London, New York, Sydney or Shanghai. Apart from a rent cap, property developers cannot simply buy up real estate and change its use, and leaving flats empty for speculation is difficult.

*Lisbon*

## LISBON & WHO IS NEXT

This dynamic is a global phenomenon. Take Lisbon, which many people think of as 'the next kid off the block' as a capital of cool. Its assets are obvious. A deep history, global connections from its past empire, regarded as a relatively safe place, sunny weather and 'undervalued' property and a start-up culture in the making with organizations like Second Home locating a major base there. Madonna buys a house and talks about it, then Phil Collins and that is in the news. You look at Chiado or the area surrounding Avenida de Liberdade then and now. The glove shop disappears and in its place comes a Burger King, the old coffee house becomes a Starbucks and the march of the major brands proceeds. Who will be next off the block? Athens? It has history, it is cheap? It is warm? The gloomy scenario looking 20 years ahead unless house speculation is curtailed is that the 25 hub cities of the world and the successful ones on the second tier will become cities of two halves or three thirds: the rich in more gated environments; a middle group struggling to keep in property ownership; and a large mixed grouping of the less well-off including swathes of young people who cannot afford to buy and whose parents cannot help them.

The three examples are large European cities, but it happens globally and in smaller places too. In Beijing, Nanluoguxiang is its best-known hutong (a narrow alleyway in a residential area). In a decade it has propelled from a quiet lane for living to a tourist hotspot where you cannot avoid someone taking a selfie. As elsewhere, it started with artists moving in, then a gallery and some unusual shops perhaps launched by an expat, then the Olympic Games happens in 2008 and people in search for the authentic discover it as the hip place, and in 2013 in moves Starbucks. Then people search for the new and suddenly Wudaoying – 'the hip hutong in Beijing' - is touted as the next Nanluoguxiang. Hutongs have the intimate, dense qualities that make it easy to make connections to the likeminded. Unfortunately in Beijing's headlong rush to development many thousand have been destroyed. If more had been left perhaps the few areas that still exist would not have become tourist traps.

## PENANG

It does not always have to be like this. Take the smaller George Town in Penang with more than 1000, often degraded, shophouses. A very diverse part of Malaysia that lay on historic trade routes, it became an intellectual hub and location for mid-level sophisticated tech manufacturing. Yet many of its best left for places like Singapore so the challenge was how to get the diaspora to come back.[21]

Here the designation as a UNESCO World Heritage site was a trigger for regeneration, with Laurence Loh playing a key role and it also offered some measure of protection. The other was the George Town Transformation Programme (GTTP) launched by Hamdan Majeed from Khazanah a government investment agency and where I played a part. Both in 2008 set the groundwork for the Think City initiative in 2009. This seeks to regenerate with a principled perspective. As it says in its grants programme:

You are empowered to change your city, we do this because we believe through small acts of positive disruption, we can create cities that value heritage, place sustainability at the core of advance and serve all people.

The programme seeks to kick start regeneration by building on the momentum of civil society-driven activities and private sector initiatives, as well as build local capacity. This programme has shifted pride in George Town, has led to shophouses being refurbished and maintained, and it has been able to bring people back.[21]

However, danger signals are on the horizon. Development is attracting tourists and foreigners and their capital. Many developments have improved George Town even though the small boutique hotels are out of reach for locals. Yet perhaps the most aggressive is World Class Land, the property arm of Singapore's Aspial Corporation. It is trying to buy 200 shophouse properties on the edge of the designated heritage buffer zone where regulation is more lax and it wishes to build a 65-storey skyscraper abutting a two-floor zone. People will be pushed out. This is Think City's next challenge: to move from being a grant giver to an advocate for a different development model.

## LAND & SPECULATION

Every popular place has to contend with the gentrification dynamic and how to keep its best aspects, such as lifting the quality of public space. Prices can only be contained ultimately by control of land or value increases in the public interest. In essence the rate of value increase should be less than the rate of interest in any given place so as to encourage investing in things other than property. There is land in built up areas and unused land waiting in the wings, examples include. The German Building Codes 165-171 enable the speedy procurement of unused land. It is used to mobilise land and to finance municipal development costs in situations where there is an increasing demand for housing, workspace, or public facilities. The uplift in land values finances the measure following development. The municipality buys land at the existing, much lower, use value, and then sells the land when it has been planned and serviced for the much higher price of undeveloped plots. The difference is used to fund social infrastructure such as schools, parking and green areas. Owners can fend off the public purchase if they are willing to carry out development in line with the plan, in which case the municipality gets some compensation.

Foundations and charities buy land to take it out of the market. In the Islamic world waqf is a popular example, an unchallengeable charitable endowment under Islamic law. It typically involves donating a building, plot of land or other assets for charitable purposes with no intention of reclaiming the assets. This can be for religious purposes or affordable housing as in Georgetown Penang. Various foundations have done this elsewhere, such as in Berlin where the Swiss Edith Marion Foundation bought the extensive, and famous, Kindl brewery as well the well know alternative hub Schokoladen with more to follow. Another Swiss foundation Abendroth has provided the loan for the large urban village the Holzmarkt, a social enterprise development along the river Spree.[22] The Kreuzberg municipal district in Berlin is buying back assets that had been previously been privatized in order to safeguard socially oriented uses. All large cities are experiencing these dilemmas and have appointed a land advisor to scour global best practice - Nicholas Falk, the founder of URBED.[23]

*Urban regeneration in Penang*

The nomadic age behaves more like a meme than an ideology. A meme, as Richard Dawkins its inventor says is an idea, a behaviour, a style that moves from person to person and affects them along the way so generating a culture. A meme acts like **a living organism and its embedded and embodied ideas seep their way into a culture** and are transmitted too from one mind to the next via media, talking or common rituals.

Those attracted to the nomad culture are similar to those interested in creative or smart city thinking and many qualities are the same. They want environments where they can be curious and where curiosity is encouraged. They believe this sparks imagination and is the soil for a more interesting life. They want a culture of creativity, or a creative milieu or quarter, or a creative ecology, if not everywhere in the city then at least in significant parts.

# THE NOMADIC MEME & CREATIVITY

## CREATIVE QUARTERS

Successful places that attract the mobile typically include many of those features listed above under Nomad Planning distilled from the best, classic practitioners: an overall balance between local buzz and global pipelines; an older fabric, with a diversity of building styles with a street pattern that is intimate, diverse and not dominated by well-known brands and chains and with built structures from different historical periods including the contemporary; an overall atmosphere that creates a multi-layered experience visually and in terms of activities, including combining the intimate and the iconic, the somewhat shabby and clean and potentially sanitized new; an environment that feels open, diverse and mixed, where the presence of different cultures and people finds expression in the built form and facilities from restaurants to cultural centres; it somewhere that is not too self-consciously orchestrated and planned, so it allows unpretentious authenticity to develop and come through; there are a variety of structures for work and living at different price ranges to ensure start-ups and young innovators have a place to live and work, as well as places for established older hands. Cheapness is key.

There is an overall physical setting that combines the high quality ordinary and small with the occasional extraordinary gesture; there is blending the old fabric and heritage with the challenging new; a landmark within the quarter is probably present, perhaps a reused old industrial structure; a good mix of uses is necessary to provide the ability to work, research, to live, to recreate and to relax, and there are buildings with flexible structures that allow for adaptable uses. **Human scale developments are crucial that encourage interaction** and mixing and a diversity of third spaces that are accessible for talking, eating and relaxing. Another balance is between production facilities and consumption, thus the quarter enables the full value chain from ideas generation, learning, through production to consuming to be present.

The district at its best combines commercial and non-commercial activities and uses, such as research centres, public entities, not for profits, cultural facilities and low cost subsidized spaces. There is lively mainstream and alternative scene, a rich set of cultural facilities from the commercial to non-commercial, such as galleries or museums which successfully blend tradition and innovation. Overall, playfulness and humour is fostered through temporary installations and unusual activities.

If we are looking at a defined area, public management structure is probably necessary, like the local authority or a public private partnership or development agency, that is alert and tries to ensure a fine balance between gentrifying and remaining accessible in terms of cost and cultures.

This also provides a marketing and promotional structure that can ensure the right level of events. Over time this may not be necessary as self- generated activity can take over. It is important to make sure the intent of the quarter is visibly communicated through its urban design or its activities.

My colleague Jonathan Hyams and I tried to explore how you could measure such interesting places and developed The Creative City Index in collaboration with Bilbao Metropoli 30.[24] We believe it is a useful tool for cities to explore. Detailed assessments have been undertaken in 25 cities and the method looks at four core areas and specific domains within them, namely how does the city:

**Nurture and identify its overall creative potential** and reinforce its cultural distinctiveness in order to generate more innovations and so make the city more resilient. Here it assesses:

> Openness, trust, accessibility and participation

> The talent development and learning landscape at all levels

**Enable and support this creative capacity** so that opportunities and prospects are maximized. The evaluation here looks at:

> The political and public framework and its regulations and incentives regime

> Strategic leadership, agility and vision

> Professionalism and effectiveness

**Exploit and harness its expertise, talents and aspirations**. The evaluation here concerns:

> Entrepreneurship, exploration and innovation capacity

> Communication, connectivity and networking

**The lived experience of the city** physically and in terms of activity in encouraging creative potential so it assesses:

Distinctiveness, diversity, vitality and expression

The place and place-making

Liveability and well-being

The Index is both a subjective and objective assessment and this distinguishes it from other ways of evaluating cities. This is valuable as it brings up issues that normally do not emerge with other assessments. It might be, for instance, that a conclusion is that confidence or collaboration is a problem, but there is no department responsible for this. The holistic approach also ensures one is always looking at the city as a totality (and not only through one lens). It combines the economic, social and cultural and looks at how the regulations and incentives regime provides conditions for the city to think, plan and act with imagination.

The evaluation looks at innovative activity and investigates the spectrum from the individual, the firm, industry sectors and clusters, networks in the city, the city itself as an amalgam of different organizational cultures and as part of a city-region. It assesses how creative the private, community and public sectors are, as well as looking at areas like education, the varying business sectors, the arts and cultural scene, specific industry sectors, science and organizations that help the city's prosperity and well-being. It highlights how important cross-disciplinary working is as organizations cannot be islands onto themselves. Levels of creativity in working across sectors and inter-organizational networking can have explosive impacts given how value added is created by inventive partnering and networking, as say between universities and local communities. Assessing the obstacles to generating creativity is significant, with mindset and behavioural change being crucial. It is increasingly recognized that highlighting obstacles, themselves targets for creative action, is as important as highlighting best practices. It addresses too one of today's greatest paradoxes: the rise of the creativity agenda and simultaneous rise of an increased culture of risk aversion.

Given that more nomadic people now have more choice and mobility about where they want to be, the physical setting, ambience and atmosphere is of upmost importance. This is the stage, the container or platform within which activity takes place and develops. It generates the milieu or environment. The milieu mixes hard and soft infrastructure. Clearly a creative milieu can be a room, an office, a building, a set of buildings, a refurbished warehouse, a campus, a street, an area, a neighbourhood and occasionally a city. These places can equally be completely uncreative. What makes a milieu attractive to the nomadic crowd is that it gives the user the sense that they can shape, create and make the place they are in, that they are an active participant rather than a passive consumer, and that they are an agent of change rather than a victim. These environments are open but they have unspoken rules of engagement. They are not wild for the sake of wildness so that things dissolve in chaos, but they accept the need to be stretched. A cautionary proviso: such environments will attract outsiders who only consume and give nothing back. They borrow the landscape, chew it, digest it and spit it out. They can drain the identity of a place if their numbers overwhelm the locals.

*Street market, Beijing*

# THE SENSORY LANDSCAPE OF CITIES

The city is a moving canvas, not only are people moving in and out but everything within it seems to be moving too. There are people walking, riding bikes, and driving cars, being driven in a bus, a metro or a train, going up and down escalators and on lifts. Seen from on high we see more movement than rest - take escalators. Remember once going on a metro escalator. Solid metal steps going clunk and click in measured rhythm and the rubber handrail juddering somewhat as it moves faster than the steps. Now an escalator moves and everything moves with it. The ads once fixed now show distracting instant video clips and these come in repetitive sequences so your eye catches fragments as you slip past. On some the handrails have ads inscribed and so you touch the ad as you move along. You may as you do this be looking at a You Tube clip on your mobile. Ads even invade the adjacent steps with messages on each riser that sometimes escape onto the treads. I have even seen fast changing, pulsating stock market information on risers the same time as they show the seconds go past. You get a ghastly sense of linear time moving you towards the end – death. And once outside the buildings themselves move with interactive interfaces. No wonder people hanker after stillness.

The city is a 360 degree, all embracing, immersive experience and it is this heightened sense of variety and possibilities that our nomadic being searches for and tries to absorb. At times this is a pleasure, you soak things in – impressed, you marvel at the creativity, enticed, it lures you into its spell. The solid urban fabric shifts and moves as more surfaces are becoming interactive and these are getting ever larger, often you can control how an urban interface operates from your mobile device. You are partly in control. Mostly, however, it is the capitalist dynamic trying to sell you something.

## THE INVERSE NOMADIC

One hundred years ago, if you were working or middle class anywhere, most of what you bought you needed. Now most of what you buy you do not need, leaving aside the two and half billion people at the bottom of the pile.

# THE CITY AS A COMMUNICATIONS DEVICE

To keep going capitalism must manufacture needs. It must pump up desire. It propels the inexorable dynamic to get you to spend, otherwise the system falls apart. It has its delights, but is emptier than its appears. The system could not survive if it was not immensely seductive, and fashion is its name and these fashion cycles are getting shorter and shorter, moving, moving, moving. It is a hedonistic treadmill, it drains energy. So, increasingly our primary sensation in cities is one of messages coming in at you down a channel located far away with no escape for you. This is a 'inverse nomadic', the commercial world chasing you and getting into your personal space wherever you are. The voluntary nomad lifestyle gives you control, but this gives you a feeling of overload and of things being out of control. This is why we sense, feel and understand through increasingly narrow funnels of perception. What might that be? Is that at 90 or even only 45 degrees? **A nomadic world can mean we see more but experience less with depth**.

Things flicker by and our personal sensory landscape is shrinking precisely at the moment when it should broaden, given what we need to engage with in the wider world. At the same time, the world of commerce in the name of experience attempts in ever more shrill tones to grab our sensory attention. This is done by constant motion, the beat and rhythms of music to make you tap to the sound or even gyrate, micro second screen grabs or clips taking you into infinity with zoom out shots. We protect ourselves often by shutting off and our perceptive capacities cramp up. In that state we cannot sufficiently recognise or practice most of the senses. Nuance goes by the wayside as does our ability to distinguish noise registers, rhythms and pitch, masked by the continuous low-level din – and often that is traffic. We do not give ourselves time to appreciate the subtleties and qualities of materials, are they soft, warm and yielding or harsh, cold and unforgiving, or even to how the patina of the ages seeps out and lets a building silently speak. We crave the overriding smells of complexity, of the freshness as you enter a market at the vegetable or fruits end as these feel 'authentic' and uncontaminated. We encounter mostly instead the powerful, heady blast of perfumes and cosmetics as they seep through department stores or their waft of warm, stale air in colder climes and in warmer ones a draught of cold.

**A city communicates through every fibre of its being** starting with its topography, climate and physical structure and then followed by its atmosphere and external reputation. Everything sends out a message. A grid-like city with its straight lines and flat roads such as Melbourne feels different from one that is curvy and hilly as in Sydney or San Francisco. An old city feels different to one that is new, an industrial city different to one based on services, an inland city to a harbour city. The buildings of a city communicate. If they are well ordered and framed into a street with varied shops this creates a contrasting experience to one where each building feels like an isolated island in the landscape, the typical rather soulless corporate feel most cities have. Size matters too. Are buildings very large or smaller and intimate, are public spaces vast and windswept or more contained so encouraging sociability. Do buildings feel accessible and open to you or are there usually guards at the entrances. Are the shops diverse and distinctive or are they brand names you know from around the world. Are cultural facilities all clustered around one place or are they spread throughout. Is there just one main centre or are there various zones in the city each with its own life. Are the suburbs lifeless or is there a local vitality too. What a city feels and looks like sends out innumerable messages with its values etched into its physical fabric as well as how the city is programmed. Places that are more authoritarian come across as distant and forbidding; a place that is open-minded will show this in a physical way too. A city wishing to be green will show its intent.

HIDDEN SENSES ON THE MOVE

The sensory landscape of a city is the totality of experiences you perceive by being in and navigating a city. Not only the obvious ones like seeing, smelling, hearing or imagining the feel of the textures you see. These are the tangibles, but there are the invisibles. The city is a vast, dense sea of electrical energy fields and waves estimated to be 100 million times stronger than 100 years ago. They are rushing around at high speed. These massive currents crisscrossing the urban environment are unseen, unfelt, unheard, without taste or smell. The accumulative, heady cocktail of magnetic and electrical fields generated by power transmission lines, pylons and masts, mobile phones, computers, television and radio, lighting, wiring and household appliances can seriously interfere with the subtle natural balances of each cell in our body. The sum of perceptions is experienced emotionally. How we experience these senses determine the mood, disposition, temperament and ultimately personality of a city. In an iterative process the effect of these tangibles and imperceptibles shapes and reinforces how we perceive the city, how we behave in a city and what it becomes.

By looking, sensing and feeling closely we can discern the overall atmosphere and specific signals of a place. These sensations often are encapsulated in a feeling of 'yes' or equally a response of 'no'. Blank walls, the inability to walk, relentless asphalt or glass reflecting back at you project a 'no' reaction like 'keep out' or 'stay away'. A good secondary shopping street with its diversity of often very local shops interspersed perhaps by a pocket park, by contrast, tends to give you a sense of 'yes' since your eyes are diverted and entertained. The street says you can join in. By observing with all senses, calmly alert, you can figure out whether people you encounter seem to be close, respectful and open or suspicious, tense and rushed. Without even speaking to anyone we can sometimes measure the pulse of conviviality - how people get on. Equally we can take in urban decline or growth, whether a place is loved or cared for, how polluting it is, how powerful it is. This is what we might call urban literacy - the understanding of how places work.

Crucially we need language to make this experience conscious, yet our language of the senses or for the nomadic world is not rich enough to describe our cities today. Literary figures or artists apart, our language is hollowed out and dry, shaped by the technical jargon of the professions, especially those in planning and the built environment. The language to describe the city remains dominated by the physical, without sufficient descriptions of movement, rhythm or smell and sound – the nomadic world in short. Our visual language comes largely from architecture and urban design, disciplines which still dominate discussion on cities. The language is broadening yet still somewhat focused on static elements rather than dynamic wholes. Urban design, meanwhile, sees and describes cities more as dynamic totalities: place, connections, movement, mixed uses, blocks, neighbourhoods, zones, densities, centres, peripheries, landscapes, vistas, focal points, and realms. But both frequently exclude the atmospherics of cities, the feeling of the look. Does it make you shrink into yourself, make you calmly reflect or fill you with passion? Does it close you in or open you out?

## OVERLOAD & DISTRACTION

Constant stimuli of images, sounds, words take on a life of their own and the city feels as if it is running away with itself. It distracts, fragments and can shatter our attention. Take adverts. There are ads on airline sickness bags, on bannisters, railings, stairs, escalators, in toilets, on tables, on chairs, on floors, on sidewalks and complete buildings as they become interactive interfaces. The urban landscape at times appears like an advert mosaic. They are increasingly converted into digital screens heightening the sense of motion, fizz and clutter. You cannot escape an ad and they are getting bigger. This helped launch the global billboard banning movement with Sao Paolo a pioneer. Mayor Gilberto Kassab launched the Clean City Law in 2007 and called adverts a form of visual pollution. The city removed 15,000 billboards and 300,000 oversized storefront signs in the first year. São Paulo is not exactly an ad-free city any longer, but it is dramatically different than before.

The non-stop blitz and pervasiveness of ads is fuelled by our experiences elsewhere from always online smart phones and ever-present spam emails or name-brands featured on social media, TV shows and films. The paradox is that the **freedom of choice projected by ads as liberation is experienced as claustrophobic** and crowds you in. A constantly repeated number is that we are bombarded by a tsunami of 5,000 messages a day, up from 2,000 a day in the 1970s. This is what market research firm Yankelovich estimated in 2007, others more recently suggested the number is anywhere between 4,000 and 10,000.

Turning ad spaces into art installations is a good move and even some counter-messaging provided by graffiti. At times amusing, clever and delightful, it is often merely an angry or ugly defacement where urban tribes mark their territory.

The irony is that the **nomadic world promises you diversity and so often offers sameness**. Surface appearances may be different, but wherever you go you see the same stores, the same brands, the same block buster films, the same cars, the same shopping centre formats, the same music genres, the same architectural styles, the same clothing, the same fashions, the same trends. The globalised market and media have ensured that is so. **The fightback will begin**, however, and some of this will be nostalgic, looking backwards before the confidence emerges to be as far as one can be oneself rather than copying.

Of course there is still local distinctiveness. The massive Indian film industry focused on Bollywood has a different aesthetic than that of Hollywood and different stars and icons.

# THE DECLINE OF DISTINCTIVENESS

India has chain stores we do not know in the rest of Asia or Europe and Africa like Big Bazaar or Reliance Retail. Korean K-Pop is different from US hip-hop. The Hispanic world has its cultural legends and the world music genres, especially from Africa and places like Mali, Burkina Faso or the Congo are rich in content. In many countries it is local bands or singers who reach the number one spot like O.S.T.R.'s *Life after Death* in Poland, or in Korea where very few of the global labels are in evidence. The Twice song *Cheer Up* was a number one song, but a reviewer said 'it begins with what sounds eerily like a musical quote from Radiohead's *No Surprises*'. Nevertheless, within the cultural sphere many of the underlying patterns are similar, for instance in music the core genre is often hip-hop. These genres, styles and trends travel the world.

Let us take three examples to describe a theme with endless illustrations: architecture; place names; and retailing. Is it beyond human ingenuity to think of a Chinese, Japanese, Russian, Nigerian, Egyptian, Brazilian high-rise building style that responds to climate, culture and local aesthetics rather than merely trying to be flashy and imitative. Architecture astonishingly has a similar palette world-wide, but exceptions exist. Here Tallinn and Estonia need a mention with their interestingly zany designs, and even in the Arab world there is some modern local flavour. And Africa's talent, such as David Adayje, Francis Kéré, Kunle Adeyemi, Mphethi Morojele and Mokena Makeka are blending an aesthetic that has a strong African flavour. We therefore expect more to come from that continent.

We have witnessed mostly a roving band of nomadic starchitects as the world globalized with renewed force. They are stepping over themselves to produce the most spectacular forms, proliferating gleaming glass towers, bold shapes breaking out of traditional square box patterns; skyscrapers exploding onto the landscape, some with good public spaces. They have built vast retailing, entertainment or cultural centres that try to bewitch, enchant and seduce you. **It will be interesting to see which of these stand the test of time**, at least they look different from the interminable monotony and low quality sameness that has invaded and dominates the urban landscape.

These are supposedly the manifestations of ambition, yet reflecting ambition is more complex. Consider Malaga or Bordeaux where instead of one 'global' icon, a hundred well-blended and co-ordinated initiatives are more effective than the one-off building. Malaga, once seen as the cheap holiday resort for the British has brought its extensive old city to life by expensively under-grounding all car parking, upgrading housing, and bringing out its Andalusian character in innovative schemes like canvas sun shading of streets.

China is now officially banning its weird buildings that are distinctive — whether truly interesting or just faddish is a different question. This propelled China onto the architectural stage. Yet according to guidelines on urban planning in 2016 from the State Council, China's Cabinet, the statement says: 'this applies to the construction of "bizarre" and "odd-shaped" buildings that are devoid of character or cultural heritage', and the directive calls for buildings that are 'economic, green and beautiful.' What beautiful means is a question for debate, perhaps the monotonous structures that line Beijing's seven ring roads - I think not. Targeted are buildings like the Sheraton Horseshoe in Huzhou, the Sunrise Kempinski hotel in Beijing, Guangzhou's Circle, inspired by a jade disc and home to its plastics exchange, the Gate of the Orient in Suzhou, and perhaps even the CCTV building by OMA and Rem Koolhaas. This is possibly why construction on the world's largest proposed skyscraper at one-kilometre high, the Phoenix Towers in Wuhan, had not started in 2017. Does it include Zaha Hadid's Soho Galaxy in Beijing, which was then copied in Chongqing. It is called the Meiquan, and the developer behind Meiquan, 22nd Century, denied accusations of pirating the building, his blog says: 'Never meant to copy, only want to surpass.'

There are so many Sohos and **if you want to be trendy just call yourself Soho - or not**. The first and real Soho name in London apparently comes from an ancient hunting call —soho —which took place on lands west of Wardour Street in the current Soho. New York's SoHo means south of Houston Street. Both these places are renowned for their vibrant cultural life and edgy feel and, in the past, some griminess, sex clubs and traditional markets. I should not be too sniffy as I had my office in London's Soho for 15 years in the 1980s and 1990s, setting up my organization Comedia and also running a social innovation hub for the Joseph Rowntree Reform Trust. I loved the area and its combination of intimacy, artiness and even sleaze.

But since then any gentrifying area in the world is in danger of being called Soho. There is Palermo Soho in Buenos Aires, Hong Kong's Soho, South of Hollywood Road. Others indirectly get the name as Trastevere is known as the Soho of Rome and Brera the Soho of Milan and both cities have Soho restaurants. Madrid has a Soho restaurant, a hotel Vincci Soho, a Soho House, and a Cambridge Soho club. The latter brings together two brands Cambridge and Soho. There are Soho hotels as in Miami, Chicago and Toronto.

Then of course there is the Soho House chain, rightly since its original location was in Greek St., Soho, London. Now it has 18 locations and is expanding across the hip centres of the world - from Barcelona, to Berlin and Istanbul with Sao Paolo, Rio de Janeiro and Hong Kong on the horizon.

There is Soho Coffee Co. started in 1999 in Cheltenham, not far from where I now live, and aiming to have 50 outlets by 2018. It has a solid ethical foundation supporting Fairtrade coffee. The name is ubiquitous and my latest find was the Soho Travel Agency in Trieste. One of the biggest Sohos is Soho China, one of the largest prime site office developers in China that has a dozen Soho branded developments. They say their 'soho originally stood for "small office, home office"'.There are copycat derivations like SoMa, South of Market San

*Sohos in London, Beijing, Trieste and Madrid*

Francisco, where the Soho sound rings in your ear. Clearly the ring 'So', 'Mo' 'No', 'Bo', 'Ho' has a rhythm to it. Boho is a bohemian and there are numerous boho brands from cosmetics to clothing, such as exploring 'the best Boho in Boston.' Noho is now North of Soho in London and New York and there is Noho North of Hollywood in Los Angeles. I am sure Nomosoho in Crosby Street New York wanted to send out a different message for this hip place as they probably overlooked that 'nomo' means not homosexual. Remember too if you are obsessed with the Soho sound there is a town called Soho in North Korea, and another area in Pyongyang called Soho-ri.

The serious decline of distinctiveness can be seen in Soho House – when visiting in Berlin not one member of staff could, was willing or apparently allowed to speak a word of German in what is now 'the hottest hotel in Berlin'. The German deputy finance minister noted: "it increasingly drives me up the wall that waiters in some Berlin restaurants only speak English," adding: "You would never find this craziness in Paris... we will only understand each other if we speak each other's language."[25]

Next up is food retailing and it is food that we imagine can be locally produced and sold. Not so. The drugstores CVS and Walgreens in the States together control between 50 and 75 per cent of the market in each of the country's 14 largest metro-areas, such as Chicago, the Bay Area, Los Angeles and New York, and together control at least half the market share in almost every major US city. Walmart currently captures around 20% of the grocery market in the US, up from around seven per cent in 2002. The top four US food retailers led by Walmart control an astonishing 40 per cent of the vast, complex US market. Grocery sales in Britain are dominated by Tesco, Asda, Sainsbury's and Morrisons. Dubbed the 'big four', they had a combined market share of 73.2 per cent in 2016. The top three food retailers in the Netherlands control 83.5 per cent of the market with Albert Heijn in the lead with 35.4 per cent, followed by SuperUnie with 29.6 per cent and Jumbo with 18.5 per cent. In Australia Woolworth has 36.3 per cent and Coles 33.2 per cent. Two companies with a 69.5 per cent market share. What they sell has travelled the world. Green beans from Kenya, tomatoes from the Canaries, potatoes from Cyprus, avocados from Israeli, asparagus from Spain, apples from New Zealand, pak choi from China, mangoes from India, dates from the Middle East and roses from Ecuador. These are the same roses the mafia gangs get immigrants to sell to diners in the restaurants of Australia, the States and Europe.

Again we see the counter-reaction, interesting new bakeries sprouting up, specialist cheese shops or old-fashioned fishmongers or butchers. Farmers markets, that attract all classes, are on the rise and a boon to new food focused start-ups. **Great as they are their force cannot contain multinational food power**. The creativity bursts out in the numerous restaurant formats and pop-up food experiences, and these are subject to the constant movements in taste, fashion and trends that sweep the globe. At one moment it is Mexican tacos, the next Japanese teriyaki, South American parillas, (iron grilled barbecues), Scandi fresh food. Then there are the craft beers, experiments with wine and even vodka made from cow's milk - Britain's Black Cow. Often it is the fusions that capture the imagination like current favourite Yotam Ottolenghi's Middle Eastern mix of cultures. Criss-crossing continues apace.

Similar examples of **the dominance of the 'constant same'** could be made with clothing. It is not only that most of the world dresses in the same Western style, it is also that you see the same clothes shops in their thousands, like Zara or H&M, both of whom are in fact well-designed.

Notable exceptions include the Arabs frequent wearing of the thawb, the generally long tunic, or the variations women wear such as the hiqab, the headscarf that covers the head and neck, but leaves the face clear, the niqÐb, a female head covering and scarf that covers all of the face except for the eyes, or the burqa which covers the whole body from the top of the head to the ground. Of course, Indian women wear the sari.

A good example of dealing with the global and the local is the most globally popular and immensely successful televised Indian Premier League cricket competition. The eight teams have a minimum of 16 players. Of these every team must have at least two players from the Indian under-22 pool, as well as a minimum of eight local players out of the total. There can be up to 10 foreign players in a team's pool and of the 11 playing in a game only up to four.

The effect has been dramatic on the development of India's young cricket talent coming through, who apart from being mentored by famous senior players would not have had such visibility.

The spread of Kolkata's idol making district Kumortuli and that of Jodhpur's blue city that follow remind us of old forms of distinctiveness. Beyond flashy towers and cafés what will the distinctiveness of our cities look like in the future?

*A very Torino day in the rain*

This section draws on issues first explored in my book *The Art of City Making* published in 2006.

3

# ZONES OF
# ENCOUNTER

*Previous page: Rome*

*This page: Brookly Heights, New York*

# MEETING & MIXING

The civic is made up of a mass of small and often insignificant – even random – encounters or transactions that grow into something more substantial. It might be a friendly gesture, a brief chat with a shopkeeper, or someone telling you the way. It would include a myriad of imperceptible small things, like facing upwards, or smiling, or looking people in the eye, being attentive. Exchanges get deeper, perhaps a longer chat about the children in the local park, perhaps revealing something more personal, perhaps doing a small favour to a passer-by or a neighbour. This spectrum of socializing can have varied impacts. Public transport is one of the most common ways that differing groups come together; in that sense it is democratic as you are forced to share space. You probably do not chat unless it is a longer train journey. With urban gardening it is easy to chat, you are doing something together in a public place and you may ask for advice. This may lead you to suggest your collaborator read a book or join a walking group. Dancing at a festival is more intimate. There can be a chat-up or pick-up dimension when it stimulates the senses. Yet it does not need to be sexual. Texting, twittering and media sharing too can be part of the civic fabric, virtual as it is.

Instances of the civic are pleasing: 'No, I don't want any tips, I'm here to help', says the Chicago Architectural Foundation guide who has talked for 90 minutes. '' Or a cluster of Chicago police officers: 'Are you enjoying the city, where do you come from? Do you know the way?'

There can be spontaneous outbursts of civic behaviour, such as flash mobs, part of the tactical urbanism repertoire which tries to change the city provocation by provocation. These are a positive version of riots. Ones I have witnessed included one that concerned violence against women in Ghent, and a gory bloody one in Bilbao against bullfighting. One I did not personally attend was the spontaneous 'Ode to Joy' event for peace, Europe and togetherness in Odessa's fish market.[1]

# CONNECTIONS: SHALLOW & DEEP

Other civic examples are more stilted, maybe even in a forced enclosure, like the doctor's or dentist's waiting room. At the latter, you know what it is about, teeth and gums, and you have common aches and especially if children are around this is an ice-breaker. If someone black, Chinese, Indian or white is in the room, at least you have a common purpose: 'get rid of that pain'. Animal problems are brilliant ways of connecting at the vet – 'what type of dog is that', 'what are they called', 'are snakes easy pets to keep', 'do frogs give you much pleasure'. And countless loves have evolved from dog walking encounters in the park.

**Never underestimate who you are meeting, never pre-judge** or let a prejudice develop from that. So you think they are 'only' a taxi driver, nothing wrong with being one. Take at random three chats on taxi journeys in one day in New York in January 2017. The first is studying chemistry and his brothers are both doctors, and from Hungary. He says: 'I only work as hard as I need too, there is more to life than striving for money'. The other, the Afghani, practices German and can hold good German conversations. The third, from Haiti, speaks multiple languages and sounds very entrepreneurial. Then surprisingly the Italian lady at the kiosk till at La Guardia airport when she sees I am buying the Harvard Business Review (I do that rarely) says: 'do you know something, my niece teaches at Harvard'. It goes on, the older Ethiopian taxi driver at Washington airport tells me how continual ads on American TV blunt the mind and that more people should study critical thinking.

It is from these myriad threads of connections, shallow and deep, that the civic is knitted together and then woven into a pattern of unspoken rules of engagement. These interactions create feelings that may develop into affinity or personal relationships that go beyond the basics as you see into another person's private life. It may lead to love or marriage. Of course, too there are the family bonds, and some of these are clan like, there are the neighbours where you live or who might own the shop nearby, there are work networks and affiliations through enthusiasms, religion or team sport. These multiple relations and friendships are what ultimately builds community, the neighbourhood feeling and then the obligations, even duties, that might evolve from that. It is a collection of incidental links, weak links and then stronger and stronger links. This civic behaviour is an antidote to the privatization of experience, it is more public.

**Being civic is about more than voting or volunteering or associational life** or formal civic participation projects or community development initiatives. It is an attitude of respecting the other too, it is about getting closer and yet keeping distance without being distanced. It cuts across class and income. How a neighbourhood feels about itself is crucial. A positive self-perception as well as image outside affects how people behave, how relaxed they feel. They become more open. Contrary to clichéd assumptions, poor people also reveal a strong appetite for participation, of course, and can be equally international in outlook and ready to be experimental and innovate.

The goal is to make better cities by creating a culture of civility. Civility is more than politeness. It is respect, affirmation on occasion, tolerance, self-restraint too. The civic is the texture of successful urban life. Behind it and the civic city lies a vast reservoir of fragile agreements about collective living: accepting the Christian church bells or *adhan*, the mosque call to worship or the atheists view that formalized religion is not central to their life. All are alright in this type of city, and this also manifests itself physically. Looking again at Chicago, there are gestures of generosity such as one of the best public space management regimes that I have ever seen. Vancouver, Melbourne, Portland, Bilbao, Malaga and Nice offer similar examples.

Too often we start with big words like 'community', as if that happens in one big hit, whereas **community is a laborious business**, it builds from the past of our locality, its reason for being, its trades and attractions and its purpose today or the network of shops that structure your needs. So a retirement community feels different from a start-up neighbourhood. Each of these needs differing resources and is shaped by encounters that have created trust (or mistrust). Community is the result of this history and might start with random acts of kindness and end with shared dependencies. Being civic helps it along.

Clearly the civic is also part of a wider decision-making realm, once called the *polis*, where we take part in political life through its mechanisms. Here we make choices together (do we want to build a metro system or a theatre) or take essential decisions (shall we build a dam). The media was once a large part of this but in good part has abandoned its fourth estate role for entertainment. 'The News' was once the water cooler - not any more. We have fragmented this political arena. We talk on Twitter, but do not bother to vote. The Reithian notion of inform, educate and entertain that set up the British Broadcasting Corporation (BBC) has also shifted to entertainment. The major channels have to compete with other media and bother less about educating - it takes too long: **precisely at a time when civic education is needed**. Additionally, when truth is malleable as with fake news or direct manipulation, it makes developing a civic culture hard. It is corrosive, it reduces trust and raises suspicions.

The notion of community changes for the nomadic those large proportion of people in a city on a temporary basis. At one extreme, places driven by their government functions like Washington DC or Canberra have large cohorts of government workers who are temporary residents who may live in the city for a government term or a time-dated contract and also many people are on a fly-in fly-out rota. At the other extreme, there are the short stay residents, typically a digital nomad, who feed the short-term rental market. For both being an integral part of a city's society is difficult and they tend to confine their relationships to their own grouping rather than mix with the indigenous population.

I experienced this fractured sense of belonging myself working with the World Bank in Washington for a year. I socialized with those in a similar position to me, always looking for congenial public hang-outs and I confess I only met a couple Washingtonians briefly through the one person from the city I knew previously. The digital nomad experience differs in that they are not part of one large organization and their tentacles more likely stretch across the networks created by social media which would include locals of a similar mindset or interests, through the incubator centres or co-working spaces or cafes that essentially play a similar function, or taking part in Pecha Kucha event (sharp short presentations, where you can present your ideas or hackathons). Our digitizing world escalates the range of people you can connect with freely.

The collective urban experience, where the settled and unsettled meet, thus takes on an added importance. With fragmented communication channels the norm, and tribal affiliation growing, there are fewer common events to be discussed over that clichéd water cooler. This is why festivals, culture, sporting and spectacular events frame an increasingly significant part of urban culture. Here locals and nomads can share an experience.

The city is increasingly a permeable thing – a built fabric with a variety of functional or municipal boundaries; a network of trading, cultural or political relationships. In addition the city extends its tentacles through its highly networked individuals across the globe. The city is then a connective node, which for its residents is either a full-time or part-time home. This shifts community in the sense of a more fixed geography and predictable patterns of links. It is more a spectrum of bonds from the light to the weighty.

**Cohesion and bonding are deep human traits that have immense survival value** and are at the core of our social behaviours, which are still essentially tribal. We are hard-wired to bond and this allows us to feel what others feel. If this is weak, it will be difficult for us to work out who we are, or how we can relate well to each other. By understanding how to engender a stronger sense of empathy we can build a more robust and coherent civil society and stronger communities. We connect better with the other when we feel at ease, and when not we become more tribal. The many 'I Heart My City' programmes are one testimony as is the 'Let's Do It – World Clean Up Day'[3], proposed for September 2018 with 150 countries and six million people taking part. This civic-led mass movement began in Estonia in 2008 with 50,000 people. There is also the 'Clean Up the World' campaign[4] started by 'a simple Australian bloke' and yachtsman, Ian Kiernan, who saw the pollution in Sydney Harbour and wanted to do something. Another is the 'We love Helsinki' programme that encourages people to dance together. In these ways cities can become engines for empathy, and urban leadership can lead the way by showing a sense of civic generosity in tone and action.

The emerging sharing economy of Airbnb, Uber and Freecycle is fundamentally reframing our sense of material ownership that might help counteract tribal tendencies and help us shift to being more engaged with others – from the sharing economy to the real sharing society. So the city could begin to address some of the biggest psychological questions facing humanity.

Cities are places where the stranger and difference meet the tribal instinct and the basic human desire to connect. Creating zones of encounter with opportunities to mix and communicate can reduce tensions, emphasising what we share as human beings more than what separates us, so building social capital.

Tensions between the wider social needs of the city as a whole and those of the tribal play themselves out, with its sharpest expressions being visible and invisible urban ghettoes, based on interests, tight relations, prejudices and culture. People look for and choose the like-minded for convenience, to avoid the complexity of mutual understanding or to feel safer, creating in-group thinking and excluding difference as a default position.

**Two forms of parallel lives, especially, threaten a city's cohesiveness: poverty and ethnicity**. We think of the city often as a place where we can go anywhere we like. Yet the reality is that poor people are often stuck in their neighbourhood, never go to the city centre and are mostly connected to people who are equally poor – reinforcing connections to the under-networked. The city centre can be intimidating and the consumerist dreams on offer can depress them. The posh brands are certainly out of bounds. The rich too often keep to themselves in their enclaves and these can increasingly be gated. There is little criss-crossing in the city. On rare occasions does the city come together.

# PARALLEL LIVES

Too often, intervention in those poorer places in difficulty treats them as sick. The tone is serious and it might need to be if crime and drugs are endemic. Yet does that work? Perhaps the playful approach incorporating fun, celebration and joy might deliver more traction. Here the British Arts Council's Creative People and Places initiative[5] has been effective in poorer locations like Stoke or St. Helens and the designation of Hull as Britain's City of Culture 2017' has boosted their sense of self and the story they tell themselves. It could be sport too that triggers transformation. Michael Brearley, the ex-captain of the English cricket team in 'what's the point of sport' discusses the power of teams with insight. In essence it goes to the heart of the civic, since it revolves around balancing egotism and collective endeavour, building a joint aim and finding a way to get there.[6]

A group mentality is great when something needs to get done without too many questions being asked, but less so when dealing with complexity and diversity, the day to day reality of urban life. This is one reason why rural dwellers tend to have far more conservative views of life than urbanites. They are simply not challenged by difference in the same way as their urban cousins.

The ethnic and social divides remain prevalent right across the world. If you are an Aborigine in Australia it is a difficult life; so is being a Uyghur in China, a Kurd in Turkey or a Palestinian in Israel, let alone one of the 200 million 'untouchables' – Dalits - in India. They are still caste out - mostly - even if the Indian constitution bans discrimination. Excluded usually from social and public spaces and prevented from drawing water from public facilities and segregated in schools there is little upward mobility. Consider too that it is 50 years since the Civil Rights movement in the USA. Yet the condition of the majority of poor, urban African Americans is bad and the chances for to get out of a vicious cycle is difficult, so drugs and crime are more likely to proliferate with more – especially young – people going to prison. The Black Lives Matter movement is a spark and the Dalits from India are trying to learn from them.

Once, the perceived wisdom was that migrants would arrive in a place and move along a continuum. This first involved being with their own people, then dispersing elsewhere by moving up and out and then assimilating into the majority culture. Here the arrival city acts as a portal. This is less true now. One group in particular, blacks, were not only staying put from one generation to the next and becoming more concentrated, stuck in stagnating ghettoes from which there seems to be no escape. This is happening to Hispanics as well especially in the USA. Alarmingly, spatial concentrations are closely aligned with indicators of poverty and deprivation[7]creating an underclass and negative neighbourhood effects that magnify problems, making it even harder for residents to leave. Housing policies and attitudes of financial institutions too can build an architecture of segregation. Concentrations of poverty generate a cycle of attitudes, behaviours and values that hinder people grasping opportunities.

**Empathy and tribal behaviour have a troubling side**. An American study[8] demonstrated that there has been a rise of special and minority interest groups since the 1970s. These have become more and more insular with members increasingly less-likely to meet people with different views. This is the echo chamber that can lead to a 'parallel society' – a phrase coined by Wilhelm Heitmeyer in 1994. It stands for an alleged failure of the integration of migrants and for the end of the idea of a multicultural society. This worry, even fear, has heightened in relation to Muslims, as some reject the culture of the majority society and its rules. In Britain this led to the 'parallel lives' concept first coined by Ted Cantle in 2004[9] and reinforced by the Casey Review surveys in Britain in 2016.[10] When people are surrounded only by those who agree with them, their views become more extreme, rigid and prejudiced. This dynamic is compounded by the limited number of close connections our brains are able to make, and once that limit is reached stereotyping, over-simplification and group-think come into play.

*Arabs and Jews, in Jerusalem*

Depending on definition, parallel societies or parallel lives exist in cities. In the strictest sense this is where people cut themselves off voluntarily, withdraw and seek alternatives for almost all the institutions of the majority society. Research in German cities, and especially the Ruhr area by Thomas Meyer[11] and later by Halm and Sauer[12], looking largely at the Turkish community, suggested that parallel societies exist, but not in the tightest definition. That latter definition would be where extreme patriarchal structures prevail overall, women have few rights and liberal-democratic structures are rejected and forced marriages the norm or where they have their own hospitals or schools and where people believe freedom of religion and the equal rights of other believers is problematic. This is reinforced if they only look at their own language media, only go to their shops, voluntary organizations, restaurants or cultural activities. Children growing up in those contexts can become open to the lure of extreme organizations.

The British Cantle report with its focus more on Pakistanis and Bangladeshi noted:

'Whilst the physical segregation of housing estates and inner-city areas came as no surprise, the team was struck by the depth of polarisation ... compounded by so many other aspects of our daily lives ... this means that many communities operate on the basis of a series of parallel lives.'

Another example is the insular Haredi community of ultra-orthodox Jews of Stamford Hill in London who do not connect in any meaningful way with non-Jews. They have persuaded the municipality to erect an *eruvim*, a symbolic enclosure marked by poles and wire across six and a half miles that converts public space into private space so allowing them to move around on Sabbath. The Haredi really do live in a parallel universe, as a community frozen in aspic[13], living life as it was lived in nineteenth century Eastern Europe. Here arranged marriages are the norm (are they forced, one asks), the commandment to 'be fruitful and multiply' is followed, so families with seven plus children are common. They have their own schools with barely any secular education and are unequipped to handle modern life. Mobile phones have texting often disabled and television is forbidden. I witnessed this too with a Jerusalem planner in its famous enclosed Mea Shearim district where ecstatic prayer rang throughout the evening. Nobody looked me in the eye. Their values depend on keeping the world at bay.

The Cantle Report notes that these issues of togetherness are exacerbated 'by **the lack of honest and robust debate as people tiptoe around the sensitive issue of race, religion and culture**.' Here political correctness can hinder debate. Thus it is defined as racist to specify that a surge of several instances of abuse and exploitation of young girls in Northern cities in the last decade was by British Pakistani men 'who have a problem with women', as is mentioning that the vast majority of sex abuse within families in Britain is by white men acting alone. No-one is saying all Pakistani men or all white men have problems with women.

**Cities clearly have parallel universes, some of these are permeable and others are not**. Some matter and some do not, as long as people try to understand the other. People separate or come together in work arrangements, around enthusiasms, ethnicity, backgrounds, class and more. All these patterns criss-cross the city. When you map the movement flows, clusters and nodes in a city you detect the type and degree of connections. Overlay on that wealth or health, and further differentiations occur. Take enthusiasms from football, dancing, to cooking or walking clubs or art buffs. How they navigate the city and who they meet is defined by that. Take volunteering from political activities to meals on wheels for the elderly to helping disengaged young people and this determines your city geography. Take work, where the garbage collectors view differs from that of the insurance broker working in the city core. Take young parents, their geography is defined by school and leisure options. The way this comes together is well described by Mitchel Resnick:

'A flock of birds sweeps across the sky. Like a well-choreographed dance troupe, the birds veer to the left in unison, suddenly they all dart to the right ... Each movement seems perfectly co-ordinated ... the flock is graceful ... and it is organized without an organizer, coordinated without a coordinator. Bird flocks are not the only things that work that way. Ant colonies, highway traffic, market economies, immune systems – in all of these systems, patterns are determined ... by local interactions among decentralised components.'[14]

This is equally true for cities, but often there is less grace than one would wish.

These social and spatial dynamics have a strong flip side in cities. There are masses of people from diverse backgrounds who integrate well and who enjoy the delights of difference, freeing up their exploratory instinct. Let us focus on Muslims as they are a big debating topic. The major multinational Bertelsmann Stiftung European *Religion Monitor* 2017 study on the integration of Muslim immigrants reveals that Western Europe is making clear progress[15] . By the second generation at the latest, the majority have integrated given their language competence, education, working life and interreligious contacts. It concludes that this

success is 'notable as none of the participating countries, France, Britain, Austria, Germany and Switzerland offer consistently good opportunities for participation, and Muslims encounter open rejection from about one fifth of the population'. Muslims seize opportunities that come, and they want to continue practicing their religion even though it is not readily accepted by mainstream society. It in itself does not hinder integration, and 'they strive for higher education levels just as much as other immigrants.' The *Religion Monitor* 2017 identified three strategies for advancing integration and cohesion: first, improve opportunities for participation, especially in the employment and educational systems; second, accord Islam the same legal status as other institutional religious groups, thereby recognizing religious diversity; and third, promote intercultural and interreligious contacts and discussion.

Just as I am writing this I read about 'My Muslim family and our foster kids'[16]. Esmat Jeraj's family has, over a period of 25 years, taken in 60 foster children. Some have been Muslim, but also many Christians, Hindus and Sikhs.

I have never found ethnicity, race or religion an issue ... if a child wants a bacon sandwich, we say you can't have it in this house but we can take you to a restaurant where you can have one ... we made space for a Hindu child to keep their idols or goddess in their bedroom ... and we always celebrate Christmas and Easter with Christians.

The Intercultural Cities network[17] that Phil Wood and I helped instigate has numerous examples. This all is encapsulated in a feeling of does this place say 'yes' or 'no'. The 'yes' city will have an enabling spirit of generosity, openness and a welcoming attitude.

*Guest workers, Doha*

*Exhibition at the National Gallery, Canberra*

# THE CIVIL & THE CIVIC

Significant concepts mostly have complex and manifold meanings - their importance causes arguments. Take the word 'value'. Do we mean values or value, that is ethics and morals or money value or worth? Take 'worth'. Is that distinction and dignity or price and assets? Take civil and civic. In everyday language the distinction is dissolving and **to be civic means to be engaged with your city** and these engagements happen across a spectrum of activities informal and formal.

The cluster of words civil, civic, citizen or civilization come from the same root. The linguistic origins are strikingly relevant today. In the Proto-Indo-European language spoken by people who lived across vast swathes of Asia and Europe from roughly 4500 to 2500 B.C a core word root is '*key'. This spread across cultures. It means: 'to lie down', 'to settle', 'to be rooted', 'a bed', but also has links to 'love' and to be 'beloved'. The idea of being the incumbent or a member of the same home or place and under the same roof is also implied. In proto-Italian it transforms into '*keiwis' where the word 'civis' – citizen - comes from and the derivations that follow. Jumping across time we detect a link between 'beloved' and civic pride.

*Civitas* is the social body of citizens, who in Roman times were bound together or united by law by a contract giving them both responsibilities and rights of citizenship. Then it was restricted to the few, of course. This agreement creates the *res publica*, literally speaking 'public matters' in which they take part. The civic is to do with a place and the nomadic with no-place or temporary place. Can they mesh well?

The words 'civil' and 'civic' can cause confusion. It is useful to unpack the terms, whose meanings are merging given the way the new media allows you to be involved in both simultaneously. Let us explore their origins for clarification and to discover its range and importance. Later we largely use 'civic' as the overarching term.

'Civil' is partly behaviour in personal interactions, such as being respectful and genial so being able to have a conversation without starting an argument in a civil manner. This capacity for debate is a strong element of the civic city, whose agreed rules of debate have broken down in public debate in many countries. Opposing views are so strong there is little common ground and vitriol, shaming or offending is no longer off-limits. Debates have coarsened.

'Civil' can describe how individuals in a community or society relate to each other as distinct from with official bodies or government. 'Civil rights' are the rights we have as a person. This freedom allows us as to do most things we wish, subject to agreed codes of behaviour that embed into the local culture. It allows us too to engage in political activity of our choosing or to demonstrate without any institutional, legal or social constraints or to set up a campaigning voluntary organization. So civil disobedience is legal and 'civil law' concerns relations between individuals and not between individuals and the state. The term 'civil society' emphasises too that there are alternatives to government or commercial services. These include voluntary organisations, co-operative or mutual societies or faith entities, as well as informal support groups such as neighbours and family.

Together these differing elements make up civil society. It is not under the direction of any authority wielding the power of the state. There are threats to these freedoms in 109 countries as of 2015, up from 96 the year before.[18]

'Civic rights', by contrast are those we have in relation to our community or city structures or our political system, such as in a democracy where we can vote or campaign for change. The broadest rights - 'human rights' are those fundamental rights or freedoms everyone on the planet should have such as free speech or the right to free assembly.

**The 'civic' in the most literal sense means relating to a city or its governance** or the opportunities or possible duties involved in running a city. So the 'civic centre' is the buildings where the local authority is housed and at times extends to cultural facilities like libraries, a park or shopping centre. The civic role of a library is that it can help prepare people to be more competent citizens, more willing to involve themselves. With civic engagement citizens might participate in some form of mechanism that makes the city work such as an ad-hoc campaign, a collective endeavour to clean a street, a lobby or more formally being on a local health, schools or community council. More

*Rome*

broadly it can refer to the responsibilities of citizens in relation to the whole of society, such as obeying the law or having 'civic duties' demanded by the state, such as in Australia the duty – not just the choice – to vote.

The grey area between the civil and civic lies at the heart of negotiating what our cities are to become. **A good city needs both a strong civil and civic city**. This deals with an interesting dilemma. At times behaviours are implicitly agreed as civil, but some people overstep the mark, such as being as being too noisy or littering the streets, so they need to be enforced, a civic action.

The creative tensions between the civic realm of the state and the civil realm of the citizen are important. **The great civic city allows space for the civil**. Places need a civic narrative to bind their people to where they live. Its role is to make the case that this specific place is worthy of allegiance. Many actors make this possible and a shift is occurring as civil society activists and business groupings seek a greater say in how the city works.

silence
démocratie
morale
écritures
à
jeu
femmes
vérité
americain
mal
acteurs
mensonges
sexe
cinéma
de
ceremonie
regards
sons
comédie
revolte
innocent
fraternité

We cannot talk of the civic in today's sense nor discuss a nomadic world until individuals move from being subjects to citizens. There are four long historic waves of individual expression, expansion of rights and empowerment and in parallel often virulent counter-reactions to these. Currently we are witnessing a 'cultural war' between 'progressives' and 'traditionalists' exemplified most starkly by the USA Trump agenda and that of Putin's Russia, both of whom are imprisoned by a 'circle of certainty' – they think they are always right. Once they are gone there will be others with exactly the same patterns of thought and equally worrying views.

# TRAJECTORIES OF EMPOWERMENT

In the *Shipwrecked Mind*, Mark Lilla sharply encapsulates the problem:

The reactionary is anything but a conservative. He is as radical and modern a figure as the revolutionary, someone shipwrecked in the rapidly changing present, and suffering from nostalgia for an idealized past and an apocalyptic fear that history is rushing toward catastrophe.

**This is the culture war we face - a battle of ideas** and what views of life and the city have cultural hegemony.

Jacques Barzun in *From Dawn to Decadence: 1500 to the Present- 500 Years of Western Cultural Life* describes the first three big long term movements as a trajectory that mirrors the process of empowering individuals. Each of these movements changes the way civic life expresses itself and how the city looks and feels, its built structures and its daily life. The first, from 1500 to 1660, was when Protestants challenged Catholicism, asserting that people could have direct access to God. They could then redefine themselves and their relations to the higher being. The second, from 1660 to 1789, was the slow pursuit of political freedom and individual rights that culminated in the French Revolution, whose slogan 'liberty, equality, fraternity' exemplifies the shift from subject to citizen. The third was between 1790 to 1920 and the big marker was Marx, who sought to turn political equality into economic and social equality. This movement exploded with the Russian Revolution and had other manifestations throughout the twentieth century.

A fourth can be added, and which has a dramatic impact on urban life and how that unfolds and how cities feel. It is the 'cultural revolution' that started in the early 1960s encapsulated by the slogan 'the personal is political' with its focus on gender, sexualities and identity. It continues until today culminating in the agendas of inclusion and cultural diversity. These sought to widen recognition, for women, with the reordering of relationships between the sexes, and for gays, transgender people and others, ultimately through constitutional rights, as well as encouraging acceptance of our diversities of colour and ethnicity.

Coinciding with this revolution are the well-known economic, political and social changes. Thus we see ascendance of the marketplace as an arbiter of value and taste from the 1980s onwards; the rise of a knowledge-driven economy; a decreased role for the state and the emergence of political formations beyond the left/right continuum; the demand by many publics to participate in defining the values and purposes of society – the social inclusion agenda; challenges to the unified canon of knowledge in many fields from science to the arts and a blurring of intellectual boundaries; the growth of multicultural national communities; a general sense of fracturing in the unity of a body politic.

The constant attempt is to widen the franchise, yet these historic processes did not happen seamlessly. It judders along, it has set backs, defeats and forward shifts. The French Revolution, for example, affirms equality regardless of class and education, but represented a threat to established interests. The Congress of Vienna in 1815 then restores the monarchies and oligarchic orders curtailing the revolution's great hopes. Yet the emancipatory drive continues, such as with the revolutionary attempt to create the Paris Commune, that was crushed in 1871. The building of the Sacré-Cœur basilica in Montmartre is a symbolic monument created as a national penance for the 'divine punishment' of the defeat in the 1870 Franco-Prussian War and the socialist Paris Commune after 'a century of moral decline' since the French Revolution , according to Bishop Fournier. This is a reassertion of a Catholic order over a secular one. That battle is mirrored in reverse by Bismarck's *Kulturkampf* in Germany between 1871 and 1879 which sought to contain the powers of the church and affirm the separation of powers between church and state.

The reform dynamic and gradual transitions continue over the nineteenth century, such as the rise of worker's movement, a widening of the franchise, more schooling, the improvement of the health conditions from which the working class benefits. With votes for women in place after World War One it is only possible to consider the civic life in its full reign at the beginning of the inter-war period after which fascism creates a backward step. An important jump is then made after 1945, for instance, with T.H. Marshall introducing the notion of the 'competent citizen', who needs education to be able to participate fully in society.

**This overall trajectory has increasingly enabled the free movement of people across the globe** and allowed them to slot into the lives of other cultures on a large scale.

Many in the West have despised this fourth wave of egalitarianism which they say liberal elites have imposed on societies, such as feminism, the gay-rights movement, identity politics, the influx of immigrants, or the questioning of the existing cultural order. Indeed any progressive direction of life. These views are mirrored by fundamentalist Islamists who decry the West's decadence and whose current most extreme form is ISIS or Al-Qaeda. Add to this the complexities of the imperialist legacy in the Middle East who feel deep long term humiliation and the mix of feelings becomes unpredictable.

They would say too that the inclusive way of representing differing identities as LGBT+ which means LGBTQQIAAP is political correctness out of control. Here it means lesbian, gay, bi-sexual, transgender, queer – in the sense of beyond binary, questioning, intersex, asexual, allies, pansexual.

Many have felt stigmatized – and often these are white men – in being seen as bigoted and intolerant if they questioned this tendency to over-define or to act against the erosion of traditional values.

The fear of collapse of 'civilization as we know it' erodes faith in democracy and a parallel yearning for someone of strength and bluntness to tell the truth who can save us. We expose ourselves then to the perils of a Faustian bargain with the world - a willingness to give up the values of civic life.

## THE ANXIOUS ZEITGEIST

We live in awkward times. The world is turning to its darker face. The Zeitgeist is one of rising anxiety. The grey zone disappears. The world best lived, for me, is by reasoning and conversation. This provides a frame within which difference can be lived and shared with mutual respect. That view has been drained of confidence. It feels exhausted and consequently it is mistakenly accused of being 'wishy-washy' with no apparent point of view.

**The confidence in the civic needs to be restored**. Civic values and rules of engagement are crucial and they include: providing settings for a continually renewed dialogue across differences, cultures and conflicts; allowing strongly held beliefs or faiths expression within this core agreement; and acknowledging the 'naturalness' of conflict and establishing means and mediation devices to deal with difference. The civic accepts different ways of living, it recognises arenas in which we must all live together and those where we can live apart. It generates structured opportunities to explore and discover similarity and difference and to learn to know 'The Other', and in cities we are always dealing with the other. It wishes to drive down decision-making on the subsidiarity principle, which implies much greater decentralisation and devolution of power. Central government takes on a more subsidiary role. This enhances participation and connectivity at local level. It helps generate interest, concern and responsibility.

**It is in the civic where the give and take of urban life unfolds**, where strangers might meet and where the rules of civic engagement are constantly negotiated. This is the culture of democracy. Remember democracy is a mental space, an intellectual space, an atmosphere and it can be a physical space especially when its physical nature resonates so it encourages cross-cutting conversations. Here the mutual sympathy of sentiments can meet and convergences can be built out of the fragments. Here we deal with the continuous tension between wanting to be autonomous and commitment to a bigger whole.

Constructing civic life within a nomadic context, which values openness and cuts across boundaries has encountered a new difficulty - unfortunately.

## THE SPECTRE OF DECLINE

The spectre of decline and moral degradation has re-emerged. It has haunted the West ever since its rise. Its recent incarnations include several right-wing organizations and politicians, some of whom have gained power. Franklin Foer in Atlantic monthly[19] writes:

Dangerous strains of apocalyptic thinking from the last century are re-emerging – the fear of cultural degeneration, the anxiety that civilization has grown unmanly, the sense that liberal democracy has failed to safeguard civilization from its enemies.

Or Steve Bannon, Trump's former strategy advisor:

'We're at the very beginning stages of a very brutal and bloody conflict ... we must fight for our beliefs against this new barbarity that's starting, that will completely eradicate everything that we've been bequeathed over the last 2,000, 2,500 years.'[20]

This dangerous approach saps and sucks the life out of civil society as any threat of imminent barbarism is always taken to justify name-calling, prejudice and extreme solutions. The danger signals are out as constant phrases like 'real Americans', 'real Russians', 'real French' or 'real Brits' testify. Or as the Breitbart website notes: 'It's war. It's war. Every day, we put up: America's at war, America's at war. We're at war.'[21] The writings seem to want to turn the culture war into a real one as the fears rise that America is at risk and its power is slipping away. 'We want a civil war for a new world order to rise, there must be a massive reckoning,' says Bannon.

Russia's Putin is an ally in fighting this cultural war and it explains the complex relationship the West had with him. Foer says that Putin is:

'... against the culturally decadent and spiritually desiccated Euro-Atlantic... against the fetishization of tolerance and diversity ... with the West becoming infertile and genderless that rejects its roots, including the Christian values - the basis of Western civilization. ... They are denying moral principles and all traditional identities: national, cultural, religious, and even sexual. ... They are implementing policies that equate large families with same-sex partnerships, belief in God with the belief in Satan. We are moving into: 'chaotic darkness' and a 'return to a primitive state.'

In these processes, the globalists (as distinct from patriots), the left, Islamists, liberal elites are all lumped into one threat as if they were an integrated entity with control over our cultural story that is a 'coordinated synchronized interactive narrative'.

**The disappointments about democracy are expressed in differing forms** including curtailments witnessed in Turkey, Hungary, Poland, Russia or the British Brexit vote and the Trump election, as well as tech-savvy new political formations such Podemos in Spain, the Five Star Movement in Italy and parties like Marie Le Pen's National Front in France and Geert Wilders Party for Freedom in the Netherlands. They reflect the exhausted dissatisfaction and fatigue about how things are. At times, you are not sure whether you are dealing with religious zealots or unprincipled nihilists.

This either/or world, where you are with us or against us is triggering riots. Disaffection in now so strong that riots are increasing across the continents, whether as a response to poverty, racism, crime or unfair police treatment. Consider 2017 and Hamburg's three days of rioting at the G20 summit against globalization. Consider the disturbances in East London over the death of young father Edir Frederico Da Costa in police custody. The French Bastille Day protests to coincide with Trump's Paris visit. Then the Charlottesville events where a Unite the Right rally was held and dominated by far-right figures and white supremacists. It left several dead and scores injured. Several anti-fascist protests then followed throughout the USA. Similarly, in Melbourne, the Australian Pride March led to violent protests, there were riots in Cape Town against lack of policing, in Nairobi because of election rigging, and in Xinjiang as Muslims were being forbidden to celebrate Ramadan.

Increasingly social, personal and political divisions are being laid bare on the streets and this is likely to be just the beginning as people with dramatically opposed views live in the same city, the same neighbourhood, the same street, the same building.

The civic city in a nomadic world has a lofty aim despite the powerful forces ranged against its principles of living together. It seeks to engender a discussion on how a different urban civilization can be constructed – a concept that includes the whole civil, civic, citizen repertoire, but also the dynamics of nomadism. Is it really new? Is it merely the same as before but with turbo-charged migration and movement patterns? Or do the agitated flows and shifting mobilities create a new scenario. My belief is that it does for two main reasons.

First, the digitizing world and the 'here and there' phenomenon create a novel relationship to place, space and time and a blending of the real and virtual as well as massive uses of artificial intelligence and self-regulating sensing systems and devices.

# THE CITY AS A CIVILIZATION

Second, there is porousness and shifting identity. People need to be porous to new influences as well as to retain their existing selves. We need both to be local and global to survive in the current world. We need boundaries and borders to ground and anchor identity as well as bridges to connect us to the outside. Identity is shaped by a variety of factors from upbringing to friendship networks to work, yet it is crucially also rooted in geography and place.

**Despite increased mobility, a sense of place remains a core value** and often acts as the pivot point from within which a person acts. There is a need to be somewhat closed, contained and located to control the gathering of influences, to reflect upon them and to energize oneself, as well as to remain open to connecting with possibilities, to generate work, to allow others to influence us and to operate effectively. These are potentially contradictory forces.

At an urban level porousness means allowing global chains or architectural styles that, although they may bring us up to date, may swamp and destroy the local vernacular or local shops. In popular places, gentrification pressures can eviscerate the local. The iconic Bizim Kiez campaign launched in Berlin after the threat to close a Turkish convenience store exemplifies the tensions.[22] One resident noted:

'I live in the middle of a bubbling pool of gentrification. Some of its effects are worrying; some, I'll admit, are welcome. But this latest move feels personal. Filou, the little bakery opposite our apartment, is being forced to close. According to the building's owners, the bakery no longer fits in with 'the concept of the neighbourhood.' Apparently, the London-based owners know more than I do about the 'concept' of my neighbourhood, where I've lived for eight years. ... If this little corner of the world is not for people who like good-quality, fresh bread seven days a week, then who the hell is it for? And who decides?'

Ironically, this supposed more choice that we have can limit possibilities if **these choices are just variations of the same thing**. We may have to be conservative, to hold back and reject and be seemingly uncreative to set the pre-conditions for maintaining a strong identity.

Tensions do, of course, arise from the complexities of trying to absorb and contain the global capital movements, the widening notions of identity and demands of identity politics plus the desire of many to create more participative politics.

## FAULTLINES & BATTLEGROUNDS

In the dynamics of this overall scenario we find faultlines, battlegrounds, paradoxes, deeper drivers of change and strategic dilemmas. Faultlines are change processes that are so deep-seated, intractable and contentious that they shape our entire worldview. They determine our landscape of thinking and decisions across multiple dimensions and can be global in scope, affecting our broadest purposes and ends. They may create insoluble problems and permanent ideological battlefields. Even if they eventually solve themselves, such problems are likely to take a very long time to resolve: 50 years, 100 years, or even more. It is then more a question of mediating and managing conflict. Currently the three most important are the battles between democratic optimism and hope often linked to secular worldviews versus *doom* and *pessimism*; between an *ethics economics* and a crude *economic rationality* as well as between creativity and risk.

## HUMANITY & HOPE

Polarization is growing rampantly. Yet hope reflects a positive view of human potential where attributes like compassion could come to the fore and where kindness is seen as a constitutional part of being. Here secular humanists align with some of best spiritual, often religious people, such as Sufi Muslims. They are heterophilic the somewhat obtuse Greek word that means 'being a friend of those who are other'. This view believes that gestures of generosity trigger a willingness to give back and to be publicly-minded. Therefore investment in the public realm and public space is crucial as an emblem and physical manifestation of intent, and this is mostly undertaken by public authorities. Sadly some fear the softness of compassion.

Hope feels there is a way of addressing grievance and humiliation without resorting to the extremes of allowing people to inflict their prejudices onto the world. It recognizes the schisms and fractures between the educated and less educated and incentivizes changes from below. It acknowledges the forgotten people of all shades and colour. It resists what some call 'stupid old men inflicting on younger people their views of life, when they do not want live this way' - the old in Britain voted to leave the European Union, the young largely wanted to stay. Optimism arising from faith in humans differs from that of optimism driven by nostalgia and a return to a glorious, purified past.

## ETHICAL ECONOMICS

The aura of inevitability that neo-liberalism is the only way has been shattered.[23][24] The trickle-down effect is more an ideal than a reality. It is no longer producing enough winners to be the dominant political idea. This is the ideology that a deregulated globally-oriented market is more competitive, where utilities are sold and public services outsourced. This spread as a set of principles across the globe. Its arguments lie at the core of the ascendancy of the free market and it is associated with Margaret Thatcher and Ronald Reagan in the latter 1970s. It was a theory that allowed Thatcher to say 'there is no such thing as society' and that shattered the confidence of those working in public service. It shifts our view of citizens to consumers and clients. There was an initial blossoming as economies started growing and more people became middle class especially in

*The great Wall of Xian*

China and India. Partly the growth was driven by new technology, there was wider property ownership, which many enjoyed, cheaper money and cheaper goods. Yet the reality was that it was largely fuelled by debt.

Neo-liberalism and its approach to city making has had huge holes blown into it, suffering its first major collapse in the 2007/8 financial crisis and then going into political crisis in 2016/17.

**Over the last three decades, critiques and alternatives have been conceived and promoted**, but capitalism is agile. It has powerful supporters especially in the mainstream media, so it has weaved its way into the mental mindscape and has conquered the realms of the thinkable. Yet now suddenly it is possible to use the word capitalism for what it is without being seen as a hardened socialist. Namely, as a system, an ideology, a project - instead as if it were the intrinsic nature of life. Its ideas have provided the warp on which the patterns of our thinking and behaviour are woven. It affects the language we use and the discourse of public affairs. It entraps us and sediments itself.

When a culture invests its faith only in the market principle and trusts the drive of capital to produce sensible choices, the logic, interests and points of view of those who control markets will count for more than those who believe market-based decision-making is an impoverished theory of choice-making.[25] Conversely, if it is held that there is something in the idea of a public, common or collective good that has value and is beyond the vagaries of the market, we can do different things, and these are often more inspirational.

Even conservatives are seeing the problem and responding to the disenchantment they see. Take the British Conservative Party manifesto of 2017: 'We reject the cult of the selfish individualism', 'we do not believe in untrammelled markets', 'the benefits of markets have not spread equally and across the generations', 'the City of London is wrongly incentivized'. Rising depression, especially in cities, is causing a rethink. It reflects the shadow side of entrepreneurial culture when 'magical voluntarism' (you can do it all on your own) confronts limited opportunities, as Mark Fisher notes.[26]

Is this revolt, witnessed across the globe, another episode or a breakthrough? Can it trigger systemic change and foster an alternative regulations and incentives regime, able to counteract inequality or embed a new ethics into the economy?

The third faultline is also a paradox. A *paradox* is an incongruity that seems to be contradictory. The major one is between *risk* and *creativity*. The evaluation of everything from a perspective of risk is a defining characteristic of the contemporary age. Risk is the managerial paradigm and default mechanism that has embedded itself into how companies, community organisations and the public sector operate. Risk is a prism through which any activity is judged. It subtly encourages us to constrain aspirations. Creativity is the currency also of our age that generates the ideas and possible solutions that become products and services. It reflects the lifestyle of the varieties of nomads. The series of major CEO surveys[27] including those in the private and public sectors by IBM have again and again reinforced the need for creativity as the primary priority.

The risk and creativity issue is part of a wider agenda concerning openness or being more closed. Is the default position of our culture more one of: 'Yes if' or more one of 'No, because'? In the first you are open to possibilities and suggestions without looking immediately at the obstacles.

## BATTLE GROUNDS

Discussions and policy debates around faultlines often become *battlegrounds* because the nature of debate is intense and contested. Four of the most important are, first, how to deal with the diversity of populations in cities who may have diametrically opposed views as to how life should be lived and the issue of porous identity. Second, whether we can move to the fourth lean, clean, green economy when so many interests are locked into the old system. Whether the regulatory and incentives regime can be constructed to encourage environmentally sustainable lifestyle, including recycling, renewable energy resources, energy efficiency and behaviour change Third, whether the social equity agenda and widening gap between rich and poor, that global capital largely exacerbated, can be forcefully addressed. Finally, in terms of urban development, how the more popular cities across the world, such as Lisbon, Vancouver or Buenos Aires, can avert the gentrification pressures. These raise prices, push out older populations due to rising rents, lead to the closure of local shops as multinational chains move in who can afford higher rents. Yet at the same time some gentrification is positive. It can create the economic conditions to renew an area, it can raise standards and increase facilities.

Other profound trends have been with us for a long time. Will they continue. This brings us back to the nexus of emancipation built around individuality, choice, and independence that has been growing since the Enlightenment. Some feel this particular driver of change is at the edge of exhaustion. Perhaps the long expansion of the individualism has reach its limit.

*Theatre piece called Disorder promoted at
the Humboldt University, Berlin*

These new patterns of change and risk, mostly global in scope, are combining to form a crisis that cannot be dealt with by business as usual approach. **Averting the worst will require cities to play a more prominent role in national life**, both practically and politically. They can act more nimbly than national governments to deliver the innovative and integrated responses required. These solutions are complex and the wandering skilled, flexible nomads of the world will be needed. Will we let them in?

Is this civic, nomadic city a new urban civilization, or simply more of the same on booster pills? Civilization is a high-level ordering device and the complex culture of a society or a place. It is a person's widest cultural identity and it shapes their psychic structures. It embodies a specific set of ideas, ethics, beliefs and ways of being as well as economic structures, a built fabric, cultural activities, and ways of running itself.

There needs to be a dramatic shift in focus. In the late 1990s, I proposed that the idea of 'civic creativity' should be a central theme to guide city progress.[28] Creativity should not be seen as restricted to the fields of science or the creative economy sector – such as web design or the arts, important as these are.

To quote:

'Civic creativity' is defined as imaginative problem-solving applied to public good objectives. The aim is to generate a continual flow of innovative solutions to problems which have an impact on the public realm. 'Civic creativity' is the capacity for public officials, businesses, large and small, or civil society organizations together to effectively and instrumentally apply their imaginative faculties... this agenda seeks to be a means and guiding principle to make this happen.'

# CIVIC CREATIVITY: THE NEXT STEP

The notions of the 'civic', the 'public interest' or 'public good' have come in for a battering over the last decades. A string of negatives is associated with them: worthy, holding things up, red tape, politically correct, inefficient, social welfare-ist spring off the tongue. 'Private' by contrast is seen as alert, quick-footed, responsive, well managed, as distinct from self-interested or unconcerned. 'Civic creativity' aims to bring out the best of public service, private initiative and civic activism as each, depending on context, has something to offer. It seeks to unlock the gatekeepers who block opportunity. This can only happen within larger agreed aims of what the city wishes to achieve.

Reading through vision statements, strategies and plans for cities, similar ideas appear again and again, such as being sustainable, well-educated and competitive. But how, and do the old models work? Twenty years on the need for social, civic and publicly focused creativity is more urgent than ever. The context has changed, the names we use will differ, yet the issues remain largely the same, such as how urban life can become more fulfilling at a personal and collective level. This links strongly to questions of fairness, opportunity, the ability to participate and civic generosity.

The urgent issues of urban life also play themselves out in the public realm: how to behave in a civilised, tolerant way towards each other so we feel safe; or how the built environment inspires or deflates. One can visibly see whether a city is unfair and uncaring. Many solutions need inventing from new forms of incentives to make public transport more sustainable to dealing with gentrification pressures and more. Here the social innovation movement comes to the fore, which Geoff Mulgan crisply describes as: 'innovations that are social in their ends and their means' or 'new ideas, products, services or models that simultaneously meet social needs and create new social relationships and collaborations ... They are innovations that are both good for society and enhance society's capacity to act." (*Open Book of Social Innovation*). Medellin, Columbia once one of the world's murder capitals has transformed through inventive solutions that changed social life, such as a linked series of escalators that take you up to the formerly inaccessible favela of 12,000 people at

*Comuna 13*. Or its well-designed libraries like *Parque Biblioteca España* that are inspiring people to learn.

This is the ambit of 'civic creativity.' It negotiates between and seeks to balance the diversity of conflicting interests that all urban development involves even though public authorities may fear it as it implies losing control. Thus, it is always involved in some form of politics. Being creative in a civic sense needs to be legitimised as a valid, praiseworthy activity. Its unique qualities centre on a passion and vision for how the city works as a whole, not only isolated projects – although these may encapsulate a broader problem, such as a local initiative to provide play areas for kids is signally to the whole city whether it cares for the young. Unleashing this collective energy can motivate and empower people and civil entities to resources, often public and private, to deliver better social outcomes, higher social value, and social capital'.[29] Yet good intentions are often thwarted by the risk-averse, inward-looking cultures.

The 'civic creativity' concept may seem incongruous, but that gives it its power: holding at a tension point two qualities we rarely associated with each other, with 'civic' seen as worthy and 'creativity' as exciting and enterprising. It should be the ethos for urban leadership.

*Escalators in Comuna 13, Medellin*

*Genova old town*

# PSYCHOLOGY & THE CITY

In the blink of an eye in evolutionary terms cities have risen meteorically to dominate our lives as have our more nomadic lifestyles. This relentless transformation of large-scale urbanisation and movement put increasing demands on our senses, attention, time, our capacity to cope with the strange or different and our mental state. Highly adaptable as we are, it stretches this ability to the limit. Adjusting to the nomadic world exacerbates this major psychological challenge, which my colleague Chris Murray and I explored.[30]

**In a constant cycle of influencing and being influenced, the city impacts upon our mind** and our emotional state impacts upon the city with untold effects. It is astonishing that psychology, the study exploring the dynamics of feeling and emotion, has not been taken sufficiently seriously as an urban discipline, not only by psychology itself but also urban decision makers, since it seeks to understand why we act the way we do. Acknowledging the 'psyche of a city' could radically shift our understanding of a place and its potential future. The current situation demands that we use its insights.

The city is not a lifeless thing with inanimate clumps of buildings and technology or like a machine. This view misses its essential human nature and our responses to it.

People have personality, identity and, as they are congregations of people, so do cities. To see the urban fabric, its dynamics and city life as empty shells devoid of human psychological content is careless. To be blind to its consequences is foolish, as the city is primarily an emotional experience with psychological effects. Cities are the most complex human invention and without cities much of the world we know could not exist. Even a cursory review shows that here is a virtually untapped, rich seam of ideas and practices in psychology that could, with relatively little effort, help cities cope with their fractures and with transformation by providing new perspectives and workable solutions.

# CITIES & THE ARCHAIC MIND

A big question emerges. Modern humans have been around for 200,000 years leading mostly a nomadic existence to survive, but settled places for only 6,000 to 8,000 years at most. It is not the place where we, or our psychological apparatus, evolved, since of the estimated 107 billion[31] of us that have ever existed, merely a fraction has lived in a city. We are an urban species living within an archaic mind.

Just as the body is the museum of human evolution so the **psyche is the mental museum of our primeval past**. We carry unwittingly anciently formed psychological elements of this into our new nomadic, urban age, the most well-known of which is the fight or flight response. Others include being wary of the unknown, protecting our territory and forming tribal groups. Adapting towards becoming *homo urbanis* has psychological consequences and as we shift, the cities that do best may well be those able to help the ancient and modern parts of ourselves to come together.

*The Dunbar Number* research invented by Robin Dunbar suggests we are hard-wired to relate closely to around 150 people – about the size of hunter-gatherer tribes and the average village population in Europe until the eighteenth Century. So, we may be living with **the mind of a village in the body of a city** and this reinforces the importance of neighbourhoods that help us relate, and build trust and community. Not surprisingly we struggle when large movements of people move in and out of cities. Seeing the city with a psychological lens can help create initiatives to deal with and heal fractures, divides or feeling overwhelmed by diversity.

**The dramatic change we are witnessing requires readjustments**. Especially mentally when **the sense of belonging linked to place disperses** across networks and geographical boundaries in more fluid, fast flowing settings. This flickering world creates an impatient mind as the screens of virtual worlds suck you in and blend with tangible, touchable realities. You are here and there simultaneously. Disruptive technologies such as artificial intelligence or sensing systems makes the city feel as if it is on a rollercoaster, as are you. It is a strange sensation, and add to this that cities are places where most of us are strangers – it can be eerie stretching coping mechanisms to the limit. How to establish civic life is then a psychological issue. That life is more than the digital platforms that connect us all across spaces and place or enable us to be in constant touch or help navigate the urban by-ways and hotspots and link us with the like-minded.

Being in the ever-moving city creates a two-way psychological process with perpetual transactions changing moment to moment as our daily lived experience unfolds, with repercussions both for us and for the places we are in, and in ways we cannot always be aware of. This civic life will be different to what went before. In cities, we are a mix of people with intensely personal histories, differing cultures and perspectives, views of life and interests who have come together to share, whether we like it or not, a collective space. Cities are the spatial-level par excellence for uniting diverse identities into a common whole, places where face-to-face interaction still really matters as a means of binding and bonding people, building a sense of shared community, citizenship, and stewardship of place.

Revealing and **working with the composite character or psychology of a city can be a powerful tool** in understanding what pushes a place forwards or holds it back. What curtails or contributes to its civic life, what creates the spirit of a place and how that embeds itself into attitudes, day to day life? We interact with cities in our work, our housing or transport and have a constant lived emotional experience in them. This impacts directly on how we develop and feel. Mental health in cities is generally worse than in rural areas, and it worsens the bigger a city gets and when more things are changing and changing fast. This increases anxiety levels and closes people in. This does not make cities bad as it is largely connected to concentrations of urban poverty.

A sense of entitled individualism has grown with consumer culture, fostered by our market driven economic system, and can be a barrier to successful city living, focusing on the singular 'I' and 'me' not the collective 'us' and 'we' that is a defining feature of what makes us human. Ultimately, the most successful cities will be those that can build psychological resilience, to adapt, to deal with adversity, diversity and complexity, to bounce back and continue to function competently, and to provide the conditions where inhabitants can achieve their larger aims.

Two influential concepts separate from psychology, are 'place identity' and 'place attachment'. Place identity explores how where we live and grow up influences our sense of self. It is instrumental in fostering belonging, purpose and meaning in one's life (or lack of it). Place here refers also to community, and the shared sense of a city's wider identity, as well as individual neighbourhoods. The extent to which a place meets people's psychological, social and cultural needs can have long term emotional impacts for individuals. Place attachment looks more specifically at emotional attachments to a place, and suggests that both the amount and quality of time spent in a place are key determinants in that relationship. Attachment can fracture when the new norm is nomadic.

*Filthy Luker, Taipei*

SCHOOLS OF PSYCHOLOGY & POTENTIAL

The many branches of psychology provide perspectives or insight and some psychological knowledge has been absorbed in urban disciplines such as urban design. Very briefly here is a summary. Psychodynamic theory reviews how emotions, thoughts, early-life experiences and beliefs shape a person's present-day life and their coping mechanisms,[32] such as how to cope with a fast-moving world. Behavioural psychology is extensively used in commercial marketing, and seeks to influence actions, feeling and thoughts. It is now commonly applied, such as to speed up tax payments by telling people that most others pay their tax on time. Cognitive psychology helps people identify problems and cope. It has been successfully applied to visual design, using the 'laws' of similarity, symmetry, proximity, continuation[33] which have influenced urban design and architecture so they understand what psychologically works for people.

# PLACE PURPOSE & WELL BEING

Humanistic psychology focuses on characteristics shared by all human beings such as love, grief, caring, self-worth and the fulfilment of human potential. Maslow's 'hierarchy of needs' developed some of the central humanistic ideas about self-actualisation - an innate drive to reach human potential. Self-esteem is key and is engendered by feeling safe, it helps people find meaning, belonging and a sense of well-being. Constant movement and change in cities disturbs this process. Positive psychologists[34] [35] focus on potential rather than the shortcomings of individuals, stressing what makes life worth living, such as joy, well-being, satisfaction, contentment, optimism, flow and feeling good. It has influenced the study of happiness and well-being now part of the urban policy repertoire. Under-explored so far is how to increase well-being when so many temporary residents live side by side with those there permanently.

Archetypal psychology was founded by James Hillman, a Jungian psychologist and an urbanist. He explored the realm of imagination, enduring metaphors, myths and the deepest patterns of psychic functioning. He notes that imagination, good and bad, is more powerful than rational beliefs and continuously seeps through into consciousness. This can clearly explain many of the populist reactions to turbo-charged globalization. Evolutionary psychology explores why and how humans act the way they do in adapting to changing environments. Greater knowledge of these forces can help us understand how the dramatic impacts of the digitized world are shaping mindscapes and how it can adapt to deep-rooted evolutionary needs, especially as the blending of virtual and real worlds proceed with developments in artificial intelligence. Social psychology studies how people act, think, and feel in the context of society and how these things change as we interact with others. Cultural psychology looks at how behavioural patterns are rooted and embodied in culture. In particular, it explores 'enculturation', the process by which people learn the requirements of their surrounding culture and acquire appropriate values and behaviours. This is highly relevant in decoding how people can adapt to the mobile world.

The 'peace psychologists', Herbert Kelman and John Burton adapted the work of Maslow[36], showing how basic **psychological needs have to be met before progress could be made on bringing people together**. They include: feeling secure; belonging; self-esteem and respect; a right to cultural identity; an ability to participate; and a sense of fairness – sometimes, a simple apology. Given urban tensions this work is increasingly important. Environmental psychology explores interactions between differing physical environments, human behaviour and perception, including the built and the natural. It asks how physical environments feel for citizens, such as the draining dullness of blank walls, jarring juxtapositions of buildings and how some environments feel cold, external or monotonous. Finally, the advances in neuroscience are transformational as it explores the brain in action and how it responds to circumstances.

The enormous potential in applying all these areas of psychology in adapting the city to the nomadic world is obvious given the challenges of groups with different outlooks living in close proximity. Understanding how personal and social networks operate and what our fundamental needs are will help successful place making. We remember that the history of city making is littered with design casualties, including failed utopias. Cities in the sky became squalid prisons, an architectural vanity that decimated social networks. Indeed, the knowledge or psychology of the designer can clearly impact on the people they design for.

## THE PERSONALITY OF CITIES

Consider cities and how they might be psychologically adept at coping with the evolving world. Some we call sober, others constrained, thwarted, stifling and reduced or edgy, 'can do' and open or welcoming, among many other adjectives. These **can be described as personality traits both in humans and cities**. Our responses to geography, location, resources and weather can all shape this sense of personality. Contrast the demeanour, attitudes and behaviours of someone from a colder northern city to a person living on the equator. Think of the difference between port cities and those inland, in mountains or on the plains. Think of a capital city or a satellite. Citizens of different places are perceived as arrogant, vibrant, self-important or subdued. Physical environments too have differing effects. Places perceived as ugly and with endless swathes of asphalt and the ever-present noise and smell of cars can drain the spirit. This can enclose people and make them anxious and uncommunicative. At the other extreme, places seen as beautiful can lift the senses and engender a feeling that the world is in order or stable and so strengthen confidence and open people up. This yearning for wholeness is powerful. Urban atmospheres differ sharply as does a sense of confidence, and we need to ask what is its deeper source.

Sydney is a place whose atmosphere is brash, determined and achievement-driven whereas, so the cliché goes, Melbourne seeks achievement at a more considered pace and is regarded as more refined.

Trieste, feeling it is always stuck at the edge, was obstructed endlessly by Venetian sea power and then later embraced protection from the Habsburgs whose glittering sea port it became. After World War I a victorious Italy moved into Trieste. The Slovene names were switched to Italian and then followed ongoing border disputes, forced Italianization, Nazi occupation, the decimation of the Jewish population and the formation of the only concentration camp on Italian soil. Today Trieste feels a little sad, like it is looking for a role and a less disturbed identity so it can face the future with clarity.

*Restful streetscape, Portland*

Mannheim in Germany, whose string of discoveries include Carl Benz's car, is seen as industrial and ugly – the core was destroyed in World War II and this external battering leads many Mannheimers to apologize too much. This shapes its self-image and can turn the city inwards. But in its undergrowth, it has one of the most vibrant German music scenes.

We think of Athens with the weight of its gloried past to which the present can never measure up, Beijing with its sense of being at the centre of the world, Tel Aviv as the first all-Jewish city in modern times which maintains its pioneering spirit and is now a global start-up hub, while Dubai's recent explosion onto the world stage is sharply shaping Dubaians' sense of self and destiny.

These city stories and their historic facts can have deep psychological effects, with the past reflected in the present, determining the future for a city as it can do for a person. They are therefore worthy of consideration.

My colleague Chris Murray and I wondered if it is possible to transfer a number of psychological tools from person to place and so we built a toolkit for 'psychologically resilient cities' and developed a city personality test. The results create a entirely different way to discuss place. See http://urbanpsyche.org/

The results of our surveys are laden with practical implications. The challenges for Lisbon's city makers are clear when it says of itself it is more introverted than extroverted, more self-absorbed than nurturing or more an improviser than a conscientious doer. Also, being more an idealistic dreamer than practical, who finds it hard to make decisions for the future is important especially when *saudade*, that nostalgia for great things past remains present in the collective psyche.

Relevant too is when Berlin comes across as having a fracture, beyond the obvious of the Berlin Wall. It says it is more introverted yet remains very spontaneous; and when it comes across as having a strong, at times grumpy, character that likes to talk things through and that with a sense of duty. We begin to understand why its civic forums and campaigning attitudes are so important. When we understand the power of centuries-long Castilian dominance over the Basque country, we grasp too Bilbao's strong entrepreneurial spirit as well as its reluctance to be self-critical. And finally, Adelaide, the only place where idealistic free settlers came in Australia, we understand too how others criticize the city for not 'walking the talk' but instead discussing things endlessly.

*Soho, London*

# SIGNALS OF THE CIVIC

The civic impulse lurks everywhere potentially – it is alive although sometimes dormant. It grows with encouragement in a virtuous cycle and declines when not nurtured. It is a renewable resource and so it can be seen as a form of capital, even a currency. There is a dramatic contrast between finance and social capital: with finance the more you spend the less you have; with social capital it is the reverse in that the more you encourage it the more you get.

**Gestures of generosity trigger positive emotion**[37]. Take the Indian woman with a sign offering me a free hug in Frankfurt airport, Shanaya was her name. When I hugged her it made me feel warm rather than cold once I overcame being self-conscious. My trillion cells seemed to open out and my next encounters were infused by the experience. She had chosen exactly the right place to offer her hugs, it was symbolic as airports are places where we are all passers-by, floating in a world of non-recognition. The large graffiti sequence in Galway, Ireland, exhorting me to do random acts of kindness was different. I felt somewhat distanced – I didn't know what to do. I recognized their intent, it was better than telling me to 'fuck off' – a graffiti sign I have seen in many places. Later, though, the message did seep into my consciousness. How – if at all – it has affected me I do not know.

These examples may seem trivial, but they remind us that you can encourage the good as well as the bad. Our instincts are both tribal and defensive as well as social, and much of this comes from the deep psyche. It is the context that encourages one or the other. I witnessed this viscerally working across Croatia, Serbia and Bosnia and especially Sarajevo – once an intercultural hub where the Orthodox church, the Catholic one and the mosque were steps apart from another in co-existence. Now that has been shattered. The Mostar bridge exemplifies it too starkly with symbolic resonance. Before the troubles Croats and Muslims criss-crossed the bridge, yet now a divide is immediately felt as the war tried to emphasize difference rather than similarity. Stories like this abound – Nicosia, Belfast, El Paso or Jerusalem. **We open out when we feel at ease**, we close in and become tribal when there is too much of the unknown that we feel we cannot control.[38] When so much is on the move it is more unstable than stable.

# RECONSTRUCTING THE CIVIC

Individuals, organizations and places are dealing with these dilemmas of whether and how to engage with their city on a daily basis. At times it is structured, as in the vast numbers of voluntary bodies, faith groups, activist or service delivery groups in any human settlement. These range from organizations helping the elderly, parents, the sick or that lobby for justice, fairness or basic needs from housing to play facilities. These can relate strongly to government institutions or fill in the gaps they have left behind. Much here is self-organized, whether to set up support groups for children in need or to care for the homeless, to improve a public park. Organizing around enthusiasms expresses and reflects clearly the vigour of urban life – the running club, football fans, the flower or art lovers, those who cherish their dogs, cats or even rodents. Their gatherings can have a messianic feel. The tentacles are like the nervous system or blood stream circulating through the city. In sum **all these activities are the texture that makes things work**. They are triggered mostly by needs, and in constant negotiations it is discussed or argued about where the onus is put - more on government or more on citizen driven entities.

In the welfare state model the balance shifts one way and provides a safety net, and some have criticized how this can reduce civic energy and create a culture of entitlement or even dependency or give the state too much power. Yet its opposite extreme can leave people forlorn and unable to cope and that is the case in many countries where people

*A place of quiet in Helsinki. A joint project by social services and the Lutheran Church*

have to rely on themselves, their families or networks. The austerity period that started after the financial crash of 2007/8 has in any case reduced the resources for states or local authorities to provide forcing the less privileged, especially, to rely on other forms of help. This is provoking a radical rethink, yet the structures, processes and mindset of public institutions remain largely unaffected and so often unable to respond or to harness the ever present civic drive.

**Most things have been reinvented**, business models or technological opportunities for example, but **less so our political procedures and democracy**. Democracy is more than occasional voting and it took centuries to develop in Europe. It relies at its core on openness, complex soft infrastructures like accepting differing points of view that are embedded in the cultural landscape. Competing models now vie with each other across the globe, for instance Asia or the Middle East have their own views or cultural perspectives. Their traditions are more directive or top down, others are more driven by entrenched interests that do not want to let others in as this would threaten power bases. It reminds us that the Western model cannot be assumed to work, think here of Iran or Iraq or China. Yet the democratic impulse from below bursts through continuously - the desire to determine one's own fate or to participate, to feel empowered.

Dissatisfaction with traditional democracy is rising, it has not delivered on its promises, it cannot operate as it is used to. The system is seen to have been captured by elites operating in their own self-interest, whilst the gap between the rich and poor grows – inexorably. This is the intrinsic tendency of capitalism and unless it is contained and framed and contained by public good imperatives the consequences will erupt and are already erupting in forms of revolt such as populism. The system is perceived as unfair. At the same time the digital revolution is generating new forms of engagement outside of traditional party politics and the young increasingly choose different ways of showing commitment to causes. Parties are perceived as machines where you have to navigate yourself up through a greasy pole. Instead you see a focus on projects, campaigns or social movements like the Occupy Movement that cuts across geographies, and some of these are revolts and there will be more. Often they are temporary alignments, but this has a weakness. How do these fragments come together as a powerful force that can challenge embedded systems? There are exceptions, of course, such as Emmanuel Macron's rise from nowhere to capture the French presidency.

Three responses are noticeable. First, there are city or national and supranational authorities seeking to change the overall system; second experimental labs either within or connected to the public authority; and, lastly, independent initiatives.

Think tanks, universities, researchers, government hybrids or supranational **organizations focusing on public sector innovation have proliferated**. An increasingly rich landscape has evolved to rethink traditional bureaucracies. Some focus on making them more efficient such as with IT, others are more radical. They include global organizations like OECD and its Observatory of Public Sector Innovation, which focuses on establishing rules and processes that foster innovation as well as breaking discipline boundaries[39]; semi-governmental organizations like MindLab, in Copenhagen[40] a cross-governmental innovation unit that involves citizens and businesses in creating new solutions for society. There are semi-independent city hall based labs like Lab para la Cuidad in Mexico City[41], which seeks to connect citizens and the city in novel ways by using the megalopolis as a proving ground. Bologna has its *Immaginazione Civica* initiative reflecting its strong traditions in civic innovation. There are universities such as the Ash Center for Democratic Governance & Innovation at Harvard[42] whose project on municipal innovation supports the replication of good practices, working closely with local officials.

Of special interest is Change@SA[43] in Adelaide, which seeks to create a culture of collaboration, continual improvement and inventiveness within a vibrant public service. Its 90-Day Project was framed around a specific challenge, sponsored by the State Premier and was a Cabinet priority. The 90-day timeframe provides a sense of urgency and a constraint. Public servants volunteer to participate. They are expected to think creativity, to take risks and to consult with users. They combine people across normal agency boundaries and they see the user or citizen context. Ultimately the aim is to transform the system itself. Projects have ranged from health, enhancing skills, environmental improvements, police operations, transport development and beyond.

The Living Lab Movement is an important development and there are several hundred across the world. Here users shape innovation in their own real-life environments, whereas in traditional innovation networks the insights of users are captured and interpreted by experts. Many initiatives focus on social innovations and look at issues from the street upwards. Belgium, the Netherlands and Finland are leaders in using Labs to harvest creativity. Flanders and Brussels have co-created funds to develop public innovations adapted to projects coming out of Labs. This has meant taking away or changing rules.[44]

A new range of think tanks is emerging like Kennisland in Amsterdam[45], which starts with the users of public services to assess whether they connect with real needs and what citizens could do themselves. On the government side they have set up customized learning platforms to help solve the problems of public organizations and individual professionals such as with the Slimmernetwerk (Smarter Network). Attached to this is the Doetank (Do-tank) whose aim is learning by doing in helping public servants innovate themselves. Another network is the Kafka Brigade[46] an international research group 'on red tape and dysfunctional bureaucracy'. It addresses what to do when citizens and public servants become tangled in a web of too complex procedures. Kafka Brigades bring together all parties from front line workers, managers and policymakers around particular cases, such as revising domestic abuse procedures, rethinking support for 18-24 year olds seeking work, or trying to overcome the barriers for green growth.

NESTA[46] in London, now a charitable body was set up by a government endowment and seeks to be: 'an innovation foundation … we back new ideas to tackle the big challenges of our time'. Such as how to use digital tools to improve the quality and legitimacy of decision-making or helping create the Second Half Fund that supports the growth of innovations that mobilise the time and talents of older people to help others alongside public services, such as becoming volunteer teachers in schools.

All these entities have similar aims namely collaborative problem solving, engaging citizens in new ways or breaking down older organizational paradigms. Collectively their methods and approaches stress openness and a willingness to re-assess assumptions, putting a focus on **social innovation as a catalyst of change, fostering an experimentation culture** centred perhaps on living labs, rethinking issues like procurement, embracing measured risks and unleashing the capacities of individuals who bring forth a form of 'bureaucratic creativity' capable of transforming organizations and systems. Crucially they highlight the need for real life experiments that, if they work well, become common practice. It implies allowing the alternative to influence the mainstream.

There is a shift too towards competitions with more complex objectives to drive new ideas. At their best they help cities to focus on what they want to achieve and to harness the collective imagination and to explore initiatives that might not be possible under normal circumstances.

They include most famously the European City of Culture, founded by Melina Mercouri in 1985, a year-long celebration of the winning city with the European Union (EU). Initially a string of capital cities were nominated but increasingly smaller cities are getting the prize. This idea has been copied in Asia, there is also one for capitals of Islamic culture and the Hispanic world. Many of these simply uncritically say a version of 'we are a great cultural capital'. Yet others allowed cities to harvest their cultural resources and to create experimental programmes especially to bring out local distinctiveness and engage their communities. Others such as UNESCO's Creative Cities Network of over 120 global cities, though a useful marketing tool especially for smaller cities, suffer as they are ultimately controlled by a supranational body that is far too distant from local creativity as expressed on the ground. The UNESCO scheme gives status but no resources. In addition, to define creativity as merely a series of art forms remains a weakness. Here we encounter a faultline and battle

between the national and the local. Other designations focus on being green, such as the European Green Capital award won by Stockholm, Hamburg, Copenhagen, Bristol or Nijmegen. Another is the World Design Capital. It has been won by Seoul, Torino, Helsinki, Cape Town, Taipei and Mexico City, where a focus has been on social design. Within all these prizes we detect a tension about who controls the agenda. Often it is the public authority that presents the bid, whereas the prize criteria highlight citizen engagement.

The better known philanthropic city competitions are the Bloomberg's Mayors Challenge, concerned with organizational change, the Knight Cities Challenge, and the J.W.McConnell Family Foundation's Social Innovation Generation (SiG) partnership. They all reflect the need to do things differently.

**Taking a helicopter view of organized or more spontaneous civic action** these are the themes we detect. Below I elaborate in more detail on some judging awards and competitions I have been involved in, such as the Robert Bosch Actors for Urban Change programme, the European Capital of Innovation scheme, the Knight Foundation's Civic Innovation awards or the New Innovations in the Creative Economy (NICE) competition or the Human Cities initiative. The level of energy, dissatisfaction and imagination is astonishing when I reviewed these hundreds of proposals.

Many focused on acknowledging local culture and going with its grain in order to counteract the flattening effect of globalization; some concentrated on arts initiatives to highlight local distinctiveness; others searched for means of engaging the under-engaged; and some focused on building capacities and confidence, There was a desire for self-organization often using digital technologies to connect disparate communities; there were clever apps that monitored the mood and atmosphere of places; there were numerous projects to address the digital divide; schemes to bring different cultural groups together so as to foster intercultural understanding; and the environment was a dominant worry. Refurbishing and reusing older buildings was a prevailing theme too. Often these were co-working spaces aimed at creating new communities and  beyond the creative hubs for new economy there were many social innovation centres proposed. Indeed, social innovation was a dominant theme. Unsung heroes were everywhere.

**Reframing problems was a consistent topic**. Groups are thinking afresh, such as 'what could a health system look like that is more patient-driven', 'how can you affect behaviour change towards more sustainable lifestyles', 'how can you rethink public procurement procedures to encourage innovations', 'what are new learning settings that are not traditional schooling', or 'how can we think of work in a robotizing world'. Many addressed the bigger capitalist dynamic concentrating on issues of justice and fairness.

As an example of the first, let us explore the European Capital of Innovation scheme, where the winner receives one million euros and it seeks to encourage city systems to be on top of the emerging world. Its language differs from the clichés of what public authorities are like.

This scheme sets interesting challenges for public administrations across Europe. Launched in 2014 it is part of the European Union's Horizon 2020 strategy. This states:

A broad approach to innovation is required not limited to bringing new products to the market, but also processes, systems or approaches, that recognize Europe's strengths in design, creativity, services and the importance of social innovation. ... Increasingly, the city can be seen as a place of systemic innovation, where the four P's - People, Place, Public, and Private - are an interconnected, interdependent systemic whole. Innovation is seen as a system linking citizens (People), the built environment (Place), public organizations and policy-makers (Public) through business (Private) – so creating an interactive innovation ecosystem of the city.

The criteria are interesting with their focus on the letter 'I'. Integrated so maximising holistic viewpoints involving people and place; innovative in its processes and how to achieve impact; inclusive by illustrating citizen engagement; inspiring so it attracts talent, funding, investment and partners; interactive in that it encourages open communication between key players. The five I's became the four E's in 2017. Experimenting with concepts, processes, tools and governance models to test drive innovation, engaging citizens in co-creating innovation processes so ensuring an uptake of their ideas or empowering the local ecosystem by implementing new practices to expand a city's attractiveness as a role model.

Competitions with good criteria are useful to get cities to think about restructuring and visioning. Over 120 cities have applied across the scale from the very large, such Paris, Berlin, Barcelona and Amsterdam, through mid-sized cities such as Torino, Grenoble, to smaller cities such as Groningen or Modena. To win the award they had to show a track record. The biggest obstacles to change identified by participating cities reflect the challenges that democracy faces world-wide in its attempt to recapture civic energy. This was the rigidity of their own municipal institutions and the need to overcome the silo mentality, as was the ability to achieve real collaboration and connectivity between the various players in order to benefit from networking.[47]

**The power of openness was evidenced in all winners:** open-data applications with strong participative elements, such as crowd-sourcing ideas for finding and funding urban solutions from crime prevention, to energy saving to dealing with traffic problems. Cities often threw out problem solving challenges to established private companies and the world of SMEs or start-ups so allowing them to use the city as a test bed for innovations. This has helped many companies to prototype inventions and to use the city brand as a marketing tool.

Many addressed the energy transition using incentives and regulations in imaginative ways to do better than the mandated global reduction targets. Some reconceptualised complete systems in the city, such as restructuring health and so empower citizens to manage and maintain their own health and wellbeing with ICT tools. The solutions seek to deliver an advanced, personalized, connected health service based on open systems and collaboration. There were model urban development schemes acting as inspiration, effectively becoming co-creative 'living labs'. These typically combined incentives to develop the creative economy, eco-city thinking or new forms of mobility, and this often required a 'quadruple helix' approach – linking citizen involvement, universities, and the public and private sectors.

Here is a flavour of some winners. Barcelona won the award in 2014 for introducing the use of 'new technologies to bring the city closer to citizens' emphasizing 'technology for people'. This scheme took the 'smart city' notion much further with significant applications in public health and social services. For instance, teaching the elderly to use smart phones to communicate with their doctors. An unintended consequence was many were able to communicate with their grandchildren in new ways.

Amsterdam argued that the fight against floods since the sixteenth century had forced the city to collaborate, but its twenty-first century version is different, embracing openness, pragmatism and adaptiveness. It was the winner in 2016 for its holistic vision of innovation that connected four areas of urban life: governance, economics, social inclusion, and quality of life. Its digital social innovation system connects citizens to the city, enabling new conversations and problem-solving, from fixing a broken paving stone to **a conscious orchestration of 'serendipity' and more 'meeting places' virtual and real**, such as *Pakhuis de Zwijger*. This is an independent platform and place for inspiration and joint problem solving. There is too the Amsterdam Institute for Advanced Metropolitan Solutions, which is a heavily funded living lab, to develop and test complex metropolitan solutions – involving the Amsterdam citizens as testers, users and co-creators.

Paris was a runner up and opened up municipally-owned property (streets, gardens, buildings, basements, schools) to experimental solutions where innovations were often encouraged by thematic calls for proposals. Their credo was that the sum of collective intelligence outside an organisation is always greater than the knowledge within and by opening out and exchanging, this collective intelligence can be channelled.

Groningen, a runner up created tools and processes to develop a user-centred smart energy ecosystem. Called the 'smart energy citizen' the aim was to shift the power in energy markets from large energy providers to groups of citizens. Imaginative communication is used to foster behaviour change, including heat maps for the whole city showing where and how much energy is used.

Espoo, part of the Helsinki city region and a finalist, established a strategic partnership uniting science, business and artistic creativity. The location of both Nokia and the new major game companies, Rovio (Angry Birds) and Supercell (The Clash of Clans), brings these elements together naturally, as does Aalto University, a unique merger of an art and design university with one focusing on science and technology and also a business school.

Torino faced a dramatic transition converting from an industrial city to a centre of innovation and culture. Consider that it was essentially a FIAT city as that company employed nearly 100,000 workers there 40 years ago but now only a few thousand. It has had to rethink how its operates by working on developing trust, horizontal partnerships, trying to be lean (as they say: 'no rigidity in the procedures, to support the fluid and risk-taking process of innovation'). In the context of Italy this is creative.

The Actors for Urban Change initiative developed by the Robert Bosch Stiftung in cooperation with MitOst e.V. has a different perspective. It aims to achieve sustainable and participatory urban development through cultural activities by using specific potentials of culture as driver and enabler of positive change. It seeks to strengthen the ability to collaborate in a cross-sector way, involving public and private partners, yet a cultural initiative drives the process. Winners receive an award, but also training. Winners include Bratislava in Slovakia, that has tried to develop a biking culture in the city through its morebikekitchen; the Urban Agora project to revive Varvakeios Square in Athens, the 'Dress up the city voids' initiative through participative placemaking in Aveiro, Portugal; the Living Archive of Childhood in Barcelona, an online platform to gather children's views on public space; another concerned transforming a traditional kiosk in Kaunas as a neighbourhood meeting point as was thinking about urban utopias in Lublin's own once social housing utopia; or reactivating dilapidated courtyards in the medieval city in Maribor, Slovenia.[48]

Mexico City's *Laboratorio para la Ciudad*[49], founded in 2013 and launched by Gabriella Gomez Mont, a former filmmaker, is exceptional. It is an experimental think-and-do tank for the city government. Politically courageous it employs a multidisciplinary team of 22 people, including political scientists, artists, planners, anthropologists, photographers and lawyers. Their views are fresh and they engage underrepresented communities across the city and make calls to gather ideas or to solve problems – for example by developing apps. One crowd-sourced a route map for the myriad official and semi-official minibuses that crisscross the city. They also acted as a negotiator to solve the escalating Uber versus traditional taxi conflict that resulted in an agreed new levy to help the transport system. A strong focus has been on creating public play areas for the nearly five million children in the city, whose needs are largely neglected. In addition their community visioning work is helping the city administration reorient its services. Naturally working with and against the bureaucracy in imaginative ways is challenging.

A similar inspirational semi-public initiative is Woensel West. It is an extension of the Strijp-S renewal project in the old Phillips areas in Eindhoven into housing, mixed use and incubation centres by a social housing company Trudo. The neighbourhood had received special 'urban renewal status' whose goal was to end 'deprivation' with extra budgets to renovate houses, improve public space and to organize social activities. It failed partly because of the decline of Philips, but also because many people leaving psychiatric institutions were housed in the district.

Trudo was convinced traditional policies would not work. They needed a dramatic game-changer as the local school had to be closed down because of heroin trading. In spite of threats it started with security and in collaboration with the police they dealt with drugs and prostitution. The clever solution was a scheme whereby students give their time freely to help the underprivileged in exchange for cheap rents. This immensely successful project has transformed a failing school to one of the best in the province.

A mass of civic activity has nothing to with public authorities or private entities and is triggered by concerned citizens. Everyone has a tendency to remain amongst themselves, bankers meet bankers, the poor tend to network with the poor and alternative types with their equivalents.

Davide Brocchi, an Italian sociologist living in Cologne wanted people to connect across differences. He invented **Der Tag des guten Lebens (The day of the good life)** or *Buen Vivir* in 2014. Its aim was to create neighbourliness. Brocchi sees it as more than just an event to talk, to play, to be together, but as a means of refreshing democracy. The initial event took 18 months to organize and was held in the more alternative area Kirchfeld, where it was more likely to get traction. To organize it in poorer areas was more difficult as it required gaining trust. The 2017 event attracted 100,000 people and the hope is that the neighbourliness does not stop on that day.

It also won the German Neighbourhood Prize, where the runner up was *Witzin macht Zukunft* (Witzin makes a future), where a village near the poor area Magdeburg, threatened by people leaving, was revitalized by local energy, partly by providing internet for all, by establishing a volunteer fire service and also an agro-business. There were 1,100 applicants. Examples proliferate once you look closely, from the popular guerrilla gardening movement to the world-wide 'parking day' started in San Francisco. Here parking spots are occupied and made into mini-parks, reminding us that cities can have less cars. Another is restaurant day launched by Helsinki, that every three months allows the community to sell food on the streets.

Across the continents we see evidence. Take the inspirational El Sistema whose motto is Social Action for Music. It is a voluntary sector music education program in Venezuela, founded in 1975 by educator, musician and activist José Antonio Abreu. Or the amusing, but serious *cebritas* programme in La Paz. It is influenced by Bogotá's then mayor, Antanas Mockus, who had an initiative to get mime artists to tease and shame city drivers for breaking traffic rules. In La Paz volunteers dress up as zebras to interact and even direct traffic, stressing that civilized behaviour and human beings count rather than cars.

## THE CIVIC COMMONS

These themes, ideas and projects have led to an interest in the civic or urban commons. Concern is rising exponentially as public space becomes privatized and **our civic assets that were once the pride of our communities are being starved** of recognition and finance. Our libraries, parks, community centres were the neutral territory where rich and poor and people of varying backgrounds could meet. They are a connective tissue. Today, too often, we spend less time together across divides and understand less about people who have a different life experience so mutual trust declines. Carol Coletta, then of the Knight Foundation, conceived of 'Reimagining the Civic Commons' and a major project is now being trialled first in Philadelphia with follow up in Memphis, Chicago, Detroit and Akron. The Actors for Urban Change initiative from Berlin has made the theme of 'urban commoning' a central thread of its work and here Bologna has been inspiring. This includes a city's civic assets, but also explores how shared spaces can be governed and managed in new co-operative ways with local communities, such as city streets, green spaces, public squares or community gardens and allotments.

Bologna has taken this further and created a regulation based on the notion of the city as a commons. The 'Bologna Regulation on Public Collaboration for Urban Commons' adopted in 2014, enables collaborative approaches to manage urban space and property including both public and private property for initially one year. The regulation is a product of "The City as a Commons" project and is being taken up by other Italian towns and cities. The Bologna Regulation states that the city wishes to share responsibility for how the goods, tangible, intangible and digital are activated and cared for to improve the collective enjoyment.

Zurich

# THE RELEVANCE OF RESISTANCE

The mood is shifting as the light and the shade of the city become apparent to all. Many feel they must resist the dominant template and narrative. They believe there can be another type of city that operates on different principles though difficult to achieve when market logic and its capital flows determine how city making flows. They ask does profit maximizing create the city we want, they say 'no' and they proffer alternatives.

Vast amounts of money are roaming the globe in search of investment opportunities and property development has a special allure. Too often it leads to gleaming towers with little character or pumped up shopping centres that can entice, excite or deflate. These actors have powerful lobbying clout, they persuade the authorities to allow one more storey or even ten. They achieve changes of land use that can be especially profitable and too often they capture the best sites, like river frontages, which should be publically accessible. The pattern is known. Contrast projects where the public good is interwoven with private initiative and where the surrounding community has a say – they mostly feel better.

Land ownership is the driver and land is a scarce resource. The principles of owners determine what can occur. Does it speak to its city or give back, does it encourage interaction or feel more gated. There is a tendency for privately projects to lack public generosity. Good places understand that their city is not a series of projects but that the city is the project.

A theme running through the concern of critics is how our current system socializes costs or losses and privatizes profits when things go wrong. The largest example in history was when governments in the Western world in 2007/8 bailed out the banks whose unsustainable financial manipulations impoverished many. The rules-based system had evaporated and this lack of regulation continues to cause more frequent financial crises. Some describe this process as governmental capture by corporations and in many countries this has led to a kleptocracy – a form of stealing, where corrupt leaders use their power to exploit their people and resources to extend their personal wealth and political power.

# THERE CAN BE ANOTHER CITY

A fightback has begun, but is it strong enough or is it only a speck of dust in the wind? To create a form of alternative urban development requires alternative finance and there are five types. Ethical banks, whose over-riding principles is not maximizing profit, but achieving a public good aim, include: Triodos, GLS, Umweltbank, Ethikbank in Europe, the Urban Partnership Bank, and the Spring Bank in the US. In Asia, banks for the poor are crucial and of these Grameen Bank is the best known. The second type is credit unions, especially popular in Australia and the US, they are member-owned and any profits return to their community. Building societies are similarly owned by their members. Originating in Britain, most were privatized under the Thatcher government, giving each member a small profit so the communal spirit was lost. By contrast in Denmark the sell-off profits were put into a new foundation Realdania, whose assets now surpass three billion euros. This resource is used to improve the Danish urban environment landscape to ensure future generations benefit. There are also community finance initiatives, such as those where locals might come together to save a loved pub, a threatened bookshop or set up a local energy company. Finally there is peer-to-peer finance and crowdsourcing.

The mistrust of traditional banks is very strong. It explains the desire for alternative financing as evidenced by a survey by the comparison website uSwitch.com. It found that 77% of British people would trust the John Lewis Partnership, which owns department stores and the food retailer Waitrose to be their bank. Their 86,000 staff are all partners in the business. This is reflected in the more positive service and atmosphere of all the stores.

Looking across the realm of cities there are innumerable initiatives that do things differently. They are part of a battle of ideas and, although they coalesce, they are not framed as a grand narrative.

The Transition Network is **a movement of communities coming together to reimagine and rebuild the world**. It is a combination of civic local engagement and a world-wide network. The first to call itself Transition Town in 2005 was Totnes in Britain and the network has spread now to over 50 countries in a myriad of groups in towns, villages, cities or schools. At the last count they identified more than 1,500 projects. The aim 'is to step up to address the big challenges we face by starting local. By coming together, we are able to crowd-source solutions.' They seek ways to promote local food production, to find means of mobility that reduce energy, to encourage cradle-to-cradle thinking in design and production of goods, and they foster alternative currencies so everything circulates within the local boundary.[49]

Transeuro Halles is a grouping of cultural centres initiated by citizens and artists and has been at the forefront of repurposing Europe's industrial buildings for arts, culture and activism since 1983. It currently has 90 members and seeks to 'strengthen the sustainable development of non-governmental cultural centres and encourage new initiatives by connecting, supporting and promoting them ... providing opportunities for learning and sharing so promoting the practice, impact and value of arts and culture'.[50] Buildings such as the famous Cable Factory in Helsinki are part of the network.

The Impact Hub network with over 100 centres across five continents and more than 15,000 members offers space, a community, and a global platform to support social innovators. They are a combination of 'an innovation lab, a business incubator and a social enterprise community centre offering you a unique ecosystem of resources, inspiration, and collaboration opportunities to grow the positive impact of your work'.[50]

The World Social Forum, founded 2001 on Porto Alegre, was until 2016 a global meeting place of those who challenge the way things are. At its height up to 100,000 people attended its meetings that later moved to places like Mumbai, Nairobi, Tunis and once to the Northern hemisphere in Montreal. It has as its motto 'Another World Is Possible', or as Arundhati Roy prefers to say '*Another world* is not only *possible*, she is on her way.' It says of itself that it is

'... an opened space – plural, diverse, non-governmental and non-partisan – that stimulates the decentralized debate, reflection, proposals building, experiences exchange and alliances among movements and organizations engaged in concrete actions towards a more solidarity, democratic and fair world to build alternatives to neo-liberalism.'

It tended to meet on purpose in January at the same time as its great rival the World Economic Forum in Davos so as to provide alternative answers to world economic problems.

These projects, organizations and networks are crucial. **They bring life, energy and solutions to our world that after struggle and time are often taken up by the mainstream**, though perhaps too late. They are like positive fragments on the globe, yet could they come together in one city.

In my time as a fellow of the Bosch Academy in Berlin I pondered whether Berlin could become such a model. Not that I believe it is the best city in the world. Copenhagen is a model too for its sustainable development and Bologna also has a rich tradition of harnessing its civic imagination. Medellin remains inspiring for a its dramatic transformation from a murder capital to a city that has tried to turn around its favelas. Curitiba remains a beacon especially under former mayor Jaime Lerner, whose urban acupuncture approach was effective. He helped make it a green capital. His first project in 1972 turned the main car thoroughfare to a pedestrian mall against strong resistance and he did it quickly in 48 hours. Since then it has become a model for urban planning innovation. And, of course, there are others too.

Indeed, many say Berlin is not necessarily creative in some respects. Its history, though, where people could avoid military service by moving to West Berlin, nurtured a tradition of resistance and an anarchic streak. Once the city was reunited, squatters moved into a large number of the borderland buildings, many of which were later formalized, and here their inhabitants pushed the boundaries of what is possible. Most well-known currently is its club culture driven by techno music, but there is more. Its tradition of civic activism meant it led local government to focus on a bike culture and forms of sustainable living. Its special circumstances of bringing East and West together means that there is far more housing in municipal ownership as is a substantial stock of industrial structures, and there is a cooperative housing tradition. With Berlin's popularity, gentrification is moving fast and threatening the city's balance. And radicals are entering politics and seeking ways to counteract these processes, even on occasion buying back properties to safeguard them from speculation. There is an intense debate on regulation and incentives and how to extend existing codes, such as broadening zoning laws to include the mix of shops in neighbourhoods. Another is to only sell municipal land to the project deemed best rather than to investors who offer the highest price. **A special development is how foundations are collaborating with community groups and activists** to buy major properties to take them out of the market. The Maryon Foundation, based in Basel, saved a large part of the massive former Kindl Brewery in the heart of hipster Neukölln for non-commercial, mostly cultural use. It had been a squat too. Another is the Ex-Rotaprint complex undertaken with the Trias foundation. The Abendrot foundation also from Basel, whose income comes from insurance and which grew out of the anti-nuclear movement, helped the emblematic Holzmarkt development, a highly unusual experiment in a world capital. The former 200-metre long riverside site included one of Berlin's major squatted night clubs, Bar 25, and it became a symbolic battle. Once Bar 25 had to leave, the city wanted to build a new high-rise quarter and put the land up for sale. The protests began including under the slogan 'Spree für Alle' (the Spree river for All) to stop the area becoming a media zone. The Bar 25 instigators found a saviour in the Abendrot foundaton who fought off competition from hedge funds and bought the site for over €10m and then leased it back to a cooperative founded by Bar25 regulars. The contract was unusual as neither the cooperative nor the Abendrot foundation are contractually allowed to sell the property for their own profit.

The project value of the Holzmarkt development is more than €100 million and it is a complex site, part of which has the railway running over it with viaducts underneath. Holzmarkt's flexibility enabled it to use these interesting structures in exchange for giving the rail company some land to store its materials. Its long term financial stability will be provided by a hotel at one end and the Eckwerk buildings at the other. This is a cluster of five of the highest wood framed buildings in Germany, each over 10 stories. These will be rented out to students and an incubation centre with the aim of creating a lively community. Holzmarkt describes itself as a village and has a mix that normally would not occur at a prime site of this nature. At its core it has a kindergarten, a production house, it runs a market, it is a venue, it has a restaurant and a bakery. Drink and food in the first stages are paying back the loan. Crucially the waterfront is accessible to all and on the opposite bank is one of Berlin's biggest cooperative housing complexes. Within the development there are 25 companies gathered in four clusters where more profitable activities can support the less profitable.

Additional **project financing was gathered from a series of sympathetic alternative banks** and a group of 150 people who each bought a share for €25,000. Everyone, including the big lenders, only has one vote and the overall project is governed by a cooperative structure. It has become so emblematic that it attracts a stream of visitors from across the globe, especially mayors. Holzmarkt is now forming a network of alternative urban development initiatives including the Venn Quarter in Tel Aviv, the Gather project in Amsterdam and the Alte Mu in Kiel. The aim is to extend this globally. One lurking danger is that Holzmarkt may become too popular and precisely trigger the gentrification of the area it set out to avoid. We shall see if it will help systemic change, certainly the hope is there.

4

PLACES OF
EMPATHY

PRO
COMMUNITY

When people organize and demand
influence they move the world.
The future is powered by strong
communities.

CLAIMING
SPACE

Generous public spaces are not
extravagant. Creating space for public life where there is none means
putting people first and pursuing
the ideal of an open society.

Previous picture: Millennium Park, Chicago

This picture: Danish Pavilion, Venice

# PATTERNS OF PROGRESS

Do you like spiders or do they frighten you. Do you like foreigners or do they do they make you feel uneasy. We have a stark choice to open out or to close in. This opening out I call civic urbanity. It is a normative idea. It is a promise for a better city. It taps into our deeper yearnings for connection and purpose. It does not come naturally. It has to be fostered and can become part of a new common sense if practiced and encouraged by cultural attitudes and revised regulations and incentives and programmes. Or put another way swayed by this it becomes self-understood behaviour or seems the right thing to do. It proceeds by negotiation about why civic urbanity should be put taken seriously - in itself a cultural project.

City-making at its core involves arguing about values and making choices based thereon. Then it entails applying values and using politics to turn values into policies and exerting power to get your way. These are shaped by our culture. So the scope, possibilities, style and tenor of a city's physical look and its social, ecological, and economic development are culturally shaped so culture moves centre-stage. If, for example, a culture invests its faith only in the market principle and trusts the drive of capital always to produce sensible choices, the logic, interests and points of view of those who control markets will count for more than those who believe market based decision-making is an impoverished theory of choice-making.[1] If a culture holds that individual choice is everything - individuals always know best - this impacts the city. Conversely, if people believe the idea of a public, common or collective good has value and is beyond the dynamics of the market a different city evolves. Any culture based argument implies or proposes a trajectory, a plan of action - even a manifesto of what to do next.

## SECULAR HUMANISM

The ethical frame that best supports civic urbanity is the secular humanist position. This privileges civic values, which in essence seek to foster competent, confident and engaged citizenship. It is concerned with the capabilities, interests and achievements of human beings. It does not decry the virtues of science or the sustenance religion or other belief systems give. In a city context its aim is to ensure that people of difference live together in relative peace and accord as the city is in part defined by people do not know each other.

The idea is to arrive at practical standards that provide principles to guide common views, behaviour and to help resolve conflicts so that difference can be lived and shared with mutual respect.

# XENOPOLIS OR COSMOPOLIS

Xenopolis, means a city with foreigners. It has a negative ring. Cosmopolis sounds more positive. Secular humanism as a core Enlightenment project has been drained of confidence. It feels exhausted and consequently it is mistakenly accused of being 'wishy-washy' with no apparent point of view. Its confidence needs to be restored. The confident secular humanist view proposes a set of civic values and rules of engagement, which include: Providing settings for a continually renewing dialogue across differences, cultures and conflicts; allowing strongly held beliefs or faiths expression within this core; and acknowledging the 'naturalness' of conflict and establishing means and mediation devices to deal with difference. It seeks to consolidate different ways of living, recognising arenas in which we must all live together and those where we can live apart. It generates structured opportunities to learn to know 'The Other', to explore and discover similarity and difference. It wishes to drive down decision-making on the subsidiarity principle, which implies much greater decentralisation and devolution of power. Central government takes on a more subsidiary role. It is an enabler and facilitator. This enhances participation and connectivity at local level. It helps generate interest, concern and responsibility.

*Secular* does not mean emotionally barren. Indeed I treasure the heightened registers of being that spirituality evokes. It is an animating force may be just the thing that makes some cities more liveable in than others. Therefore, civic urbanity stakes a claim to playing a part in developing a new cosmopolis. The latter is not a defined project with a specific end result, but an attitude that we need to work on - continuously.

*Louise Bourgeois sculpture at the Guggenheim Museum, Bilbao*

265

Urbanity and to be urbane has a combined economic, social, political and cultural history which is useful to retrace for today and to recapture its best features. The tradition of urbanity is essentially European reflecting an attitude that emerged in the late Middle Ages and the Renaissance in Italian city states and in Northern Europe and especially the Hanseatic League cities. It was led by merchants who tried to escape from the shackles and constrictions of feudalism to do their trades in less impeded ways. It marked the movement towards meritocracy. In so doing they became a vigorous group with their own political, economic and cultural interests that successfully competed with the existing medieval order. They developed what became the bourgeois style of life including their own learning and cultural institutions and norms and values.

# URBANITY: ITS PAST & FUTURES

They were anti-feudal and in their context more democratic, they were open and cosmopolitan and proud of their city and invested in it. They reflected a new emerging economy based on trade, new methods of production, there were new professional bodies, education and science institutions and a focus on rational calculation. This gave citizens a sense of collective identity and shared solidarity reflecting an attitude to life. The city became at times more important than familial ties, clan bonds or ethnicity. This allowed for greater mobility. This was a completely different worldview. It represented an emerging civic culture.

In time as the nation states evolved the role of cities changed, their independence declined as capital cities like London or Paris began to dominate. Equally with the rise of states the force of identity shifted to the nation so diminishing the power of cities. The rise of a more centralized welfare state in some countries exacerbated this situation.

It is unwise to idealize this original bourgeois urbanity since it became more superficial and consumption oriented. The notion of urbanity even degraded ending with the idea of the *flâneur*, someone who watches urban life go by, but uncommitted to the needs of the collective whole. So today we sometimes interpret urbanity or associate it as a synonym for being suave, refined or well-mannered. Others see it as something to do with café culture, being somewhat cool or a place with many cultural choices. Others of a more post-modern bent think that whatever a city is this represents its urbanity. So if a place is a concrete jungle and dreadful so be it.

*Two elderly people looking at an advert of a young woman in Bilbao*

The German phrase 'Stadtluft macht frei' (city air makes you free) encapsulates this idea. To use a more modern term it focuses both on 'the right to the city' and 'responsibility for the city'.

## BARRIERS TO URBANITY

Urbanity here is not merely a descriptive term but a programme for action. Today the world is more mobile, we identify with various places and cities increasingly focus of attracting this work force. These itinerant citizens have a different relationship to their city. It is less intense or deep or long term and there is less commitment to place. Equally the city usually has less power over key issues that determine its fate, such as education, transport, social welfare or its ability to create its own rules, such as creating its own citizenship with appropriate rights. At the same time many independent voluntary and community structures, which were historically vital as the nervous system and mediating institutions of a city, have been in danger of weakening relatively as they are more reliant on national governments for survival. This makes our urban culture a reduced one, because it has fewer levers to help develop citizens and so the civic. This decline of traditional forms of engagement is visible everywhere. It is reflected in low voting rates or the decline in trust and so the invisible threads of connection that make community work weaken. Not surprisingly therefore when we think of urban culture we think merely about the atmosphere, events and arts of a city. However, new forms of engagement are evolving.

Our notion of civic urbanity has lofty aims. Yet how in this overall context do you develop an urbanity where place or our sense of anchoring is different and where virtual and real worlds blend more readily and where globalization changes the social life of communities in often negative ways so that they feel fragmented.

*Chess in public encapsualtes civic life: Mexico City*

*Hanging out and a casual
chat in Mexico City*

## BEING CIVIC

Being civic is to be a full citizen, which is a person engaged with their city in multiple ways on an on-going basis in order to improve their own lives and those of others. It is about feeling that 'you' and the 'city' merge into one as if it were part of you as is every brick or blade of grass. The city owns you and you own the city. Small day to day things, like the regular breakfast at a local café or the local dentist that you have seen for years, and occasional larger events weave a web that over time feels like community. This familiarity happens imperceptively and step by step as associations with place and people build up. These create memories, meanings and histories. This identification takes time. It is why people often like places that to others are faceless, ugly or soulless because they can draw in many experiences. The bench where you had your first kiss, for instance, is why so much of peoples' identity is invested and embodied in them. There is a danger that this can entrap you and become claustrophobic as it closes you in especially if the city in question is static and unchanging.

The young and especially the ambitious prefer to escape and may prefer a place that is on the move. This signals excitement, stimulation and being where the action is. Yet acting in a civic way can in principle both deepen identity whilst develop and change the city so making it feel alive and alert. The focus can be vast from shifting the city to be green, to fostering local entrepreneurship or getting different groups to mix or celebrate. Being civic throughout history has been linked to the democratic impulse. This implies being active and so fosters a realm of debate and public discussion. Citizens thus at their best are makers, shapers and co-creators of their evolving city. They are producers of their place rather than merely consumers. The danger for most cities that need to attract the semi-permanents and itinerants with talent is that those have little time to build commitment, direct involvement, participation and loyalty. Instead the buzz and liveliness is created for them so reinforcing the consumption bias.

To be civic often involves challenging the status quo and official institutions and being an activist. This builds up a civic society as a collection of engaged individuals often acting voluntarily, or as organizations and institutions that work together in a way that official bodies cannot or will not.

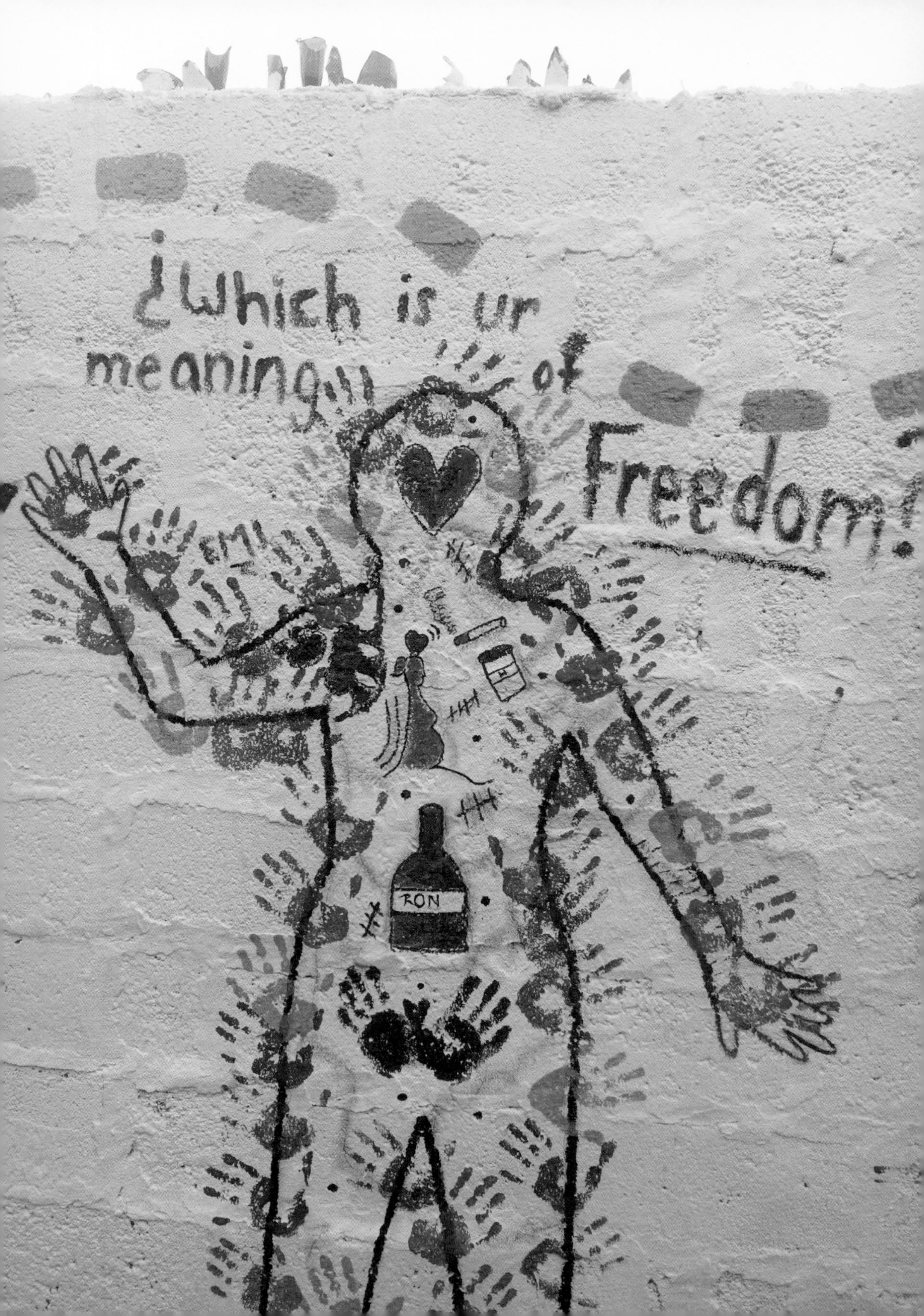
¿Which is ur
meaning!!! of
Freedom!
RON

Ten themes shape the dilemmas, challenges and opportunities for the 21st century city. Each has relevance to how we live and shape our places. They provide an urban narrative that seeks to contain the explosive mix of centrifugal and centripetal forces we increasingly find in cities. They help reshape how we can rethink urbanity.

The interlinked concepts to rethink urbanity are: holistic thinking, planning and acting; the shared commons; eco-consciousness; healthy urban planning; cultural literacy; inclusivity; inter-generational equity; the aesthetic imperative; creative city making and an invigorated democracy. Together they frame the modern idea of civic urbanity. This idea seeks to realign individual desires and self-interest within a collective consciousness focused as much on responsibilities for 'us' or 'our joint world or city' rather than choices that are only for 'me' and my more selfish needs.

# THE TEN THEMES OF URBANITY

### THINKING IN THE ROUND

The starting point is to think in an integrated and connected way. Only then can we discern the linkages and dependencies that help us understand the deeper dynamics of cities and how to make the most of their potential. This requires a changed mindset and is difficult to prescribe. Often it is a mental transformation. Yet increasingly decision makers realize that silo thinking and strict departmentalism does help create the complex solutions we need.

### A SHARED COMMONS

There is a demand for a reinvigorated public and shared commons. This is a social ethos that argues against our increasingly tribal and self-centred public culture. It fosters amongst other things spaces and places from parks to libraries that are free, non-commercial and public. Places underpinned by this ethos can help retrofit conviviality and the habits of solidarity so helping to nurture our capacity to bond and to build social capital. In time the urban civility this fosters encourages individual and collective gestures of generosity. In turn this self-generating process can create a virtuous cycle.

### ECO-CONSCIOUSNESS

All cities talk of sustainability. Every vision statement mentions combating the effect of climate change. Taking a helicopter view of cities worldwide there are many good initiatives. Yet few cities make the hard planning choices to counteract an economic dynamic, spatial configurations and physical forms that continue to make cities less sustaining. Cities have not been sufficiently imaginative in changing behaviour patterns, nor have they developed a new environmental aesthetic to inspire people to think afresh. Equally 360° thinking has not embedded itself into decisions so it becomes a new common sense able to drive change. The necessary and dramatic retrofitting process still has a long way to go even though there are vast economic opportunities from being part of the 4th lean, clean, green industrial revolution. 'Cradle to cradle' decision making remains far off.

## HEALTHY URBAN PLANNING

Urban planning that helps makes you healthy by just navigating the city in day to day ways has not imbued planning disciplines. The cities we have built and continue to create make us unhealthy. We know about unhealthy urban planning. Rigid 'land use zoning', which separates functions and gets rid of mixed uses such as blending living, working, retail and fun; 'comprehensive development' that loses out on providing fine grain, diversity and variety; 'economy of scale thinking' with its tendency to think only the big is efficient. Lastly the 'inevitability of the car' can lead us to plan as if the car were king and people a mere nuisance. Walkable cities give you time and space to experience the city in visceral ways. Part of being healthy is sensory satisfaction. A healthy place is one where people feel an emotional, psychological, mental, physical and aesthetic sense of well-being; where doing things that make you healthy happen as a matter of course and incidentally. A healthy place throws generosity of spirit back at you. This makes you feel open and trusting. It encourages us to communicate across divides of wealth, class and ethnicity. It makes for conviviality.

## INTERCULTURAL THINKING

All bigger cities are becoming more diverse. Multiculturalism is the predominant approach that acknowledges these differences. It highlights the need to cater their diverse needs. Interculturalism goes one step further and has different aims and priorities. It asks 'what when we are sharing a city can we do together across our cultural differences'. It recognises difference, yet seeks out similarities. It highlights that in reality most of us are hybrids and so downplays ideas of purity. It stresses that there is one single and diverse public sphere and it resources the places where cultures meet. It focuses less on resourcing projects and institutions that act as gate-keepers and instead encourages bridge-builders. It acknowledges conflicts and tries to embrace, manage and negotiate a way through them based on an agreed set of guidelines of how to live together in our diversity and difference. In sum it goes beyond a notion of equal opportunities and respect for existing cultural differences in order to achieve the pluralist transformation of public space, institutions and our civic culture.

## INEQUALITY & INCLUSIVENESS

Unequal societies create tension, resentment and lead to unfulfilled potential. A society of have and have-nots does not harness the collective imagination and intelligence of its citizens nor capture their energy and aspirations sufficiently. The trickle-down effect, it is increasingly recognized, is ineffective and the gap between the rich and poor is exacerbating. From the OECD to the Davos summit there are grave warnings of the looming effects and impacts of severe income disparity. It is seen as the most dangerous risk to social stability and well-being. It is corrosive, divisive, inefficient and ethically unsound. Some degree of inequality may be good for an economy, creating incentives to work hard and take risks, but a high concentration of income gains among the most affluent is damaging. The Occupy protests demonstrated the increasing public anger that it has gone too far. It can be addressed, but only if we bend the market mechanism to public good objectives.

## INTER-GENERATIONAL EQUITY

The demographic time bomb hangs over everything cities do. There will be pressure to isolate the ageing population into retirement zones with housing adapted to their needs. More innovative places will seek to think through city making from an inter-generational perspective and develop adaptable housing forms that can be transformed through the lifecycle anad where the young and the old can be together.

## THE AESTHETIC IMPERATIVE

There is the aesthetic imperative. The city is a 360° immersive experience and it communicates through every fibre of its being, its built structures, its natural forms, its activities and overall atmosphere. Its aesthetics engender an emotional response with psychological impacts. We can argue about ugliness and beauty and we should. This heightens our awareness of our surroundings and in time creates standards which of course are re-negotiated. Mostly there is alignment on what works and what doesn't aesthetically. This reminds us that every physical structure has an aesthetic responsibility to the environment and to the people in which it sits. Remember the pinpricks of ugliness spilling out from horrible buildings, misplaced urban design or insensitive infrastructures throughout their lives. These have a negative impact leading to depression and other diseases.

## CREATIVE CITY MAKING

Creative city making seeks to address the escalating crisis cities face that cannot be solved by a business as usual approach in order to survive well and to manage increasing complexity. It argues that curiosity, imagination and creativity are the pre-conditions for inventions and innovations to develop as well as to solve intractable urban problems or create interesting opportunities. Unleashing the creativity of citizens, organizations and the city is an empowering process. It harnesses potential, it searches out what is distinctive and special about a place and is a vital resource. It is a new form of capital and a currency in its own right. Creativity has broad based implications and applications in all spheres of life. It is not only the domain of artists or those working in the creative economy or scientists, though they are important. It includes too social innovators, interesting bureaucrats or anyone who can solve problems in unusual ways. Cities need to **create the conditions for people to think, plan and act with imagination**.

This requires a different conceptual framework. The capacity of a place is shaped by its history, its culture, its physical setting and its overall operating conditions. This determines its character and mindset. There has been an 'urban engineering paradigm' of city development focused on hardware for too long. Creative city making by contrast emphasizes how we need to understand the hardware and software simultaneously. In turn this effects the 'orgware' of a city, which is how manage the city under these new conditions. The dominant 'culture of engineering' has a positive and negative mindset. It is logical, rational and technologically adept, it learns by doing, it tends to advance step by step and through trial and error. It is hardware focused. It gets things done. Its weakness is that it can become narrow, unimaginative, inflexible and forget the software aspect. This is concerned with how a place feels, its capacity to foster interactions and to develop and harness skill and talent.

## AN INVIGORATED DEMOCRACY

Most things have been reinvented such as how we do business, how we build cities or how we entertain ourselves and technology has moved apace in gigantic leaps enabling to connect across the world in completely unforeseen ways. Yet our forms of representative democracy have remained largely the same for hundreds of years. We vote for politicians to speak on our behalf every four years with little involvement in between, even though substantial efforts are made to consult citizens on local plans or at times to hold referenda on major issues. Low participation in voting shows it is not enough. Cities need to explore ways of communicating with citizens to reignite civic engagement and to co-create policies. The open data movement is important here. By making hitherto hidden information freely available, new ways of decision making are possible, such as citizen juries or other forms of participative democracy from on-line voting to town hall meetings. Overall, these themes highlighted involve caring for oneself and others, celebrating and fostering distinctiveness and identity and being open minded.

Civic life needs good public bureaucracies and these need reinventing to tap the potential of cities, their citizens and businesses. They require a different mindset that shapes their organizational culture. Its two main features are to shift from a **'no, because' culture to a 'yes, if' culture**. This is the glass half full approach that listens and sees opportunities rather than problems and tries to help. This implies it should operate in **a strategically principled and tactically flexible way**. These principles encourage elastic more flexible planning to address the converging, escalating crisis globally. There is a massive, urgent task ahead for bureaucracies to help create a fairer more equal world buttressed by the right rules or incentives and regulatory. This needs a bureaucracy that can draw on all its ethical, creative and intellectual resources and reclaim a distinctive leadership role, but framed in a 21st century context. However, decades of reform and challenge have enfeebled many bureaucracies - filling them with doubt about their legitimate role and authority relative to elected government and other interest groups.

# THE CREATIVE BUREAUCRACY

'Creativity' and 'bureaucracy' are two words apparently in tension. Creativity focuses on resourcefulness, imagination, responsiveness, adaptability and flexibility. Say the word 'bureaucracy' to yourself. What does it conjure up? Mostly we have succumbed to knee jerk prejudices and clichés about who bureaucrats are and of the public sector. Mindless rules, lazy complacency, incomprehensible forms, red tape, inefficient, convoluted, overpaid, wasting resources - a string of negative connotations. This is not the full story. The very things bureaucracy is criticised for are also insurances against the abuse of power. Those working in public service are often its good defenders. So whilst we criticize many workings of most current bureaucracies we believe there can be another bureaucracy.

The standardised rules, hierarchies and procedures of a bureaucracy were initially designed to be positive, or at least efficient and fair. Bureaucracies were developed to solve the problems of their time and so reflect the culture of their age. These cultures were more deferential, more top down and hierarchical, more expert driven, less emotionally intelligent. At their best they sought systematic procedures to bring transparency and equity to decision making. They were once seen as benign and modern, if somewhat technocratic. Yet as they evolved, weaknesses appeared. Problem solving seemed mechanical and planning ahead seemed achievable in a 'predict and provide' fashion.

In a world of wicked interconnected problems and a complex risk nexus this approach is at best sub-optimal and at worst dysfunctional. The new bureaucracy will use the best of digital potentials, but will not let technologies dehumanize developments. Its 'modus operandi' will be to stimulate itself and its environment by a more co-creative, equal exchange with its communities. This demands new ways of thinking and problem solving and especially the ability to partner across public, private and community divides.

Bureaucracies created solely in pursuit of efficiency or **too fixed on administrative rules are extraordinarily wasteful of human effort** and talent. It is the discretionary effort, an unrealised resource that can make organizations more or less successful. Every individual has a vast storehouse of "discretionary" effort that they either give or withhold on a daily basis. Discretionary effort is the difference between how people are capable of performing and how well they actually perform. Systems can encourage or prevent people making this contribution. Studies, including our own, show that when people feel thwarted the organisation can lose between 30% to 50% of their potential contribution. People instead of performing more strongly, having ideas, solving problems, making the work environment better, helping others out, are potentially frustrated, bored, stressed or close themselves in.

Fundamental to triggering this effort is an attitude of leadership that sees the organisation as a joint endeavour where everyone's contribution in and outside the organization is essential. This requires systems that allow rather than curtail and a dynamic which leverages strengths. Most studies say this involves widespread leadership rather than management. Systems are managed; people are led.

In principle **there is a reservoir of hidden potential and talent locked up in public bureaucracies**. People can do much more if given the chance yet most feel underutilised and stymied into expressing themselves narrowly. Hard wired, rigid approaches within and across administrative systems, organizations, and individuals constrain what is possible. There is a direct link between the creativity of the bureaucracy and the success of a city. It's impossible to have an economically and socially successful city that is agile, attractive and sustainable without an inventive, creative, engaged bureaucracy.

Indeed **behind many great projects there is a creative bureaucrat**, finding ways to shape the rules they operate with in positive directions. Individuals with agency can shift an organizational culture and, over time, even the bureaucratic system. Things are beginning to break out and some changes are being forced by citizens who are prepared to defy rules to do so. We find examples of heroic courage but also of misery unfortunately. Creative bureaucrats can, as individuals, shape cities. But a critical mass can reshape the bureaucratic system itself embodying the values and qualities expressed by the best individuals. Bureaucracies shape and influence the mood of cities and their civic creativity can help communities bridge divides and find 'the common'.

Amongst the many I remember two interesting bureaucrats. The quiet and unassuming Jair Lin is one. He was the number two in urban planning in Taipei and understood the subtle ecology of how creative milieux work. He knew how to 'bend' the market and create rules to both encourage young start-ups as well as rescue the famous, traditional Dihua St. area in Dadaocheng. His Urban Regeneration Office (URO) was open to experiments. It connected with progressive developers and sought to control the development of key small sites determined to contain the speculative dynamism present in the city. One strategy was to transfer some property rights in exchange for keeping the original buildings.

Another is Athens Vice-Mayor for Civil Society Amalia Zepou, formerly a documentary filmmaker. She created the platform "synAthina" to trigger a new energetic relationship between citizens and the public domain. This was more than voluntarism, but a co-creative process of active citizenship and an open-minded administration. It developed into an idea that won one of the five Mayors' Challenge awards from Bloomberg Philanthropies in 2014. SynAthina is now part of a social innovation unit, a systematic mechanism between the municipality, local organizations and citizens. The aim is to facilitate citizens' creativity to modernise local governance to improve citizens' lives and strengthen the democratic process.

*The Bosch Stiftung, Berlin*

# WHAT IF....

So we come to the end. Great places, beyond providing for basic needs such as work and good facilities have five significant qualities, they are:

• Places of anchorage and distinctiveness. Somewhere that feels like home and that generates a sense of the known, the familiar, the stable, the predictable; it feels safe and so is comforting. This place celebrates where it comes from and acknowledges its past, its heritage, its traditions and core assumptions about who it is. This makes people feel rooted, yet ironically it gives the confidence to be more relaxed in where it is going and the changes that may unfold. It dares to be innovative

• Places of connection and reconnection. Somewhere that is locally bonded, where communities of difference can connect and mesh. This place is at ease with the wider world and the global including its diversity. It makes no distinctions between patriots and globlai It has seamless connectivity physically within and beyond the city confines, it is digitized reaching out to the virtual worlds stretching out far and wide.

• Places of possibility and potential: this city fosters open-mindedness and encourages a culture of curiosity. This provides choices, options and opportunities in differing phases of life. It is a place with an experimental culture so ensuring it remains flexible and adaptive to emerging changes.

• Places of learning: Here there are many possibilities to self-improve from the formal to the informal. This is a lifelong learning environment and a place where a discussion culture is vibrant and things are thought about afresh when necessary. Here you can develop personally and professionally.

• Places of inspiration: There is a visionary feel, where aspiration and good intent is made visible in interesting ways through the built fabric or through the vitality of culture and urban programming. Each reinforces the other and this creates a positive virtuous spiral.

This place is sum manages to add values and value simultaneously in any major initiative it undertakes. So its economic and social drive is framed by an ethical value base.

*Buildings in Tirana*

**Can the issues raised in the Civic City help create a way forward?**

# REFERENCES

## SECTION 1

1 https://www.creativespirits.info/aboriginalculture/people/aboriginal-population-in-australia#axzz4mhnbEUam

2 Many think that gypsy is pejorative name given its connotation of illegality, yet some Romani organizations themselves use it.

3 http://www.thegreynomads.com.au/

4 https://beunsettled.co/medellin-colombia-coworking-retreat/

5 http://www.dnxhub.com

6 https://levels.io/future-of-digital-nomads/

7 http://www.goingmobo.com/

8 http://becomenomad.com/about/

9 http://www.hackerparadise.org/

10 https://www.remoteyear.com/remote-year-2?utm_expid=90911645-86.4PxK1NSBQ_-Sk9SGJezseg.1

11 http://www.oecd.org/edu/education-at-a-glance-19991487.htm

12 http://monitor.icef.com/2015/11/the-state-of-international-student-mobility-in-2015/

13 http://www.nafsa.org/Policy_and_Advocacy/Policy_Resources/Policy_Trends_and_Data/NAFSA_International_Student_Economic_Value_Tool/

14 http://www.universitiesuk.ac.uk/policy-and-analysis/reports/Pages/briefing-economic-impact-of-international-students.aspx

15 http://www.rferl.org/a/athletes-switching-nationalities-in-spotlight-at-london-olympics/24645792.html

16 http://www.cnbc.com/id/47599766?view=story&$DEVICE$=native-android-tablet

17 https://www.researchandmarkets.com/reports/4176844/the-2017-global-wealth-migration-review

18 https://www.theguardian.com/technology/2017/jan/29/silicon-valley-new-zealand-apocalypse-escape

19 http://ftnnews.com/other-news/31537-italy-to-offer-residency-by-investment.html

20 https://henleyglobal.com/files/download/hvri/HP_Visa_Restrictions_Index_170301.pdf

21 https://www.passportindex.org/byRank.php

22 https://nomadlist.com/

23 http://becomenomad.com/trending-digital-nomad-locations-cities-hubs/

24 https://www.amazon.co.uk/Intercultural-City-Planning-Diversity-Advantage/dp/1844074366

25 http://www.coe.int/en/web/interculturalcities/origins-of-the-intercultural-concept

26 https://www.oecd.org/migration/OECD%20Migration%20Policy%20Debates%20Numero%202.pdf

27 http://en.ccg.org.cn/

28 https://www.theguardian.com/world/2015/nov/26/japan-under-pressure-to-accept-more-immigrants-as-workforce-shrinks

29 https://jakubmarian.com/immigration-in-europe-map-of-the-percentage-and-country-of-origin-of-immigrants/

30 https://en.wikipedia.org/wiki/Immigration_to_Europe

31 http://www.unhcr.org/uk/news/latest/2016/6/5763b65a4/global-forced-displacement-hits-record-high.html
   http://www.firstpost.com/world/worlds-stateless-people-where-do-people-with-no-country-go-1787075.html

32 http://www.aljazeera.com/news/2016/05/china-uk-welcoming-refugees-russia-160519044808608.html

33 https://www.theguardian.com/world/2017/mar/30/syrian-refugee-number-passes-5m-mark-un-reveals

34 http://www.pewresearch.org/fact-tank/2016/10/05/key-facts-about-the-worlds-refugees/

35 http://www.un.org/esa/ffd/wp-content/uploads/2016/01/Promoting-safe-migration_IOM_IATF-Issue-Brief.pdf

36 http://www.gallup.com/poll/148559/one-five-first-generation-migrants-keep-moving.aspx

37 http://www.telegraph.co.uk/expat/expatfeedback/4201967/So-you-think-youre-English.html

38 http://ec.europa.eu/eurostat/statistics-explained/index.php/Tourism_statistics_-_expenditure
   https://carleton.ca/fass/2016/gringo-gulchsex-tourism-and-social-mobility-in-costa-rica/
   http://www.traveldailymedia.com/247813/indian-domestic-tourism-surges-in-2016/
   http://www.goldmansachs.com/our-thinking/pages/macroeconomic-insights-folder/chinese-tourist-boom/report.pdf

39 https://www.wttc.org/-/media/files/reports/economic-impact-research/regions-2017/world2017.pdf

40 https://www.theguardian.com/travel/2012/dec/04/berlin-fights-anti-hipster-tourism-abuse

41 http://nypost.com/2014/08/12/is-travel-addiction-a-real-thing/

42 https://decorrespondent.nl/3138/a-love-letter-to-all-the-tourists-of-amsterdam/567685513296-340f8980

43 https://carleton.ca/fass/2016/gringo-gulchsex-tourism-and-social-mobility-in-costa-rica/

44 https://en.wikipedia.org/wiki/Prostitution_in_the_Netherlands

45 http://www.bbc.co.uk/news/magazine-40829230

46 https://www.mtqua.org/2016/09/27/pt1-size-medical-tourism-industry/

47 http://www.bbc.co.uk/news/world-latin-america-37009138

48 https://en.wikipedia.org/wiki/History_of_malaria

49 http://edition.cnn.com/2013/10/16/health/cholera-fast-facts/index.html

50 http://fortune.com/2014/09/14/biggest-organized-crime-groups-in-the-world/

51 https://en.wikipedia.org/wiki/List_of_criminal_enterprises,_gangs_and_syndicates

52 https://www.fbi.gov/investigate/violent-crime/gangs

53 https://heatst.com/culture-wars/worlds-most-feared-street-gang-sacrificed-underage-girls-in-satanic-rituals-police-found/?mod=fark_im

54 http://www.slate.com/blogs/behold/2015/09/21/adam_hinton_photographs_members_of_the_ms_13_gang.html

55 https://www.theguardian.com/world/2017/jan/12/el-salvador-homicide-rate-murder-two-years

56 http://www.bbc.co.uk/news/world-latin-america-39436568

57 http://www.bbc.co.uk/news/world-latin-america-39934676

58 https://www.unodc.org/toc/en/crimes/organized-crime.html

59 https://www.theguardian.com/global-development/2015/jul/31/people-smuggling-how-works-who-benefits-and-how-to-put-stop

60 http://www.newyorker.com/science/maria-konnikova/why-do-we-admire-mobsters

61 http://www.bbc.co.uk/news/world-15391515

62 http://www.worldatlas.com/articles/countries-with-the-highest-rates-of-contraceptive-use.html

63 https://www.theguardian.com/environment/2017/jul/12/want-to-fight-climate-change-have-fewer-children

64 https://www.theguardian.com/world/2017/jan/23/trump-abortion-gag-rule-international-ngo-funding

65 https://esa.un.org/unpd/wpp/publications/files/key_findings_wpp_2015.pdf

66 https://overpopulationisamyth.com/content/episode-5-7-billion-people-will-everyone-please-relax

67 http://news.mit.edu/2017/technological-progress-alone-stem-consumption-materials-0119

68 http://www.independent.co.uk/life-style/health-and-families/features/the-loneliness-epidemic-more-connected-than-ever-but-feeling-more-alone-10143206.html  https://www.forbes.com/sites/carolinebeaton/2017/02/09/why-millennials-are-lonely/#605864527c35

69 http://www.heraldsun.com.au/news/opinion/we-face-huge-challenges-but-melbourne-will-thrive-martine-letts/news-story/e123b466c140c9e40250369dec631af6

70 http://www.independent.co.uk/life-style/gadgets-and-tech/features/meme-theory-do-we-come-up-with-ideas-or-do-they-in-fact-control-us-7939077.html

71 https://w3techs.com/technologies/overview/content_language/all

72 http://english.fullerton.edu/publications/clnArchives/pdf/cardenas_crystal.pdf

73 https://qz.com/208457/a-cartographic-guide-to-starbucks-global-domination/

74 https://www.theguardian.com/news/datablog/2013/jul/17/mcdonalds-restaurants-where-are-they

75 http://www.huffingtonpost.com/uloop/all-about-haute-couture_b_6746770.html

76 http://www.fashiontimes.com/articles/25400/20160229/vogue-devotes-405-pages-march-2016-issue-ads-tapped-more.htm

77 http://www.businessrevieweurope.eu/marketing/856/Top-20-companies-with-the-biggest-advertising-budget

78 http://www.chinadaily.com.cn/business/2016-02/03/content_23367831.htm

79 http://www.transport-research.info/sites/default/files/brochure/20140117_205136_81493_PB05_WEB.pdf
www.clusterobservatory.eu/eco/uploaded/pdf/1381913190425.pdf
https://ec.europa.eu/transport/sites/transport/files/com20170283-europe-on-the-move.pdf
http://www.prnewswire.com/news-releases/global-logistics-market-to-reach-us155-trillion-by-2023-research-report-published-by-transparency-market-research-597595561.html  https://www.statista.com/statistics/274375/commercial-vehicles-in-use-in-the-us/

80 https://www.pwc.com/gx/en/transportation-logistics/pdf/pwc-tl-2030-volume-5.pdf

81 https://www.theguardian.com/technology/2016/jun/17/self-driving-trucks-impact-on-drivers-jobs-us

82 hhttp://www.telegraph.co.uk/news/science/science-news/8316534/Welcome-to-the-information-age-174-newspapers-a-day.html

83 International Data Corporation  https://www.idc.com/

[84] https://www.ssauk.com/industry-info/history-of-the-industry/
https://www.selfstorage.org/LinkClick.aspx?fileticket=fJYAow6_AU0%3D&portalid=0

[85] https://www.ssauk.com/media/1287/jll-and-fedessa-self-storage-report-2016.pdf

[86] https://www.sparefoot.com/self-storage/news/1432-self-storage-industry-statistics/

[87] https://fivethirtyeight.com/datalab/how-many-times-the-average-person-moves/

[88] https://www.zoopla.co.uk/discover/property-news/the-average-brit-will-move-house-8-times-801377088/#4gBMFBOKSRwBG3KC.97

[89] http://www.pewresearch.org/fact-tank/2017/02/13/americans-are-moving at-historically-low-rates-in-part-because-millennials-are-staying-put/

[90] http://www.dailymail.co.uk/sciencetech/article-452046/Pace-life-speeds-study-reveals-walking-faster-ever.html
http://www.cbc.ca/news/canada/how-technology-is-turning-us-into-faster-talkers-1.1111667
http://jalopnik.com/5975008/information-in-america-moves-33480000-times-faster-than-it-did-200-years-ago
https://www.theguardian.com/science/2015/jan/18/modern-world-bad-for-brain-daniel-j-levitin-organized-mind-information-overload

## SECTION 2

[1] See Edward Glaeser The Triumph of the City ETC or Cities are good for you

[2] The two narratives text draws The Fragile City written by Charles Landry & Tom Burke http://charleslandry.com/panel/wp-content/themes/twentyeleven/books/Fragile-City.pdf

[3] The Structural Transformation of the Public Sphere: An Inquiry into a Category of Bourgeois Society, Cambridge, Mass.: MIT Press, 1991

[4] Nancy Fraser, Rethinking the Public Sphere: A Contribution to the Critique of Actually Existing Democracy Social Text No. 25/26 (1990)

[5] https://www.nytimes.com/2016/08/26/world/middleeast/saudi-arabia-islam.html

[6] http://www.worldurbancampaign.org/sites/default/files/reports/utc_25_-_urban_citizenship_-_mannheim_germany.pdf

[7] http://www.cities4pointzero.com.au/the-big-idea

[8] Landry, C. 2016. The Digitized City: Influence and Impact. U.K. Comedia.

[9] http://www.un.org/sustainabledevelopment/sustainable-development-goals/

[10] http://mirror.unhabitat.org/downloads/docs/The%20City%20We%20Need.pdf

[11] http://www.cityofsound.com/blog/2013/02/on-the-smart-city-a-call-for-smart-citizens-instead.html

[12] Eurocities, 2015. Ever smarter cities: Delivering sustainable urban solutions and quality of life for Europe. Eurocities statement on smart cities. Brussels, Eurocities.

[13] Oldenburg, R. 1999. The Great Good Place: Cafes, Coffee Shops, Bookstores, Bars, Hair Salons, and Other Hangouts at the Heart of a Community. New York, Marlowe & Co.

[14] https://eu-smartcities.eu/content/urban-platforms    [15] https://www.jisc.ac.uk/guides/developing-digital-literacies

[16] https://www.thelocal.de/20170124/this-graph-shows-how-much-berlin-rent-has-skyrocketed-in-past-decade

[17] http://www.dw.com/en/berlin-property-market-shifts-from-renters-to-buyers/a-19449663

[18] https://www.irishtimes.com/business/commercial-property/berlin-bubble-property-is-booming-and-rents-are-rising-1.3013491

[19] http://www.salon.com/2017/06/30/how-the-berlin-government-could-rein-in-airbnb-and-protect-local-housing_partner/

[20] http://airbnbvsberlin.com/   [21] https://thinkcity.com.my/about-us/what-we-do/

[22] https://www.theguardian.com/cities/2017/apr/30/berlin-clubbers-urban-village-holzmarkt-party-city   [23] http://urbed.coop/team/nicholas-falk-0

[24] http://charleslandry.com/panel/wp-content/themes/twentyeleven/books/The-Creative-City-Index.pdf

[25] https://www.theguardian.com/world/2017/aug/14/berlin-restaurants-german-english

## SECTION 3

[1] https://www.youtube.com/watch?v=rwBizawuIDw   [2] Bazalgette, P; The Empathy Instinct: A Blueprint for Civil Society; 2017

[3] https://www.letsdoitworld.org/ [4] http://www.cleanuptheworld.org/en/

[5] http://www.creativepeopleplaces.org.uk/  [6] http://www.espncricinfo.com/magazine/content/story/681907.html

[7] The Intercultural City: Planning for Diversity Advantage

[8] Bishop, B; The Big Sort: Why the Clustering of Like Minded America is Tearing us Apart; 2008

[9] http://www.tedcantle.co.uk/publications/012%20The%20end%20of%20parallel%20lives%20the%202nd%20Cantle%20Report%20Home%20Off.pdf

[10] https://www.gov.uk/government/publications/the-casey-review-a-review-into-opportunity-and-integration

[11] http://fes-online-akademie.de/fileadmin/Inhalte/01_Themen/05_Archiv/Dialog_der_Kulturen/dokumente/FES_OA_Meyer_PARALLELGESELLSCHAFT_UND_DEMOKRATIE.pdf

[12] https://www.bertelsmann-stiftung.de/en/topics/aktuelle-meldungen/2017/august/clear-progress-for-integration-of-muslims-in-western-europe/

[13] http://www.telegraph.co.uk/news/religion/8326339/Inside-the-private-world-of-Londons-ultra-Orthodox-Jews.html

[14] Resnick, M. (1997) Turtles, Termites, and Traffic Jams. Cambridge, MA: MIT Press, pg.3

[15] https://www.bertelsmann-stiftung.de/en/topics/aktuelle-meldungen/2017/august/clear-progress-for-integration-of-muslims-in-western-europe/

[16] http://www.bbc.co.uk/news/uk-41085638   [17] http://www.coe.int/en/web/interculturalcities/icc-newsletter

[18] http://www.civicus.org/documents/reports-and-publications/annual-reports/annual-report-2016-en.pdf

[19] The Atlantic monthly – How to build an autocracy March 2017 https://www.theatlantic.com/magazine/archive/2017/03/its-putins-world/513848/

[20] https://www.theguardian.com/commentisfree/2016/dec/07/why-steve-bannon-wants-to-destroy-secularism

[21] https://www.theguardian.com/commentisfree/2017/feb/06/some-of-trumps-advisers-want-a-new-civil-war-we-must-not-let-them-have-it

[22] http://www.bizim-kiez.de/en/

[23] For a longer discussion see: https://www.theguardian.com/news/2017/aug/04/how-britain-fell-out-of-love-with-the-free-market?utm_source=esp&utm_medium=Email&utm_campaign=The+Long+Read+-+Collections+2017&utm_term=238074&subid=233044&CMP=longread_collection

[24] https://www.theguardian.com/books/2016/apr/15/neoliberalism-ideology-problem-george-monbiot

[25] For a review of these arguments see Amin Ash: Cultural Economy and Cities, Progress in Human Geography

[26] https://www.theguardian.com/commentisfree/2012/jul/16/mental-health-political-issue

[27] https://www-935.ibm.com/services/us/ceo/ceostudy2010/multimedia.html

[28] Landry Charles, 2000, The Creative City: A Toolkit for Urban Innovators, p.177-179, Earthscan London

[29] See Charlie Leadbeater and Sue Goss in Social Entrepreneurship, Demos, 1998

[30] This chapter draws on a book 'Psychology & the City' written in collaboration with Chris Murray see link: http://charleslandry.com/panel/wp-content/themes/twentyeleven/books/Psychology-and-the%20City.pdf

[31] Washington Population Statistics Bureau

[32] Containing Tensions: Psychoanalysis and modern policy making; Cooper, A; in Juncture; IPPR; London; Vol 22, 2015.

[33] Gestalt Principles; how are your designs perceived? http://vanseodesign.com/web-design/gestalt-principles-of-perception/

[34] https://positivepsychologyprogram.com/founding-fathers/

[35] http://www.positivedisintegration.com/positivepsychology.htm

[36] Kelman, H; Conflict Resolution and Reconciliation: A Social-Psychological Perspective on Ending Violent Conflict Between Identity Groups; 2011

[37] Empathy, the Emotional Intelligence Series, 2017, Harvard Business Review, Boston,   [38] See Psychology & the City – mentioned above

[39] https://www.oecd.org/governance/observatory-public-sector-innovation/   [40] http://mind-lab.dk/en/   [41] http://labcd.mx/labforthecity/

[42] http://ash.harvard.edu/   [43] http://publicsector.sa.gov.au/culture/

[44] http://www.openlivinglabs.eu/news/living-labs-guiding-sustainable-cities-innovations-europe

[45] https://www.kl.nl/en/   [46] http://www.kafkabrigade.org/   [47] http://www.nesta.org.uk/

[48] http://ec.europa.eu/research/prizes/icapital/index.cfm   [49] https://prezi.com/fgg7n-ggulog/actors-of-urban-change-en/

[50] http://citiscope.org/story/2014/mexico-city-experimental-think-tank-city-and-its-government

## SECTION 4

[1] For a review of these arguments see Amin Ash: Cultural Economy and Cities, Progress in Human Geography

# ACKNOWLEDGEMENTS

Writing a book is a difficult task. It is never a lone endeavour, you need help, inspiration and insights from others as well as emotional support and resources. First I want to thank Jab Taylor and the C.B. & H.H. Taylor 1984 Trust; Roger Martin and Robin Maynard from Population Matters; and the Robert Bosch Stiftung, who gave me a fellowship in Berlin.

Many individuals have helped through their conversations and our joint projects, they include Benjamin Barber, Margie Caust, Lynda Dorrington, Timo Cantell, Anja Pilipenko, Carol Coletta, Chris Murray, Margaret Shiu, Hamdan Majeed, Peter Kurz, Rainer Kern, Christian Hübel, Saskia Sassen, Tom Burke, Richard Brecknock, Gabriella Gomez-Mont, Franco Bianchini, Duarte Lima de Mayer, Rodin Genoff, Agnieszka Surwillo-Hahn, Darius Polok, Martin Schwegmann, Lucy Garcia, Justyna Jochym, Geoff Mulgan, Sir Peter Hall, Peter Kageyama, Bernd Fesel, Susan Richards, Eric Corijn, Leoluca Orlando, Marc Pachter, Michele Beint, Marcel Witvoet, my helpful publisher, David Hills my designer with whom I co-created this book. A number of writers have influenced me including James Hillmann, Richard Tarnas, Arjun Appadurai. Oddly perhaps I need to thank the inventors of the Internet as well as Wikipedia as they make many things easier and not to forget the guys from our book club, where we are only allowed to read novels – Bill, Jab and Phil.

Susie, Max, Nancy and Roxana have given me emotional support and much more.

**Books by Charles Landry**

**Shorts:**

01: **The Origins & Futures of the Creative City**
02: **The Sensory Landscape of Cities**
03: **The Creative City Index with Jonathan Hyams**
04: **Culture & Commerce**
05: **The Fragile City & the Risk Nexus with Tom Burke**
06: **Cities of Ambition**
07: **The Digitized City**
08: **Psychology & The City with Chris Murray**

**The Art of City Making**

**The Creative City: A toolkit for urban innovators**

**The Intercultural City: Planning for the Diversity Dividend with Phil Wood**

**The Other Invisible Hand with Geoff Mulgan**

*Portland, life as we would*
*wish it on a sunny day*

'The Civic City' is perceptive, important and clearly written. Charles manages the difficult task of providing us with a global overview of the dynamics affecting cities and what we need to do about them.'

Professor Lord Robert Skidelsky
Emeritus professor University of Warwick


'Utterly timely. Charles takes on the some of the most urgent subjects of our time, using imagery to tell a powerful story. Unless we recapture the best of our civic nature, cities will inevitably struggle.'

Carol Coletta
Senior fellow with the Kresge Foundation and formerly Vice-President of the Knight Foundation


'Charles' book is very timely especially as it is a dark time globally in a world of ever increasing uncertainty. He reminds us that city making is the work of everyone. We as citizens need to come to grips with the creative tension of living in close proximity whilst respecting differences so as to build places we want to live in.'

Lynda Dorrington
Executive Director. FORM - Building a State of Creativity, Perth, Western Australia


'The visual experience of Charles' book brings the urgent issues facing our cities alive. All of us can and need to participate more directly with our surroundings to shape where our cities are going in the future. Only then will we unlock their potential as they grow. This ground breaking book is essential reading.'

Martin Parr
Photographer